Love IS A CHOICE

Love IS A CHOICE

Making Your MARRIAGE
and FAMILY *Stronger*

LYNN G. ROBBINS

DESERET
BOOK

SALT LAKE CITY, UTAH

Library of Congress Cataloging-in-Publication Data

Robbins, Lynn (Lynn G.), author.
   Love is a choice : making your marriage and family stronger / Lynn G. Robbins.
      pages cm
   Includes bibliographical references and index.
   ISBN 978-1-62972-086-9 (hardbound : alk. paper)
   1. Marriage—Religious aspects—The Church of Jesus Christ of Latter-day Saints.
2. Families—Religious aspects—The Church of Jesus Christ of Latter-day Saints. I. Title.
   BX8643.M36R63 2015
   248.4'89332—dc23   2015008070

Printed in the United States of America
LSC Communications, Harrisonburg, VA

18 17 16 15 14 13 12 11 10 9

In honor of my father and mother,
Grant and Evelyn Robbins,
who raised their children in righteousness.

To Jan, my wife and love of my life.

And "for the learning and the profit
of my children" (2 Nephi 4:15).

CONTENTS

ACKNOWLEDGMENTS

First, I am grateful to the Lord, the true author of love. I am also eternally grateful to my wife, Jan, for her willingness to read through and comment on more drafts of this book than I care to admit and for her constant love and support for the last forty years of marriage. I am also eternally grateful to my children and their spouses, not only for their feedback on the manuscript but also for their forgiveness of my shortcomings as a parent. Heartfelt thanks to my mother, Evelyn, and my sisters, who have been so willing to provide feedback. Several friends and associates have also been instrumental with many helpful suggestions.

My profound gratitude goes to Dennis Higbee, a beloved cousin, who has invested countless hours reviewing the manuscript and helping me improve and refine it.

Appreciation is clearly due and gladly given to those secretaries who have helped so much with their insights, editing, and feedback—Rose Chibota, Janet Egbert, Linda Cornett, and Pam Wheelwright. Deep and heartfelt thanks to Max Molgard and Brian Garner for their expert assistance, keen insights, and valued suggestions in helping polish the book.

The publishing team at Deseret Book has been marvelous. I am grateful to Cory Maxwell for inviting and encouraging me to write this book; Lisa Roper for overseeing the project; Emily Watts for her expert counsel and editorial assistance early on; Tracy Keck for her kind and enthusiastic help in editing and preparing the manuscript for publication; Heather Ward for design; Rachael Ward for typography.

The opinions and views expressed in this publication are solely my own. They do not represent the official position of The Church of Jesus Christ of Latter-day Saints. Notwithstanding the aforementioned disclaimer, I have diligently sought the guidance of the Spirit and strived to please the Lord, with the hope that this work will have an inspiring impact on all who read *Love Is a Choice: Making Your Marriage and Family Stronger.*

The author's proceeds from the sale of this book will be donated to the Temple Patron Assistance Fund of The Church of Jesus Christ of Latter-day Saints. This Church fund provides financial assistance to those who otherwise could not afford the travel expenses associated with attending a temple and participating in the sacred blessings available only in the House of the Lord.

It's All about Families

In the beginning God created the heaven and the earth."[1] The first five days of the Creation were all in preparation for the sixth, which brought forth the ultimate purpose and crowning event of the Creation—earth's first family. Likewise, the crowning ordinance of the gospel is a sealing in the temple, or the creation of an eternal family. "The family is central to the Creator's plan for the eternal destiny of His children" or *His family.*[2] With the family being the central part of God's plan, it shouldn't surprise us that the first commandment He gave to Adam and Eve was to have a family: "Be fruitful, and multiply, and replenish the earth."[3]

As the first family, Adam and Eve became the divine archetype for all other men and women who would follow: "And they twain shall be one flesh, and all this that the earth might answer the end of its creation."[4] The standard works repeatedly teach us that without eternal families, "the whole earth would be utterly wasted at his coming,"[5] because it would not have answered the end of its creation. The plan of salvation is all about families.

"NOT GOOD" TO BE ALONE

From the beginning the Lord declared that "it [was] *not good* that the man [or woman] should be alone."[6] Being *alone* is an antonym of *family* and is contrary to God's plan of happiness. Therefore "Adam fell that [families] might be; and [families] are that they might have joy."[7] Having an eternal family is the only way to achieve ultimate joy.

Some are alone not by any fault or choice of their own but because the opportunity to marry has eluded them. "Faithful members whose circumstances do not allow them to receive the blessings of eternal marriage and parenthood in this life will receive all promised blessings in the eternities, provided they keep the covenants they have made with God."[8] In the meantime they enjoy the association of friends and loved ones, including their ward family.

There are times when a person may want to be temporarily alone, such as in those moments set aside for prayer and meditation, but few desire to be alone long-term. It must have been frightening for Adam to contemplate the imminent separation from Eve after she partook of the forbidden fruit and would be expelled from the Garden of Eden. As hard as it may have been for Adam to say good-bye to the Garden of Eden, losing Eve would have been the real "paradise lost." Mark Twain phrased it beautifully: "Wherever Eve was, there was Eden."[9]

If Adam had not chosen wisely, he would have become a lone man in a dreary Eden, with a self-imposed sentence of eternal solitary confinement, and "must have remained in the same state . . . forever, and had no end."[10] Could it be eternal aloneness that in great part makes hell what it is? The garden was Adam's house, but Eve was his *home* and his companion in achieving his true purpose. Earth's first love story is not only its most famous but also its most tender and inspiring. It is a story about the use of agency, love, companionship, and the making of a home.

COMPANIONSHIP OF THE HOLY GHOST

Clearly neither Adam nor Eve could be without the other and still experience joy and fulfillment. In addition to the physical and emotional companionship found between husband and wife, a third kind of companionship is vital for two hearts to be knit together in everlasting love and to achieve a fullness of joy. President Henry B. Eyring taught, "It is only with the companionship of the Holy Ghost that we can hope to be equally yoked in a marriage free from discord. I have seen how that companionship is crucial for felicity in a marriage. The miracle of becoming one requires the help of heaven."[11]

Just as ultimate joy is to be together forever as loving families in "an exceeding, and an eternal weight of glory,"[12] ultimate sorrow is destined to come from eternal separation. "For these angels did not abide my law; therefore, they cannot be enlarged, but remain *separately and singly,* without exaltation, in their saved condition, to all eternity; and from henceforth are not gods, but are angels of God forever and ever."[13]

After the Savior visited the Nephites, they achieved a glorious state of unity, love, and righteousness. Of them it was said, "There could not be a happier people among all the people who had been created by the hand of God."[14] A couple who achieves that kind of unity and righteousness is also on the path to eternal bliss. The Atonement makes it possible to be reunited with our Heavenly Parents in our heavenly home and to be together forever with our own families, united in righteousness—happily ever after.

PURPOSE AND CONTENT OF THIS BOOK

The purpose of this book is to share many of the Lord's teachings on how to wisely use our agency to nurture and strengthen the unity and love that can and should exist in families. This book will also explore how to make choices that lead us to becoming more like the Savior and, in turn, help our family members to acquire Christlike attributes as well.

In this book insights are shared on the powerful role that agency plays in matters of love, patience, forgiveness, and the development of other divine attributes that help to make a house a home. You will learn the power and impact of agency on feelings and emotions—things that much of the world believes to be outside of one's control. My hope is that by the end of this book you will have a far greater respect and deeper sense of gratitude for the Lord's gift of agency to His children and the role it plays in the success of a family. His doctrine to act "and not to be acted upon" is powerful, and a correct understanding of it changes lives in wondrous and happy ways.[15]

PART I: CHOOSING LOVE

Chapter 1, "Agency and Love in Marriage," studies doctrines of the Savior that will help you understand the role of agency in matters of love, including love between a husband and wife. It will also examine what *true love* is, according to Christ's doctrine. After all, how can you develop something that you don't fully understand?

Chapter 2, "Love and 100% Responsibility," will illustrate very clearly the power and control a person and family can achieve in life by wisely accepting the responsibility that comes with agency, including the responsibility we have to repent and forgive. It further explores the role of agency and responsibility with respect to justice and mercy and the peace and joy that result from these powerful doctrines

Chapter 3, "Agency and Virtue," shares insights into the power of agency in developing Christlike virtues that not only help eliminate vice, but also help to eliminate negative emotions and feelings that impact lives and families in such damaging ways. It outlines the principles and pattern in developing Christlike virtues.

Chapter 4, "'Even as I Am,'" shares how to strengthen home and family by choosing to follow the Savior's incomparable example and continually striving to become as He is. It also provides counsel on ways to encourage your spouse and children in their quests to become more like the Savior.

Chapter 5, "Love and Self-Reliance," helps spouses understand the role of agency in making self-reliance a priority. It also uncovers the important and fundamental interconnectedness of love and self-reliance. The chapter shares advice for increasing self-reliance within the family and raising responsible children.

Chapter 6, "Agency and Love in the Family," will help parents understand that effectively teaching their children is the very essence of parenting. It will help them understand the vital importance of respecting their children's agency and the need to guide them in its use. It teaches how love and joy are increased in a home when each family member exercises his or her agency for good.

Chapter 7, "Choosing Happily Ever After," illustrates doctrine and principles that govern happiness. It explains why the plan of salvation is also known as the plan of happiness and how one can choose greater happiness in this life. It also shares how these choices give one the hope of truly living happily ever after.

PART II: RESOURCES FOR PRACTICING GREAT CHOICES

Chapter 8, "Of One Heart, Mind, and Bank Account"

Chapter 9, "Family Home Evening Helps"

Appendix, "Christlike Virtues"

The doctrine and principles that the Savior taught and lived are powerful. His way is the only way to make a house a home—"Except the Lord build the house [home], they labour in vain that build it" (Psalm 127:1). Such a home and marriage endures *happily ever after.*

NOTES

1. Genesis 1:1.
2. "The Family: A Proclamation to the World," *Ensign*, Nov. 2010, 129.
3. Genesis 1:28.
4. Doctrine and Covenants 49:16; see also 88:19–20.
5. Doctrine and Covenants 2:3; see also 27:9; 98:16; 110:15; 138:48; Joseph Smith—History 1:39; 3 Nephi 25:6; Malachi 4:6; Luke 1:17.
6. Genesis 2:18; emphasis added.
7. 2 Nephi 2:25.
8. *Handbook 2: Administering the Church* (2010), 1.3.3.
9. Mark Twain, *Eve's Diary,* (London and New York: Harper and Brothers, 1906).
10. 2 Nephi 2:22.
11. Henry B. Eyring, "To My Grandchildren," *Ensign*, Oct. 2013, 70.
12. Doctrine and Covenants 132:16.
13. Doctrine and Covenants 132:17; emphasis added.
14. 4 Nephi 1:16.
15. 2 Nephi 2:26.

PART I:
Choosing Love

CHAPTER 1

AGENCY AND LOVE IN MARRIAGE

Can one choose to love, or is love something you *fall* in? Is agency involved, or is love something that just happens to you, like being smitten with Cupid's arrow without any say-so? If love is something you fall in or are smitten by, how can you act rather than be acted upon (see 2 Ne. 2:26)? How much of a role does agency play in matters of love?

FALLING IN LOVE

Falling in love is an incredibly powerful thing. There have doubtless been more books written, more movies made, more songs sung about love and falling in love than about any other topic. Finding a person to love is the ultimate treasure hunt. Falling in love is finding "someone just right, someone you love like the best pal you ever had and the worst crush you ever had."[1] It is an indescribably deep, euphoric feeling of excitement, giddiness, and anticipation. When you're in love, there is an unrelenting desire to be together, occupying your every thought, your every desire, your every minute of the day. It's intense! It's exhilarating!

To fully portray the feeling on paper has always eluded even the most adept poets. To comprehend it, love has to be experienced. And oh, what a wonderful experience! He captures her heart, she captures his; there is a mutual victory and surrender for both.

"The Lord has ordained that we should marry," said President Gordon B. Hinckley, "that we shall live together in love and peace and harmony. . . . The time will come when you will *fall in love.* It will occupy all of your thoughts and be the stuff of which your dreams are made. . . . You will know no greater happiness than that found in your home . . . *The truest mark of your success in life will be the quality of your marriage.* . . . This choice [of a companion] will be the most important of all the choices you make in your life."[2]

FALLING OUT OF LOVE

While the expression "fall in love" is a beautiful idiom, there are inherent risks involved in using the verb *fall,* because it could imply that love is accidental, involuntary, with no choice involved. And subtly, the expression has also led to the use of its distressing corollary, "we fell out of love," an all-too-common phrase heard nowadays as an excuse for a failed marriage. "Falling in love" and "falling out of love" make it seem as if love were something that cannot be controlled, in which people are being acted upon more than choosing to act.

If we live in a world of agency, where people are to act for themselves, wouldn't it make sense that the most important decision made in mortality, that of choosing a spouse, would be our choice and not left in Cupid's hands?

When newlyweds begin living under the same roof, they begin

to encounter a multitude of irritants unknown to singles. On the less serious end of the spectrum it might be terrible snoring, or amateur cooking skills, or socks on the floor. On the more serious end it might be disagreements on how to manage joint financial accounts. Over time these irritations can fester and stress the relationship, impacting feelings so deeply that some couples believe they are *falling out of love.* They become easy targets for Satan, who tempts them to turn to the anti-responsibility list, which will be discussed in the next chapter. Once they go to that list they are being acted upon and may throw their hands up in resignation as if they were victims of some outside influence that controls them. They may begin to doubt the decision they made to marry in the first place. They may ask themselves, "Do I really want to be married to this person for eternity?"

Eventually, having supposedly fallen out of love, they begin to drift apart, often saying things to hurt one another. "I don't love you anymore" is a common assertion. They may tolerate one another for the children's sake, resenting one another; or they may separate, believing their differences to be irreconcilable. The result is a damaged or destroyed family, another casualty of one of Satan's foremost battle stratagems.

How could something so glorious and beautiful as falling in love end up in misery for so many marriages? What goes wrong?

It is almost humorous to observe a young unmarried couple in love. After spending an entire day together, they are back together again on the phone that same night. It's sheer torture for them to be separated. They can hardly focus on anything else. Love begins to disrupt their studies or work. Everything else in life becomes a nuisance and an interruption that keeps them apart until they can be together again. In their minds there was never in the history of the world a truer love than theirs. We call this level of pre-marriage intensity "infatuation."

After the couple marries, this intensity tapers off. Living under the same roof, they each begin to discover some irritating idiosyncrasies in the other. Goethe remarked long ago, "Love is an ideal thing, marriage is a real thing; a confusion of the real with the ideal never goes unpunished."[3] When the ideal gives way to reality, familiarity can easily turn to faultfinding and enmity. "Where is that level of passion, the fire I had during courtship?" they may ask themselves. The man is no longer Superman, merely Clark Kent. The infatuation begins to fade.

Those who have confused infatuation for love may unwisely believe they are falling out of love when problems arise. The resulting doubt might cause them to wonder if they made a mistake and if their real soul mate might still be out there somewhere. Satan will do everything he can to cause further uncertainty and tempt them to separate. Their relationship is at a critical crossroad.

This is when a dose of real love is needed to rekindle the relationship. It may not restore the same emotional intensity of early courtship or change Clark Kent back into Superman, but it will completely change the direction in which the marriage is headed. As infatuation yields to charity, true love begins to blossom. Forty years later, Grandpa can love Grandma more than ever but more easily endure a short absence from her than he could at a youthful age when smitten with infatuation. Their love is maturing and growing stronger each day.

If a husband and wife are willing to apply the scriptural definition of love to their relationship, even a stale marriage and romance can be revived. Stephen R. Covey relates the following experience:

"At one seminar, after I'd spoken on the importance of demonstrating character within the family, a man came up and said, 'I like what you're saying, but my wife and I just don't have the same feelings for each other that we used to. I guess we don't love each other anymore. What can I do?'

"'Love her,' I replied.

"He looked puzzled. 'How do you love when you don't feel love?'

"'My friend,' I responded, 'love is a verb. The *feeling* of love is the fruit of love. So love your wife. You did it once, you can do it again. Listen. Empathize. Appreciate. It's your choice. Are you willing to do that?'

"Of course, I was asking this man if he was willing to search within himself for the character required to make his marriage work. All our relationships follow the contours of life; they have ups and downs. This is why our families provide a critical measure of our character—and the opportunity, again and again to nurture it."[4]

GROWING IN LOVE

For many people, falling in love is an enchanting, at-first-sight encounter. For others, it isn't so much "falling in love" as it is "growing in love," a budding friendship that blossoms over time. Though the first type may also bloom like the second, it often begins as a glandular infatuation and fantasy—a cotton-candy kind of love that has no substance.

On the other hand, "divine" love, as President Spencer W. Kimball called it, "is not like that association of the world which is misnamed love, but which is mostly physical attraction. When marriage is based on this only, the parties soon tire of each other. There is a break and a divorce, and a new, fresher physical attraction comes with another marriage, which in turn may last only until it too becomes stale. The love of which the Lord speaks is not only physical attraction, but also faith, confidence, understanding, and partnership. It is devotion and companionship, parenthood, common ideals and standards. It is cleanliness of life and sacrifice and unselfishness. This kind of love never tires nor wanes. It lives on through sickness and sorrow, through prosperity and privation, through accomplishment and disappointment, through time and eternity."[5]

Many popular songs and films make reference to an everlasting love. For the world, these lyrics are simply poetic; for us, they are genuine expressions of our divine potential. We believe that eternal love, eternal marriage, and eternal families are "central to the Creator's plan for the eternal destiny of His children."[6] However, every couple will encounter some struggles on their journey toward this glorious destiny. A happy and successful marriage depends on two people who are good at forgiving, or as President Gordon B. Hinckley pointed out, have learned "a high degree of mutual toleration."[7] True and mature love is manifest after we discover each other's imperfections and still commit to one another.

There are no perfect marriages in the world because there are no perfect people. But the gospel of Jesus Christ teaches us how to nurture our marriages toward perfection and how to keep the romance in them along the way. No one need ever "fall out of love." Falling out of love is a cunning myth that causes many broken hearts and homes.

"The family is falling apart all over the world," President Hinckley said. "The old ties that bound together father and mother and children are breaking everywhere. We must face this in our own midst. There are too many broken homes among our own. . . . Can we not do better? Of course we can."[8]

LOVE—A CONSCIOUS CHOICE

Too many believe that love is a condition pertaining solely to the heart, something that happens to you. They disassociate love from the mind and, therefore, from agency.

We know that any commandment of God involves agency. We can obey or disobey, but there is always a choice. Therefore, when the Lord puts love in the command form: "Thou shalt love the Lord thy God with all thy heart, and with all thy soul, and with all thy mind," and "Thou shalt love thy neighbor as thyself,"[9] He is not saying, "I hope you fall in love with your neighbor." The command is a directive, an appeal to the mind to make a conscious choice, involving the mind in reasoning and decision-making. The Savior made it clear that love was a command to be obeyed—a command upon which "all the law and the prophets" hang.[10] To achieve a Christlike love we must overcome the natural man (see Mosiah 3:19), control natural impulses, and even love our enemies (see Matt. 5:44). This is a command that requires a conscious decision.

In commanding us to love, the Lord refers to something much deeper than infatuation, a love that is the most profound form of loyalty—a covenant.

The Book of Mormon prophet King Benjamin also teaches that love had much to do with agency. In his counsel to parents, he proclaimed, "Ye will teach [your children] to love one another, and to serve one another."[11] How can something be taught that cannot be learned? Once again, the scriptures are teaching us about a love that involves choosing to act, as opposed to being acted upon.

LOVE AND MARRIAGE

What about love between spouses, which involves the additional elements of romance and intimacy? Does this principle of agency in love, or the command to love, apply to marriage as well?

Once again, the Lord uses the command form of the verb *love* in His instruction, "Thou shalt love thy wife with all thy heart, and shalt cleave unto her and none else."[12] It doesn't require any guesswork here to discern that the Lord is giving us a directive with a presupposition of agency.

As recorded in the book of Matthew, the Lord said, "Thou shalt love thy neighbour *as thyself.*"[13] In His mortal life, He demonstrated a perfect kind of love, and then said, "A *new* commandment I give unto you, That ye love one another; *as I have loved you,* that ye also love one another."[14] Loving as He loved is an even higher form of love than loving "as thyself." It is a pure love that puts another higher than the self. This pure love is the same love that should exist between husbands and wives. In Ephesians 5:25, the Apostle Paul exhorts, "Husbands, love your wives, [How?] even as Christ also loved the church, and gave himself for it." How, then, did Christ love the Church? His perfect example teaches us what true love, *charity*, really is. Only when we understand true charity can we fully follow the Lord's command to love.

UNDERSTANDING LOVE

How could something as universal as love be so hard to define, and for many, to find? In part it is because love is such a far-reaching and all-encompassing principle and emotion. From another perspective, it is because the world usually searches for it by starlight, moonlight, or candlelight, rather than by that "true light" (D&C 88:50) who is the "light of the world" (John 8:12). He is the one and only author of *true love,* the kind needed for a love story that truly has no end. He calls this love *charity,* and it endures "forever" (Moro. 7:47). Without charity, none of the loves mentioned by philosophers, or authors, or movies, or songs, or books can be complete or everlasting.

Jesus Christ is the only person who ever fully understood charity and lived it. As Elder Jeffrey R. Holland has stated, "True charity has been known only once. It is shown perfectly and purely in Christ's unfailing, ultimate, and atoning love for us."[15] One can begin to understand this kind of love "by study" (D&C 88:118) when searching and pondering the scriptures and words of the prophets on charity. However, to fully comprehend it, one must also learn "by faith," which requires a disciple of Christ to follow His example and learn of charity through sacrifice.

Elder Bruce C. Hafen stated it well: "Perhaps those who seek apprenticeship with the Master of mankind must emulate his sacrificial experience to the fullest extent of their personal capacity. Only then can they taste His empathy and His charity. For only then are they like him enough to feel his love for others the way he feels it—to love, 'as I have loved you' (John 13:34). That is a deeper, different love from 'love thy neighbour as thyself' (Matt. 19:19)."[16]

As the one perfect marriage and family Counselor, the Lord is the only one who can help us find the happily-ever-after kind of love—not only in the poetic sense but also in its literal and ultimate sense at Judgment Day.

CHARITY—THE GREATEST ATTRIBUTE

Of all Christlike attributes, charity is referred to as "the greatest" (1 Cor. 13:13) and is the only one used scripturally to portray the Lord's divine nature in a single word—"God is love" (1 John 4:8).

So much meaning is packed into this one word that Paul says, "All the law is fulfilled in one word, even in this; Thou shalt love thy neighbour [or spouse or family] as thyself."[17] The love of God is the meaning of the tree of life in Lehi's dream.[18] The Father sent the Son because He "so loved the world" (John 3:16), and the Son "so loved the world that he gave his own life" (D&C 34:3). The entire chapter of 1 Corinthians 13 is filled with Paul's teachings on charity and its preeminent position among virtues. The chapter heading reads, "Paul discusses the high status of charity—Charity, a pure love, excels and exceeds almost all else."

Fourteen qualities from 1 Corinthians 13:1–8 help us better define charity, the Lord's greatest attribute. As you study each attribute, I invite you to consider two things:

- Is each part of the definition describing something within our control? Can we choose to comply with each of the behaviors? For example, can you fall out of kindness, or is being kind a choice?
- How can you better fulfill the scriptural directive to love your spouse as Christ loved the Church? How can you improve in each of these areas?

THE LORD'S WAY		THE WRONG WAY	
Attribute	Christlike Love	Obvious	Not So Obvious
"Suffereth long" (1 Cor. 13:4)	• Is patient and tolerant with spouse and does not criticize. • Recognizes that spouse is progressing, is patient with imperfections.	• Is intolerant, ill-tempered, critical, cranky. • Despite staying with spouse, has no close relationship.	• Is impatient, complains, gives the silent treatment.
"Is kind" (1 Cor. 13:4)	• Is amiable, thoughtful, and interested in spouse's happiness. • Is mindful of spouse's needs and feelings, complimentary and praising, gracious. • Is a good Samaritan, comforts, is merciful.	• Is mean, miserly, cruel, inconsiderate, unmerciful. • Has a scowling countenance. • Is sarcastic or makes fun of spouse.	• Is indifferent, remote, negligent, unconcerned, uninterested, unresponsive. • Is careless, thoughtless, distracted, preoccupied.
"Envieth not" (1 Cor. 13:4)	• Is content, grateful for blessings. • Rejoices in another's gifts, talents, success. • Is generous and offers help to those in need. • Lives frugally. • Knows the difference between needs and wants, avoids unnecessary debt.	• Is resentful, jealous, greedy, covetous. • Fails to pay an honest tithe. • Is selfish and withholds help. • Has a "my," not "our," money mentality. • Incurs excessive debt.	• Is ungrateful. • Is a partial tithe-payer. • Is vain—sets heart on costly apparel, etc. • Lives beyond income. • Allows interest on credit cards to accumulate. • Does not try to save food or money for future needs.

THE LORD'S WAY		THE WRONG WAY	
Attribute	Christlike Love	Obvious	Not So Obvious
"Is not puffed up" (1 Cor. 13:4)	• Is humble, meek, teachable. • Does not speak vainly or seek attention. • Happily serves wherever called. • Lifts, praises, encourages spouse. • Seeks the will of God. • Willingly takes suggestions and even correction.	• Is proud, eager for attention, self-centered, pompous, boastful. • Murmurs against leaders. • Is condescending with spouse or "holier than thou." • Is offended when advice is given.	• Does not praise or give due credit to others. • Aspires to positions. • Is a know-it-all, is unteachable. • Considers own knowledge superior to others'.
"Doth not behave itself unseemly" (1 Cor. 13:5)	• Is courteous, well mannered, tactful, tasteful, reverent, respectful, mindful of others. • Is clean, neat, orderly. • Uses appropriate language and exercises good judgment.	• Is discourteous, crude, disrespectful, indecent, improper, irreverent. • Enjoys dirty jokes. • Is boisterous: loud and inappropriate laughter. • Is vulgar and profane.	• Doesn't say "please" or "thank you." • Has forgotten everyday courtesies. • Is disorderly and unkempt. • Makes light of sacred things.

| THE LORD'S WAY | | THE WRONG WAY | |
Attribute	Christlike Love	Obvious	Not So Obvious
"Seeketh not her own" (1 Cor. 13:5)	• Is tenderhearted, sensitive, compassionate, merciful, generous. • Seeks unity, kneels with spouse in prayer, listens with empathy, avoids contention. • Thinks "we" and "ours." • Is approachable. • Seeks to please God. • Selflessly serves spouse's needs.[19]	• Is demanding, controlling, selfish, manipulative, blaming. • Lacks unity, is contentious. • Thinks "I" and "mine." • Seldom listens, is aloof. • Seeks self-gratification, is self-indulgent. • Seeks the praise of others.	• Finds it hard to say "I'm sorry," "you were right," or "please forgive me." • Is reluctant to render help (as with household chores). • Is guilty of self-pity. • Withholds intimacy. • Is uncaring. • Complains.
"Is not easily provoked" (1 Cor. 13:5)	• Is forgiving, patient, calm, gentle, respectful. • Understands that anger is a decision and can be controlled. • Is a peacemaker.	• Is irritable, spiteful, vengeful. • Is easily angered, often hostile and abusive. • Is defensive, responds with disgust or contempt. • Swears, has a bad temper. • Blames spouse for all family problems.	• Argues over every silly, little thing, is not open-minded. • Disciplines in anger. • Does not bridle passions.

(continued on next page)

21

THE LORD'S WAY		THE WRONG WAY	
Attribute	Christlike Love	Obvious	Not So Obvious
"Thinketh no evil" (1 Cor. 13:5)	• Is nonjudgmental, respectful, helpful, pure, obedient. • Has "no more disposition to do evil" (Mosiah 5:2). • Is modest in dress, thought, speech. • Virtue garnishes thoughts unceasingly. • Is anxiously engaged in good causes. • Acts without guile. • Controls thoughts.	• Is cruel, conniving, deceitful, dishonest. • Indulges in pornography and inappropriate music. • Dresses and behaves immodestly. • Is motivated by ulterior motives.	• Is judgmental, prejudiced, faultfinding. • Holds grudges, gossips. • Participates in jokes about intimate or sacred things. • Tolerates evil influences.
"Rejoiceth not in iniquity, but rejoiceth in the truth" (1 Cor. 13:6)	• Stays close to the Spirit through regular scripture study, prayer, obedience. • Has discovered that truth leads to joy and happiness. • Suggests wholesome activities. • Enjoys Church attendance, worships regularly at the temple.	• Has an "eat, drink, and be merry" mentality. • Is indulgent, unfaithful, disobedient. • Is addicted to vices. • Justifies self, makes excuses.	• Is light-minded. • Is casual with prayers. • Is not diligent about gospel teaching or scripture reading in the home.

THE LORD'S WAY		THE WRONG WAY	
Attribute	Christlike Love	Obvious	Not So Obvious
"Beareth all things" (1 Cor. 13:7)	• Has moral courage, is bold in truth. • Is happy and content regardless of circumstances. • Turns the other cheek, is calm (this does not mean that abuse victims should silently bear cruelty or follow a disobedient spouse). • Is able to see the big picture from the Lord's perspective. • Trusts in the Lord's timing.	• Is insulting, defensive, irritable, touchy, grouchy, moody. • Is a coward. • Is ashamed of righteousness. • Blames God for problems.	• Is ungrateful. • Yields to peer pressure in compromising situations. • Is apathetic. • Is weary in well-doing.
"Believeth all things" (1 Cor. 13:7)	• Clearly sees the eternal potential of spouse and forever families and is tolerant of shortcomings. • Sees others as children of God. • Holds fast to the gospel of Jesus Christ. • Is generally positive.	• Doubts spouse's potential, is critical and cynical. • Is unfriendly to spouse. • Is condescending, intolerant. • Has let go of the iron rod, is not active in the Church.	• Is distanced, remote, inattentive, insensitive. • Is a hypocrite, lives a lie. • Goes to church but wishes to be elsewhere.

(continued on next page)

23

	THE LORD'S WAY	THE WRONG WAY	
Attribute	**Christlike Love**	**Obvious**	**Not So Obvious**
"Hopeth all things" (1 Cor. 13:7)	• Is an optimist. • Looks for the best. • Praises, builds up, expresses affection. • Continues courting spouse after marriage.	• Is a pessimist. • Is a nagger. • Is a faultfinder. • Is unrepentant, in denial.	• Is a fatalist. • Is bored. • Is neglectful. • Doesn't feel worthy to pray for forgiveness.
"Endureth all things" (1 Cor. 13:7)	• Doesn't complain or murmur. • Is responsible and gladly accepts callings. • Sees growth in adversity. • Has a desire to learn and progress. • Is steadfast, knows life is a test.	• Is always complaining, murmuring. • Shirks or avoids responsibility. • Makes excuses.	• Is lukewarm or gives half-hearted effort. • Is lazy or spends too much time on hobbies, TV, internet, etc. • Is afflicted with self-pity.
"Charity never faileth" (1 Cor. 13:8)	• Loves as Christ loves us. • Doesn't give up on loved ones. • Is supportive.	• "Falls out of love." • Flirts with individuals other than spouse. • Is an adulterer. • Loves conditionally, based on spouse being healthy, successful, slender, maintaining good looks.	• Has wandering eyes. • Views spouse more as a burden than a blessing. • Daydreams or fantasizes about individuals other than spouse.

UNDERSTANDING LOVE THROUGH ITS SYNONYMS

"Charity is love."[20] The word *love* is a synonym of charity when coupled with the modifiers, "the pure love of Christ" (Moro. 7:47), "unfeigned" (2 Cor. 6:6; D&C 121:41), "perfect love" (Moro. 8:16, 26), or "everlasting love" (Jer. 31:3; Moro. 8:17). Charity is the *to be*, or the noun; love is the *to do*, or the verb. To love as Christ loved is the virtue of charity. Love, however, is also a noun and often used in the place of charity, such as in the scripture "God is love" (1 John 4:8). Perhaps the scriptures use them interchangeably, in part, to call attention to the verb aspect of love. Several scriptural passages illustrate how the Lord taught us that love is not something you *fall in,* but a choice, a verb that we are to act on.

Because of charity's encompassing nature, all other virtues might also be considered its synonyms. To all of the virtues listed in the scriptural definition of love, we could add all other positive attributes—charity is honest, it is patient, it is friendly, it is easily entreated, it is diligent, it is considerate, it is forgiving, it is of one heart, and so on. The manifestation of these contributing virtues in our life is strong evidence that we are growing in charity.

UNDERSTANDING LOVE THROUGH ITS ANTONYM—PRIDE

The antonym of a word not only helps define it, but also reveals the wisdom, truth, and power of it, and in the case of charity, helps us to understand its greatness and prominence among virtues.

The antonym of charity is pride. In his classic talk "Beware of Pride," President Ezra Taft Benson identified pride as the "universal sin" and enmity as the "central feature" of pride. He defined enmity as hatred, hostility, or a state of opposition toward *God* and our *fellowmen*.[21]

If hatred, hostility, or opposition toward God and our fellowmen is the central feature of the universal sin, then we could conclude that a love of God and our fellowmen would be the central feature of the universal virtue. The Savior taught the universal nature of charity when He commanded us to "love the Lord thy God with all thy heart, and with all thy soul, and with all thy mind. This is the first and great commandment. And the second is like unto it, Thou shalt love thy neighbour as thyself. On [this **virtue**]," He said, "hang all the law and the prophets."[22] Charity is the Savior's way, and the only way, to overcome pride.

We sometimes say that humility is the opposite of pride, and that is certainly true in part. But humility is only one component of what it means to love God. Loving God also means submitting our will to His, obeying His commandments, serving our fellow man, and so on. The more comprehensive opposite of pride is charity, which encompasses humility and every other aspect of loving God.

CHARITY		PRIDE
A love of God	vs.	Enmity toward God
A love of our fellow man	vs.	Enmity toward our fellow man

Is it any wonder, then, that Christ identified charity as the greatest virtue? Elder James E. Talmage called it the "first and great and all-embracing commandment . . . on the basis of the simple and mathematical truth that the whole law is greater than any part."[23]

"And if there be any other commandment, it is briefly comprehended in this saying, namely, Thou shalt love thy neighbour as thyself. Love worketh no ill to his neighbour: therefore love is the fulfilling of the law."[24]

In his talk on pride, President Benson spoke of a fear that is induced by pride: "The proud stand more in fear of men's judgment than of God's judgment. (See D&C 3:6–7; D&C 30:1–2; D&C 60:2.) 'What will men think of me?' weighs heavier than 'What will God think of me?' . . . Fear of men's judgment manifests itself in competition for men's approval. The proud love 'the praise of men more than the praise of God' (John 12:42–43)."

When fear is induced by pride (as opposed to a fear of spiders or heights or other phobia), it is an antonym of love, with crippling side effects. With this pride-induced fear there is a "reluctance to face or meet a person . . . cowardice and inhibition of action or utterance."[25] When pride is replaced by love, fear is also eliminated, because "There is no fear in love; but perfect love casteth out fear: because fear hath torment. He that feareth is not made perfect in love."[26] One indication that a person is growing in the attribute of charity is their overcoming pride-induced fear.

An examination of love and fear quickly reveals the many ways they are antonyms. Love is confident and long-suffering, while fear is angst-ridden and impatient. Love is kind, while fear is suspicious and evasive. Love "envieth not," while fear is ill-content. Love is meek and humble, while fear vaunts itself and is puffed up. Love "seeketh not her own," while fear is selfish and inward thinking. Love is not easily provoked, while fear offends easily. Love is not judgmental, while fear can't help but make comparisons. Love rejoices in truth and openness, while fear retreats into dark corners. Love looks and hopes for the best, while fear expects the worst. Love gives, while fear with-holds. Love seeks to understand and is forgiving, while fear blames and resents. Love is easily entreated or warm and welcoming, while fear is aloof. Love is expressive with a smiling countenance, while fear is glum. Love is filled with faith and optimism, while fear is hopeless and pessimistic.

It is insightful that the scripture doesn't say "love casteth out hate." That is because hate is nothing more than fear in disguise. Just as love, the universal virtue, blossoms into all its component virtues—joy, forgiveness, compassion, etc.—likewise pride, with its ever-present companion, fear, masquerades itself in a host of negative emotions, such as hate, prejudice, anger, envy, and so on.

For example, when a person is angry, what does he or she fear that actually brought on the anger? When a parent is angry with a child, what is it the parent fears—failure as a parent? fear of losing control? fear of the child going astray? fear of appearing an inept parent to others? Fear of a loss of property or wasted time due to damage or inconvenience caused by a child?

If a person cannot forgive, what is it that he or she fears? If people are prejudiced, what is it that they fear? If they are covetous or en-vious, what is it that they fear? In human relationships fear is the primary emotion of pride, but it usually reveals itself in a host of sec-ondary emotions.

Pride-induced fear causes us to commit both sins of commission and sins of omission. An example of a pride-induced sin of omission is mentioned in the parable of the talents: "And I was *afraid,* and went and hid thy talent in the earth."[27] At least one instance of hiding talents is those who "will not open their mouths, but they hide the talent which I have given unto them, because of the *fear* of man. Wo unto such, for mine anger is kindled against them."[28]

We also hide our talents through a sin of omission when we abstain from helping someone who is in need of loving correction. President Boyd K. Packer has taught the General Authorities, "If you see a need to correct [help] someone and you don't, you are thinking only of yourself." It may be human nature in such situations to hesitate in correcting others for *fear* of causing offense or hurt feelings. President Packer taught us to love a person enough to overcome whatever fears may be keeping us from providing the needed help and good deed.

On one occasion, President Packer invited me to his office to correct an error I had made. He asked, "Do you want this straight or sugar-coated?"

I said, "Please give it to me straight." He then sugar coated it and lovingly taught me. I love him because he loved me enough to help me and teach me, at the risk of possibly hurting my feelings. President Packer is a marvelous example of one who appears to have overcome all fear through love. Like Mormon, he speaks with "boldness, having authority from God; and [does not fear] what man can do; for perfect love casteth out all fear."[29]

A GIFT FOR ALL

The Lord counsels us, "Seek ye earnestly the best gifts . . . for there are many."[30] In referring to charity as "the greatest," Paul ranks it above all other gifts of the Spirit. Peter says we should have charity "above all things" (1 Pet. 4:8), and Mormon declares, "If ye have not charity, ye are nothing. . . . Wherefore, cleave unto charity, which is the greatest of all" (Moro. 7:46). Joseph F. Smith called charity "the

LOVE IS A CHOICE

greatest principle in existence."[31] The witnesses naming charity as the greatest among the gifts of the Spirit are many. After the gift of the Holy Ghost itself, there could be no greater gift to aid us in the pursuit of a happy personal, family, and home life.

The Lord is selective in the bestowal of many gifts of the Spirit: "To some is given one, and to some is given another"[32] However, there is no selectivity when it comes to the greatest gift of the Spirit. The Lord bestows it "upon *all* who are true followers of his Son, Jesus Christ."[33]

It is a good thing that charity is bestowed upon all followers of Christ, because to live as happily-ever-after families in the presence of God, we must become like Him and love as He loved. "Except ye have charity ye can in nowise be saved in the kingdom of God."[34]

From these scriptures and teachings, it should be obvious that the Lord defines love as a verb with corresponding behavior. Logically, then, it should be clear that true and mature love isn't something into which you fall. We are responsible for making it grow, and we have the capacity through our choices and actions to build loving eternal families. True love is to be discovered as a decision.

CHARITY: PRAY AND ACT

Elder David A. Bednar has powerfully taught that praying with faith must include getting up off our knees and acting:

"The classic example of asking in faith is Joseph Smith and the First Vision. As young Joseph was seeking to know the truth about religion, he read the following verses in the first chapter of James:

"'If any of you lack wisdom, let him ask of God, that giveth to all men liberally, and upbraideth not; and it shall be given him.

"'But let him ask in faith, nothing wavering' (James 1:5–6).

Please notice the requirement to ask in faith, which I understand to mean the necessity to not only express but to do, the dual obligation to both plead and to perform, the requirement to communicate and to act."[35]

Concerning the gift of charity, the Lord instructs us through the prophet Mormon to "pray unto the Father with all the energy of heart, that [we] may be filled with this love, which he hath bestowed upon all who are true followers of his Son, Jesus Christ."[36]

If we pray in faith for the gift of charity, then we must get up off our knees and seek for and develop the character traits listed by the Apostle Paul in 1 Corinthians 13. If we do not, our prayer is in vain, since "faith, if it hath not works, is dead, being alone."[37]

"I LOVE YOU": A COMMITMENT

Because love is as much a verb as it is a noun, the phrase "I love you" is as much a promise of behavior and commitment as it is an expression of feeling. When we choose to love (the verb) and decide to act by expressing and showing it, only then can the noun of love begin to blossom. That is the way faith works: "Ye receive no witness until after the trial of your faith."[38]

"I love you" is a phrase we should be using in our homes much more than we do. If we don't teach our children to use this phrase, they'll be uncomfortable with it throughout their lives and may not use it very much in their own marriages or with their own children. As my wife and I raised our children, we concluded our family prayer and scripture study each morning with everyone hugging each other person. Each said, "I love you"—brothers to sisters, sisters to brothers, parents to children, husband and wife to each other. It is a wonderful way to start the day and a good way to fulfill King Benjamin's advice to teach our children to love (see Mosiah 4:15). Scripturally, the Lord is very clear with us on this doctrine—you can't "fall out of love," because love is something you decide. Agency plays a fundamental role in our relationships with one another. This being true, we must make the conscious decision that we will love our spouse and family with all our heart, soul, and mind; that we will build, not "fall into," strong, loving marriages and families. Remember, "Don't just pray to marry the one you love. *Instead, pray to love the one you marry.*"[39]

Let us hearken to President Hinckley's counsel: "I lift a warning voice to our people. We have moved too far toward the mainstream of society in this matter. Now, of course, there are good families. There are good families everywhere. But there are too many who are in trouble. This is a malady with a cure. The prescription is simple and wonderfully effective. *It is love.* It is plain, simple, everyday love and respect. It is a tender plant that needs nurturing. But it is worth all of the effort we can put into it."[40]

It is only by our constant, committed effort that we will make the love we share with our spouse a constant for eternity.

SUMMARY

- Because love is a choice, you can't "fall" out of love. True love is not something you fall in, but *grow* in. It is not happenstance as much as something you control, choose, and act upon.
- If love can be taught, it can be learned.
- Christlike virtues are necessary to convert infatuation into a lasting love, one "that never faileth" (1 Cor. 13:8).
- Because love is a commandment, we are expected by the Lord to choose to love.
- True love is defined by the Savior.

- Charity, or the pure love of Christ, is the greatest gift of the Spirit and the foremost gift in forging a happy life and a successful marriage and family.
- Charity is the universal virtue and embraces all other virtues.
- Charity is the opposite of pride and casts out fear.
- We are to pray in faith for the gift of charity, acting upon the virtues included in the definition of charity.
- The phrase "I love you" is a promise of behavior as much as it is an expression of feeling. As an act of faith, we must first choose to love before love can grow.

NOTES

1. Mary Roach, "Much 'I Do' about Mr. Right," *Reader's Digest,* Dec. 1998, 162.
2. Gordon B. Hinckley, "Living Worthy of the Girl You Will Someday Marry," *Ensign,* May 1998, 51; emphasis added.
3. Johann Wolfgang von Goethe, 1749—1832.
4. "Why Character Counts," *Reader's Digest,* Jan. 1999, 135.
5. *The Teachings of Spencer W. Kimball,* ed. Edward L. Kimball (1982), 248.
6. "The Family: A Proclamation to the World," *Ensign,* Nov. 2010, 129.
7. Gordon B. Hinckley, "A Conversation with Single Adults," *Ensign,* Mar. 1997, 60.
8. Gordon B. Hinckley, "Look to the Future," *Ensign,* Nov. 1997, 69.
9. Matthew 22:37, 39.
10. Matthew 22:40.
11. Mosiah 4:15.
12. Doctrine and Covenants 42:22.
13. Matthew 19:19; emphasis added.
14. John 13:34; emphasis added.
15. Jeffrey R. Holland, *Christ and the New Covenant* (Salt Lake City: Deseret Book, 1997), 336.
16. Neal A. Maxwell's "Wintry Doctrine" as shared by Elder Bruce C. Hafen in "The Story of *A Disciple's Life*: Preparing the Biography of Elder Neal A. Maxwell."
17. Galatians 5:14.
18. See 1 Nephi 11:25.
19. A *Deseret News* article from Wednesday, March 20, 2013, titled, "BYU, USU study says marriage thrives on shared chores, strong dad-child bond" states, "Husbands who work alongside their wives on household tasks and who participate in child

rearing are more apt to be in marriages described by both spouses as happy and high-quality, according to researchers from BYU, the University of Missouri and Utah State University. The researchers found that the 'very strongest effect' on whether either moms or dads viewed the marriage as happy was the woman's perception of the quality of dad's relationship with the kids . . . , [This was followed by] the wife's perception of how her husband takes care of the kids, [and] whether dad helps her with them." An apron may very well be the purchase that gives you the greatest return of all investments.

20. 2 Nephi 26:30.
21. See Ezra Taft Benson, "Beware of Pride," *Ensign,* May 1989, 4; emphasis added.
22. Matthew 22:37–40.
23. James E. Talmage, *Jesus the Christ* (1981), 551.
24. Romans 13:9–10.
25. *Merriam-Webster's Collegiate Dictionary.* 11th ed. (Springfield, MA: Merriam-Webster, 2003).
26. 1 John 4:18; see also Moroni 8:16.
27. Matthew 25:25; emphasis added.
28. Doctrine and Covenants 60:2; emphasis added.
29. Moroni 8:16.
30. Doctrine and Covenants 46:8, 11.
31. Conference Report, April 1917, 4.
32. Doctrine and Covenants 46:12.
33. Moroni 7:48; emphasis added.
34. Moroni 10:21; see also Ether 12:34.
35. David A. Bednar, "Ask in Faith," *Ensign*, May 2008, 94.
36. Moroni 7:48.
37. James 2:17.
38. Ether 12:6.
39. Spencer W. Kimball, quoted in Joe J. Christensen, "Marriage and the Great Plan of Happiness," *Ensign,* May 1995, 64.
40. Hinckley, "Look to the Future," 69; emphasis added.

CHAPTER 2

LOVE AND 100% RESPONSIBILITY

L et me return to one of the fourteen attributes of true Christlike love: "charity seeketh not her own." Look at the cartoon of this couple in a bookstore. It is a powerful, five-second sermon. The spouse improvement section is sold out, but the self-improvement section has scarcely sold a book. Does it remind you of any of the Savior's teachings, perhaps dealing with "motes" and "beams" in eyes?

Your success in marriage will largely depend on your ability to reverse the trend shown in this cartoon and focus on taking responsibility for improving *yourself* rather than trying to reshape your spouse. Your marriage will be improved if you focus on strengthening your own weaknesses and making your spouse happy rather than expecting your spouse to make you happy. There is greater power in giving than in getting. This is counsel that comes from the wisest of all marriage counselors.

> # The eyes=
> # They see

This clever anagram appears to speak a truth, but according to John Medina, author of *Brain Rules,* "The eyes don't see. We do not see with our eyes; we see with our brains."[1] For example, in a very simple way, optical illusions and magic tricks demonstrate how the eyes can be deceived into believing something that is not true. Conversely, the scriptures are full of examples of people who *saw* but still would not believe that which was true—"But though he had done so many miracles before them, yet they believed not on him" (John 12:37). The scriptures disprove, over and over again, the popular adage that "seeing is believing."

"FOR AS HE THINKETH IN HIS HEART, SO IS HE" (Prov. 23:7)

The brain's imaging system creates our dreams by night and interprets what we see by day. Because everyone's brain is different, people simply do not always see eye to eye. Each person sees and interprets the world differently. That is why opposing fans at a sporting event can have two totally different opinions regarding a call made by the referee. It isn't that one side is lying; it's just that people's desires can easily become their perception and reality, or what many psychologists call *confirmation bias* or *myside bias.*[2] Demosthenes, an ancient Greek statesman and orator, phrased it well: "Nothing is easier than self-deceit. For what each man wishes, that he also believes to be true."[3] In defending their wishes, biased people tend to only see and gather evidence in support of their own opinion, while being blind to any contrary evidence, often resulting in a self-fulfilled prophecy.

It is because of this human frailty that when relationships are stressed or fail there is a tendency for each person to believe the other is at fault. Logically, every problem can't always be the other person's fault. The reason political parties exist, courts convene, and marital misunderstandings occur is that there always seem to be two sides to a story. None of us are exempt. We have all had disagreements with others; most likely with loved ones more than anyone else, since that is with whom most of our time is spent and where we tend to let our guard down. "We see in the world what we carry in our hearts," said Goethe, the German poet and philosopher. And because people's hearts hold different beliefs, views, and opinions, there will always be two or more sides to a story and tension in relationships. Without love in the home, Satan can easily turn *tension* into con-*tention,* resulting in destructive finger-pointing, hurt feelings, and estrangement.

ELIMINATING CONTENTION WITH 100% RESPONSIBILITY

We can increase love in our relationships, especially in the home, by better understanding what causes contention and how to use our agency to eliminate it. We must learn the wise use of agency in contentious situations and understand the power that comes with the scriptural directive to the children of men "to act for themselves and not to be acted upon" by contentious devices (2 Ne. 2:26).

The gift of agency is the ability and privilege to make our own choices—to be in *control* of our lives. The battle in premortality was not for "partial agency" but total, complete—*100% agency*. Stated differently, the one perfect parent never forces His children. He shows us the way, and may even command us, but "nevertheless, thou mayest choose for thyself, for it is given unto thee" (Moses 3:17).

Assuming responsibility for our choices is agency's complementary doctrine.[4] Agency and responsibility always go together. *Responsibility* in agency consists of recognizing oneself as the cause for the effects or results of one's choices. Gospel doctrine teaches us that all people are responsible for the use of their agency and will be "punished for their own sins" (A of F 1:2).[5]

- The doctrinal corollary to 100% agency is 100% responsibility. We are wholly responsible for our choices and their consequences. "If we choose the wrong road, we also choose the wrong destination."[6] It isn't just a heavenly principle, but a law of nature—we reap what we sow. We repeatedly read in President Thomas S. Monson writings that "decisions determine destiny. One can't make eternal decisions without eternal consequences."[7]
- "And now remember, remember, my brethren, that whosoever perisheth, perisheth *unto himself;* and whosoever doeth iniquity, doeth it *unto himself;* for behold, ye are free; ye are permitted to act for yourselves; for behold, God hath given unto you a knowledge and he hath made you free" (Hel. 14:30).
- We control choice but not the consequences of that choice.

When the Savior said, "And ye shall know the truth, and the truth shall make you free," he was referring to the liberating blessings of the Atonement—not only freedom from sin, but freedom from the embarrassing, shameful, painful, or enslaving effects of poor choices, as well as sin.[8] "We are free, not because we can choose, but because we have chosen well."[9] Ultimately it isn't our abilities and talents that make us who we are, but our choices.

When conflict occurs in relationships, we must rely on the Savior's teachings to help us navigate the turbulent waters. One gospel principle to keep in mind is that we have zero control over other people's agency. We do, however, have 100% control over the way we respond to them.

A loving mother once gave some wise counsel to her daughter, who was upset and unhappy with a struggling marriage. She had her daughter draw a vertical line down the middle of a sheet of paper and write down on the left side all the things her husband did that bothered her. Then on the right side of the paper the daughter was to write down her usual response to each offense. The mother then had her daughter cut the paper in half, separating the two lists. "Now throw the paper with your husband's faults in the garbage," she instructed. "If you want to be happy and achieve marital success, stop focusing on your husband's faults and focus instead on your own behavior and reaction. Examine the way you are responding to the things your husband does that bother you, and see if you can respond in a different, more positive way." This mother understood the power and wisdom of 100% responsibility. (A different approach is needed in cases of abuse, as will be discussed later.)

AGENCY WITHOUT RESPONSIBILITY

A common strategy of each Book of Mormon anti-Christ was to separate agency from responsibility. We could call one version of agency without responsibility the Korihor principle: "Every man conquered according to his strength; and whatsoever a man did *was no crime*" (Alma 30:17; emphasis added). With negative consequences discarded, agency is unbridled, as if there were no day of reckoning. Another version could rightfully be labeled the Nehor principle: "All mankind should be saved at the last day, and that they need not fear nor tremble, but that they might lift up their heads and rejoice; for the Lord had created all men, and had also redeemed all men; and, in the end, all men should have eternal life" (Alma 1:4). What an attractive offer for those inclined to see things only through their own bias! The Nehor principle depends entirely on mercy and *denies justice,* or responsibility, altogether. Still others separated responsibility from agency by saying, "Eat, drink, and be merry; nevertheless, fear God—he will justify in committing a little sin" (2 Ne. 28:8).

The Savior labeled faith without works as "dead, being alone" (James 2:17). Faith without works, mercy without justice, and agency without responsibility are all different verses of the same song. With each, the natural man discards accountability in his attempt to remove guilt from the forbidden. It is akin to paying for indulgences, but much easier—this way it is free! No wonder the broad path is filled with so many—it is a no-holds-barred pleasure fest! (3 Ne. 14:13).

Sadly for those deceived, there are *two* days of reckoning—the day-after hangover they experience in this life when they discover for themselves that "wickedness never was happiness" (Alma 41:10) and again at Judgment Day when they "shall confess before God that his judgments are just" (Mosiah 16:1).

Agency without responsibility is one of the foremost anti-Christian doctrines, very cunning in its nature and very destructive in its results.

THE ANTI-RESPONSIBILITY LIST

We have identified fear as the common emotion of pride. Overcoming pride requires us to be responsible for our feelings and behavior by loving others and overcoming those fears.

The following is a very cunning list of the antonyms of responsibility, each resulting in significant damage to a person's life and relationships. This anti-responsibility list consists of things people commonly say or do to avoid responsibility, along with some scriptural examples. You will find that fear is a common element in each:

- **Blame others**—Saul blames others for his disobedience: "But *the people took* of the spoil, sheep and oxen" (1 Sam. 15:21; emphasis added).
- **Self-justify**—Saul justifies his disobedience: "*To sacrifice* unto the Lord . . . And Samuel said, Hath the Lord as great delight in burnt offerings and sacrifices, as in obeying the voice of the Lord?" (1 Sam. 15:21–22; emphasis added).
- **Make excuses**—"Laman and Lemuel again began to murmur, saying: *How is it possible* that the Lord will deliver Laban into our hands? Behold, he is a mighty man, and he can command fifty, yea, even he can slay fifty; then why not us?" (1 Ne. 3:31; emphasis added).

- **Hide**—"And Adam and [Eve] went to *hide themselves* from the presence of the Lord" (Moses 4:14; emphasis added).
- **Cover up**—The prophet Nathan rebukes David: "Thou hast killed Uriah . . . and hast taken his wife to be thy wife . . . For thou *didst it secretly*" (2 Sam. 12:9, 12; emphasis added).
- **Flee/Avoid**—"But Jonah rose up to *flee* unto Tarshish from the presence of the Lord" (Jonah 1:3; emphasis added).
- **Abandon**—Alma to his son Corianton: "Thou didst do that which was grievous unto me; for thou didst *forsake* the ministry" (Alma 39:3; emphasis added).
- **Deny/Lie**—"And Saul said . . . *I have performed the commandment* of the Lord. And Samuel said, What meaneth then this bleating of the sheep in mine ears . . . ?" (1 Sam. 15:13, 14; emphasis added).
- **Rebel**—Samuel rebukes Saul: "For *rebellion* . . . Because thou hast rejected the word of the Lord, he hath also rejected thee from being king" (1 Sam. 15:23; emphasis added).
- **Complain/Murmur**—"And all the children of Israel *murmured* against Moses and . . . said . . . Would God that we had died in the land of Egypt!" (Num. 14:2; emphasis added).
- **Find fault and get angry**—"And it came to pass that Laman was *angry* with me, and also with my father; and also was Lemuel" (1 Ne. 3:28; emphasis added).
- **Make demands/entitlements**—"We will not that our younger brother shall be a ruler over us. And it came to pass that Laman and Lemuel did take me and bind me with cords, and they did treat me with much harshness" (1 Ne. 18:10, 11).
- **Doubt, Despair, Give up, Lose hope, Quit**—"They began to

murmur against me, saying: Our brother is a fool . . . for they did not believe that I could build a ship" (1 Ne. 17:17–18).

- **Wallow in self-pity**—"Behold, these many years we have suffered in the wilderness, which time we might have enjoyed our possessions and the land of our inheritance; yea, and we might have been happy (1 Ne. 17:21).

- **Undecided**—"And Elijah came unto all the people, and said, *How long halt ye* between two opinions? if the LORD *be* God, follow him: but if Baal, *then* follow him" (1 Kgs. 18:21; emphasis added).

- **Procrastinate**—"But behold, your days of probation are past; *ye have procrastinated* the day of your salvation until it is everlastingly too late" (Hel. 13:38; emphasis added).

- **Enable**—Eli does not discipline his sons for their sins: "Wherefore kick ye at my sacrifice and . . . *honourest thy sons above me* . . . ?" (1 Sam. 2:22, 29; emphasis added).

- **Fear**—"And *I was afraid,* and went and hid thy talent in the earth. . . . His lord answered and said unto him, Thou wicked and slothful servant" (Matt. 25:25–26; emphasis added).

A PERSON'S CHARACTER AND THE ANTI-RESPONSIBILITY LIST

When reading 1 Nephi and 2 Nephi, we can only try to imagine how difficult it was for the members of Lehi's family to face their trials. Leaving their home in Jerusalem, like the Saints leaving Nauvoo, would have been heart-wrenching. Obtaining the brass plates seemed impossible. Hardships that they endured in the wilderness for eight years would have been tough for anyone. The responsibility that their prophet-father was placing upon Laman, Lemuel, and Nephi was extremely difficult. As difficult as a responsibility may be, "difficulty is the one excuse that history never accepts,"[10] as is so graphically illustrated in the case of Laman and Lemuel.

Difficult situations often become the foremost trials of one's faith. Part of these tests is seeing whether we will go forward with a believing heart (see D&C 64:34) or a doubting heart (see D&C 58:29), or if we will go forward at all. A difficult situation reveals a person's character and either strengthens it, as with Nephi, or weakens and corrupts it, as with Laman and Lemuel, who were guilty of nearly every item on the anti-responsibility list. They are the epitome of irresponsible.

It is important to recognize that excuses never equal results, nor do they correct mistakes. In the case of Laman and Lemuel, all the excuses in the world could never obtain the plates. The reason Nephi obtained the plates and Laman and Lemuel didn't is because Nephi never turned to the anti-responsibility list. He was a champion, and champions don't resort to a list of excuses. As Elder David B. Haight stated, "A determined man finds a way; the other man finds an excuse."[11] Using the excuses on the anti-responsibility list destroyed Laman and Lemuel. It is an extremely dangerous list.

Because the natural man is selfish by nature, he only thinks of himself. Going to the anti-responsibility list is his prideful defense mechanism against the fear of failure and the pain and negative consequences of his mistakes and sin. He uses the anti-responsibility list:

- **To avoid shame or public ridicule**. He doesn't want to appear wrong and be embarrassed in front of others. He hopes it will keep others from examining his behavior. It makes his unsatisfactory behavior or performance seem acceptable or tolerable.

- **To eliminate guilt.** Shame is embarrassment before others; guilt is shame before God. It is the internal pain or private awareness and disappointment in oneself. Rather than repent to eliminate the guilt, Satan tempts the natural man to go to the list to displace it. Doing so gives guilty parties a false sense that someone else is to blame, and therefore, they are still in alignment with God's will.
- **To avoid stress, distress, and anxiety.** However, the list is a false sedative, and only masks the true problem.
- **To justify inaction.** If he is not responsible, then there is no wrong to correct and no repentance needed.
- **To take an easy path.** It is easier to do nothing—the natural man is lazy and takes the path of least resistance.

The anti-responsibility list could also be called the anti-faith list, because it halts progress dead in its tracks. Pride paralyzes progress with fear. It is a cunning strategy used by Satan to cause a person to subtly surrender his or her agency. The person is no longer in control or "acting;" rather, he or she becomes a victim who is being acted upon, and Satan cleverly begins to take control. Using this list is a form of self-deception and self-betrayal.

THE POWER AND REWARD OF BEING RESPONSIBLE

Everyone occasionally fails in their attempts at success, just as Nephi did with his brothers on their first two trips to try to obtain the brass plates. But achievers accept responsibility for their mistakes and sins. They repent, get back on their feet, dust themselves off, and continue forward in faith. They may give an explanation or a reason for their lack of success, but not an excuse.

With an *excuse* an individual is avoiding responsibility. With a *reason* the individual is accepting responsibility but is explaining what went wrong. At first glance it may appear that Adam was blaming Eve when he said, "*The woman thou gavest me, . . .* she gave me of the fruit." However, when Adam subsequently adds, "And I did eat," we are given to understand that he accepted responsibility for his actions and was giving an explanation, not blaming Eve. Eve in turn also said, "And I did eat" (Moses 4:18–19; emphasis added).

When people avoid taking responsibility in their lives, they are "following the lines of least resistance, that makes rivers and men crooked."[12] Take a high-school dropout, for example. What appeared to be the easy road initially almost always ends up being the most difficult and least rewarding. Not being responsible is being short-sighted. It is self-betrayal and a means of giving up on oneself and sometimes others.

The following examples illustrate the power and reward of being responsible.

THE DISTRIBUTION CENTER

In 1983 a few partners and I started a new company originally called The Franklin Institute, which taught time-management seminars and created and sold the Franklin Day Planner. The company grew fast, and it wasn't long before we were teaching hundreds of seminars each month.

For corporate seminars, our consultants traveled to the client's headquarters and taught at their corporate training facilities. Prior to the seminar, two employees in our distribution center would prepare and ship several boxes of training materials to be used during the seminar.

The two distribution center employees would normally send the seminar shipment 10 days before the seminar. Upon arrival at the seminar location, our consultants needed only to open the boxes, distribute the materials to the participants, and teach the seminar. With up to 250 seminars being taught each month, these two employees would often commit errors such as not shipping sufficient quantities or omitting certain materials or not shipping on time, etc. This became an irritating and often embarrassing frustration for the consultants. The seminar division of our company was more than a little bothered by the situation.

When these problems occurred and we spoke with these two employees about errors and system improvements, they never wanted to accept responsibility for their mistakes. They would blame others, saying things like, "It's not our fault—the seminar division filled out the Seminar Shipment Request form incorrectly. It's their fault. You can't blame us!" Or they might say, "We shipped it on time, but the freight company delivered it late. You can't blame us!" Another excuse was, "A subsidiary packaged the individual seminar kits with errors, and we shipped the kits as they were given to us—it's their fault." It seemed these two employees were never responsible for the errors, and so the errors continued.

Then something critical happened. The director of training for a large international company attended one of our seminars and was so thrilled with it that she invited us to teach a pilot seminar to her company's top fifty executives. When the day of the seminar arrived, our consultant opened the boxes of materials and discovered that the seminar guidebooks were missing. Without the seminar guidebooks, how would the participants follow along and take notes? The training director was panic-stricken. Our consultant did the best he could by making sure each participant was given a pad of paper on which to take notes, and the seminar turned out reasonably well even without the guidebook.

Extremely embarrassed and angry, the company's training director called our seminar division and said, "You will never teach here again! How could you have made such an inexcusable error with our pilot seminar?!"

An upset senior vice president called me: "This is the last straw—we are just about to lose a million-dollar account because of the distribution center's errors. We can't tolerate these errors!"

As one of the owners of the company, I couldn't tolerate such errors either. At the same time, I did not want to see these two bread-winners fired. After pondering possible solutions, I decided to implement an incentive system to motivate these two employees to be more careful. For each seminar shipped correctly they would receive one additional dollar, for a possibility of an extra $250 each month—not a huge bonus, but nothing to sneeze at, either. However, if they made one error, a one-dollar loss wasn't a big deal. I therefore decided to also include two $100 bonuses for no errors. If they committed one error they lost not only one dollar, but the first $100 bonus. I wanted the first error to hurt. If they made a second error, they lost the second $100 bonus.

I also told them, "If there is an error, you will lose your bonus, regardless of where the error originates. You are 100% responsible for the shipment."

"That's not fair," they responded. "What happens if the seminar division fills out the Seminar Shipment Request incorrectly?"

I said, "You will lose your bonus. You are 100% responsible for that shipment's success."

"That's not fair! What happens if we send the shipment on time, but the freight company delivers it late?"

"You will lose your bonus. You are 100% responsible."

"That's not fair! What happens if a subsidiary commits errors in pre-packaging the individual seminar kits? You can't blame us for their mistakes!"

"You will lose your bonus," I once again responded. "You are 100% responsible for that shipment's success—do you understand?"

"THAT ISN'T FAIR!"

"Well, it may not seem fair, but that's life—you will lose your bonus."

They were unhappy with the conditions, but they finally accepted the responsibility—they had no choice if they wanted that bonus. In setting these conditions, I eliminated the self-defeating anti-responsibility list that destroyed Laman and Lemuel. The employees now understood that they could no longer blame, make excuses, or justify errors—even when they were right and it *was* someone else's fault!

What happened next was fascinating. When the employees received an order from the seminar division they would call the division to review the form item by item. They took responsibility for correcting any errors committed by the seminar division. They began to read the freight company's shipping/delivery form to make sure the correct delivery date was entered. They changed their shipping schedule and began to send the shipment three or four days earlier than their customary schedule. A few days before the seminar, they would call the client company to verify receipt of the shipment and the contents. If they somehow omitted any materials, they had three or four extra days to send missing items by express shipment. Errors finally stopped, and they began to earn their bonus month after month. It was a life-changing experience for them to learn firsthand the power, control, and reward of 100% responsibility.

What these two employees learned is that when they blamed someone else, they were essentially saying, "We don't control the shipment's success. Control is in the hands of the seminar division, or in the hands of the freight company, or subsidiary companies, and until they straighten up their act the errors will continue." They learned that responsibility is as much a blessing as is agency—they always go hand-in-hand. They learned that all excuses are avoidance techniques that keep you from taking control of your life.

> **Empowering principle:** It is self-defeating to blame, make excuses, or justify mistakes or failure, *even when you are right!* This is worth repeating—*even when you are right!* The moment you do any of these self-defeating things, you lose control of the positive outcomes you are seeking. You surrender your power and influence when you use the anti-responsibility list.

PUTTING MY MARRIAGE BEFORE MY PRIDE

"Like any couple, my husband and I have had disagreements during our marriage. But one incident stands out in my mind. I no longer recall the reason for our disagreement, but we ended up not speaking at all, and I remember feeling that it was all my husband's fault. I felt I had done absolutely nothing for which I needed to apologize.

"As the day went by, I waited for my husband to say he was sorry. Surely he could see how wrong he was. It must be obvious how much he had hurt my feelings. I felt I had to stand up for myself; it was the principle that mattered.

"As the day was drawing to a close, I started to realize that I was waiting in vain, so I went to the Lord in prayer. I prayed that my husband would realize what he had done and how it was hurting our marriage. I prayed that he would be inspired to apologize so we could end our disagreement.

"As I was praying, I felt a strong impression that I should go to my husband and apologize. I was a bit shocked by this impression and immediately pointed out in my prayer that I had done nothing wrong and therefore should not have to say I was sorry. A thought came strongly to my mind: 'Do you want to be right, or do you want to be married?'

"As I considered this question, I realized that I could hold on to my pride and not give in until he apologized, but how long would that take? Days? I was miserable while we weren't speaking to each other. I understood that while this incident itself wouldn't be the end of our marriage, if I were always unyielding, that might cause serious damage over the years. I decided it was more important to have a happy, loving marriage than to keep my pride intact over something that would later seem trivial.

"I went to my husband and apologized for upsetting him. He also apologized, and soon we were happy and united again in love.

"Since that time there have been occasions when I have needed to ask myself that question again: 'Do you want to be right, or do you want to be married?' How grateful I am for the great lesson I learned the first time I faced that question. It has always helped me realign my perspective and put my husband and my marriage before my own pride."[13]

> **Empowering principle:** In a marriage or compan-ionship, a 50% attitude on both parts may seem logical, but only a 100% attitude will close the door to the anti-responsibility list.

In this story, the sister learned that *even if she may have been right, blaming was counterproductive,* causing her to lose control over posi-tive outcomes. Insisting on being right is prideful and often the road-block to peace. In the repentance process, a responsible person says "I am sorry" as a vital part of asking for forgiveness in the steps of remorse and restitution.

In being the first to forgive, this sister followed the incomparable example of the Savior in being the first to love.

THE DINNER EXCUSE

A husband arrived late at a restaurant for a dinner appointment with his wife—not the first time he had done this. But he explained that he had a good excuse—a client meeting had run over. When he arrived at the restaurant, he apologized and told his wife he hadn't meant to be late but couldn't help it. This explanation did not soothe her—in fact, it seemed to make things worse.

The man described this experience later to a friend, who ex-plained that he had made a classic mistake. The friend replied, "Your mistake was that you were stuck in your own perspective. It doesn't matter that you didn't mean to be late—your lateness still affected your wife and her feelings." In such situations we tend to focus too much on the facts and completely ignore how our spouse feels, which is the more important issue.

Even though the husband's explanation sounded responsible and sincere, it was still an *excuse*. He was trying to *justify* himself and convince his wife that being late is acceptable if you have a good enough excuse. If he had really been sorry, he would have been thinking more about how he inconvenienced her and acknowledged her feelings. He would have empathized more (loving and responsible thinking) rather than justifying (selfish and irresponsible thinking).

> **Empowering principle:** For the expression "I'm sorry" to be truly sincere it has to be expressed with love and empathy, not merely to excuse oneself. Resolution to conflict is best achieved when we are selfless enough to truly see our partner's point of view. When disagreements arise, strive to understand before trying to be understood. True love "seeketh not her own."

He then realized that what he should have said to his wife was, "I understand that you're angry. I'm sorry you've been waiting for me for so long, and not for the first time. It must seem that I give client meetings higher priority than plans with you. That must be frustrating. It will not happen again." And then he should stick to that promise.

In their book *How to Improve Your Marriage Without Talking*

About It, Patricia Love and Steven Stosny share this insight: "Any attempt to talk about [a problem] while you [and your partner] are disconnected will make it worse. The trick to achieving the kind of connection you want is to develop the advanced relationship skill of binocular vision, the artful ability to see your partner's perspective as well as your own."

THE GREATEST EXAMPLE OF ALL

The Savior clearly never turned to the anti-responsibility list. He was the most responsible person in the history of the world. Even in His moments of deepest pain and anguish He showed no self-pity, one of the dysfunctional items on the list. He was always thinking outwardly with His ever-selfless care and concern for others; restoring a soldier's ear in Gethsemane and later on the cross praying for those who despitefully used Him.

Charity is a deep sense of responsibility for the temporal and spiritual welfare of another. The more we are like Jesus Christ, the less likely we are to judge unrighteously, to give up on someone, or to quit a worthy cause. We will be reluctant to blame others. Christ is perfect, we are not. He was innocent, we are guilty. Yet out of love, He became responsible for us. Because He is perfect in His long-suffering, He never gives up on us. People may give up on themselves, but He doesn't give up on them: "I will have compassion upon you" (D&C 64:2); "Notwithstanding their sins, my bowels are filled with compassion towards them" (101:9); "I will be merciful unto your weakness" (38:14); "As often as my people repent will I forgive them" (Mosiah 26:30).

We learn from the Savior that compassion, patience, and long-suffering are opposites of blaming and that responsibility for the spiritual welfare of others is among the most important elements of charity.

In His relationships with others the Savior always saw clearly and perfectly because there was never a mote in His eye.[14] Truth was always on His side, 100% of the time. With His perfect discernment, He was able to accurately see the weaknesses in others. With truth on His side, He could have been impatient with or critical of the shortcomings of His disciples, but He wasn't. His disciples said of Him, "We love him, because he first loved us" (1 John 4:19). What a powerful principle for us to adopt in our families! He did not come to find fault, criticize, and blame. He came to build up, edify, and save.[15] President Boyd K. Packer said it this way: "As you give what you have, there is a replacement, with increase!"[16]

ELIMINATE THE ANTI-RESPONSIBILITY LIST FROM YOUR LIFE

- It doesn't help a student to blame the teacher for a poor report card, even if the teacher is mediocre. Blaming is a form of self-pity and usually involves a surrendering of one's initiative and control over positive outcomes.
- It doesn't help the teacher to blame a student for poor performance. Even if the students are uncooperative or lack motivation, the moment the teacher blames them she or he surrenders power to improve the class, because the burden to improve now rests upon the students.
- Poor results in a missionary companionship should never be blamed on a lazy companion. The moment a missionary blames a companion (or the area, or the ward, or the weather, etc.) for lack of success; his or her own victim mentality allows failure to become a self-fulfilling prophecy.
- Even if your spouse manages money poorly or is not as neat

and orderly as you are, you lose control over possible happy outcomes when you conclude that he or she is the one who must change before you can be happy. In what ways can you be more responsible for happier outcomes?

- Even if your spouse is not as romantic as he or she used to be, or is a poor communicator, or seems more interested in business, hobbies, sports, or socializing than the family, you lose control over possible happy outcomes when you think your spouse is the only one that needs to change. There may be many creative solutions to these challenges when you begin to ponder on things you can do to improve the situation rather than hoping all positive change must come from the other person.

Whatever your circumstances may be, it is time to eliminate the anti-responsibility or anti-faith list from your life. It is not a list for winners or champions. It is an anti-success list. The day you eliminate the list from your life is the day you take back control of your life and when positive outcomes begin to increase and love begins to blossom. Being 100% responsible is the love-induced courage to confront your fears—or your shame, guilt, pain, and failure—head-on. It is accepting yourself as the person in control of your life and destiny. If others are at fault and have to change before further progress is made, then you are at their mercy and they are in control of the outcomes in your life. Agency and responsibility are inseparably connected. You cannot avoid one without also losing or negatively impacting the other.

The only way to close the door on the anti-responsibility list is by accepting 100% responsibility. Anything less leaves the door open for a retreat to the list. We should be of the attitude, "I'm in charge of my life and I wouldn't have it any other way!" It was with this same enthusiasm that we shouted for joy in our premortal life as we contemplated the use of agency and responsibility in mortality.[17]

RESPONSIBILITY TO REPENT AND FORGIVE

When we consider the ultimate in clean places of the world, laboratory cleanrooms used for scientific research are the epitome. But even the most sterile of labs is not 100% free of contaminants. Some level of impurity must be tolerated of necessity.

Now consider the possibility of spiritual impurities in heaven. We know that "no unclean thing can enter into his kingdom" (3 Ne. 27:19). Does that mean zero tolerance? Can the Lord look upon sin with some degree of allowance—maybe a miniscule or infinitesimal amount? Doesn't mercy allow for a little bit of impurity, a spot or two?

The Lord's answer is unequivocal: "For I the Lord cannot look upon sin with the *least degree* of allowance" (D&C 1:31; emphasis added). However, the Lord doesn't want that declaration of absoluteness to leave us hopeless: "Nevertheless, he that repents and does the commandments of the Lord shall be forgiven" (D&C 1:32). His grace is upon all "those who love [him] and keep *all* [his] commandments, and him that *seeketh so to do*" (D&C 46:9; emphasis added).

If the Lord cannot look upon sin with even the least degree of allowance, what law of the gospel demands 100% responsibility for sin? "For behold, justice exerciseth *all* his demands, and also mercy claimeth all which is her own; and thus, none but the truly penitent are saved. What, do ye suppose that mercy can rob justice? I say unto you, Nay; *not one whit*. If so, God would cease to be God" (Alma 42:24–25; emphasis added).

RESPONSIBILITY AND REPENTANCE

Not in the "least degree" and "not one whit" are other ways of saying that God holds His children 100% responsible for the use of their agency. The extreme danger of the anti-responsibility or anti-faith list is that it blinds its victims to the need for repentance. Laman and Lemuel, for example, didn't see a need to repent, because everything was Nephi's fault. We may ask, "If it's not my fault, why should I repent?" The one blinded can't even take the first step in the repentance process, which is to recognize sin or mistakes.

It has been said that "the greatest of faults is to be conscious of none."[18] If you are not conscious of a fault, how can you possibly correct it? Pride is the universal and underlying sin to all items on the anti-responsibility list. President Ezra Taft Benson defined pride as enmity toward God and man. He then defined enmity as hatred, hostility, or opposition.[19] Which of these three—hatred, hostility, or opposition—involves blaming others? All of them do—think about it.

Clearly, all items on the list are very prideful. Whenever there is contention in a relationship, there pride will be also. Any contention, whether it was gossip by the Pharisees or the less hostile Martha-judging-Mary kind of opposition, always brought forth a rebuke from the Savior.

President Benson taught that pride is easy to see in others but difficult to see in ourselves.[20] Pride is like bad breath—obvious to everyone except the offender. Pride blinds people to their own faults and thus takes them to the anti-responsibility list, the enemy of repentance. Only those who are humble and rely on the help of the Spirit can recognize how the list might be negatively impacting their life, family, or marriage. Once we eliminate the list from our lives, then repentance, change, and progress begin to accelerate, and we draw nearer to the Savior. In drawing nearer to Him we simultaneously discover we are drawing nearer to our families and growing in love. He is not only the way to eternal life, but the way to marital bliss.

RESPONSIBILITY AND CONFESSING

What does confessing a serious sin have to do with 100% responsibility? Which words on the anti-responsibility list are synonymous with not confessing? Not confessing begins with fear, which leads to many other items on the list, including hiding, procrastinating, and possibly blaming, making excuses, self-justifying, or covering up.

We have defined 100% responsibility as the love-induced courage to confront our fears, embarrassment, shame, and guilt. That kind of courage is especially needed for confession. Confessing is vocalizing the sorrow you are feeling in your heart. Only then come the priceless gems of forgiveness, cleansing, and sanctification as you accept responsibility and exercise faith unto repentance.

As a bishop I learned that confessing is more of a gift from a loving Father in Heaven than it is discipline. He knew He could forgive truly penitent people, but He also knew they might have a difficult time forgiving themselves. Confessing is a catharsis that finally helps them purge their mind and heart of the mental garbage that has been yoking them. Even though they may be facing some measure of discipline, they are finally able to "dump" the garbage in the bishop's office, and they experience a peace and joy that has been missing from their life for a very long time. This "unyoking" is perhaps, in part, what the Savior meant when He said, "For my yoke is easy, and my burden is light" (Matt. 11:30).

Discipline and *chasten* are synonyms. They both imply love and teaching, never contempt or condemnation. The word *chasten* comes from the Latin *chastus,* meaning morally pure. It signified purification by sacrifice or suffering and causing to be more humble."[21] When the Lord chastened Joseph for losing the 116 pages, it was with a love for him and a concern for his future. As He said, "Verily, thus saith the Lord unto you whom I *love,* and whom I *love* I also chasten that their sins may be forgiven, for with the chastisement I prepare a way for their deliverance in all things out of temptation, and I have *loved* you" (D&C 95:1; emphasis added). The Lord used the word *love* three times in this verse on chastening. Parents and priesthood leaders would be wise to keep that in mind when chastening or disciplining.

A BISHOP'S LOVE

Every person who humbly confesses should leave the bishop's office feeling the love of the Savior and the hope of His grace, never held in contempt or feeling condemned. Some bishops have been tempted to condemn, as the Apostles James and John did in the following scene:

"And it came to pass, when the time was come that he should be received up, he steadfastly set his face to go to Jerusalem,

"And sent messengers before his face: and they went, and entered into a village of the Samaritans, to make ready for him.

"And they did not receive him, because his face was as though he would go to Jerusalem.

"And when his disciples James and John saw this, they said, Lord, wilt thou that we command fire to come down from heaven, and consume them, even as Elias did?

"But he turned, and rebuked them, and said, Ye know not what manner of spirit ye are of.

"For the Son of man is not come to destroy men's lives, but to save them" (Luke 9:51–56).

The Pharisees similarly condemned sinners: "And the Pharisees and scribes murmured, saying, This man receiveth sinners, and eateth with them" (Luke 15:2). And just as with James and John, the Savior rebuked the Pharisees and scribes with three parables that illustrated a love for the sinner: the lost sheep, the lost coin, and the prodigal son (see Luke 15).

Faith, hope, and charity are usually listed in that order. When disciplining, try reversing the order and you will learn an additional insight into why these three virtues are linked. *Loving,* and not condemning transgressors, allows them to experience *hope* through *faith* in Jesus Christ and His grace.

THE ATONEMENT—MERCY, JUSTICE, AND JUSTIFICATION

The Guide to the Scriptures[22] contains the following definition under the heading "Justification, Justify":

"To be pardoned from punishment for sin and declared guiltless. A person is justified by the Savior's grace through faith in Him. This faith is shown by repentance and obedience to the laws and ordinances of the gospel. Jesus Christ's Atonement enables mankind to repent and be justified or pardoned from punishment they otherwise would receive."

Christ's *justification* must not be confused with the *self-justification* found on the anti-responsibility list. With self-justification, the person is essentially saying, "I don't need a Savior; I have a good excuse that I will use at Judgment Day" The excuse keeps them from repenting and accessing the Lord's grace and *His* justification. It exposes them to the whole law of the demands of justice as taught in this verse from the book of Alma:

"And thus mercy can satisfy the demands of justice, and encircles them in the arms of safety, while he that exercises no faith unto repentance is *exposed to the whole law of the demands of justice;* therefore only unto him that has faith unto repentance is brought about the great and eternal plan of redemption" (Alma 34:16; emphasis added).

Alma understood very well how excuses (the anti-responsibility list) keep us from repenting, as we learn from the account of his disciplining (teaching) and cautioning his wayward son, Corianton:

"What, do ye suppose that mercy can rob justice? I say unto you, Nay; not one whit. If so, God would cease to be God . . . O my son, I desire that ye should *deny the justice* of God no more. Do not endeavor to *excuse yourself in the least point* because of your sins, by *denying the justice* of God; but do you let the justice of God, and his mercy, and his long-suffering have full sway in your heart; and let it bring you down to the dust in humility" (Alma 42:25, 30; emphasis added).

Those who use excuses are denying the law of justice, believing it doesn't apply to them. Alma is pleading with his son not to go to the anti-responsibility list: "Do not endeavor to *excuse* yourself in the *least point.*" He was teaching his son to be 100% responsible.

As mentioned before, the strategy of the anti-Christs was to also *deny the justice* of God. To deny His justice, or to say we are not accountable for sin, is to also deny His justification in the forgiveness of that sin: "The Lord surely should come to redeem his people, but that he should not come to redeem them *in* their sins, but to redeem them *from* their sins (Hel. 5:10; emphasis added).

Hearing and understanding the true doctrine as taught by his father changed Corianton's behavior and his life. He returned to the ministry and eventually became a valiant missionary (see Alma 49:30).

DENYING THE LORD'S JUSTICE TOWARD
THOSE WHO SIN AGAINST US

Corianton had denied the Lord's justice in regard to his own sins. A second and equally damaging denial is not trusting in the Lord's justice or His wisdom in dealing with the injustices of others committed against us.

In the masterfully written classic *The Count of Monte Cristo*, by Alexandre Dumas, Edmond Dantès, the protagonist, is an honest and loving man who turns bitter and vengeful after three covetous men bear false witness against him and frame him in a treasonous plot. When a corrupt public prosecutor becomes complicit, Dantès is arrested on the very day he is to be married to his beautiful fiancée, Mercedes. At age 19 he is given a life sentence in the infamous island prison of the Chateau d'if for a crime he did not commit.

After many tortuous years in solitary confinement, he finally meets another prisoner, the elderly Abbe Faria, who in his search for freedom has miscalculated and tunneled his way to Dantès's cell rather than outside to freedom. With a tunnel connecting their cells, and nothing but time on their hands, Faria begins to teach Dantès history, science, philosophy, and languages, turning him into a well-educated man. Faria also bequeaths to Dantès a treasure of vast wealth hidden on the uninhabited island of Monte Cristo and tells him how to find it should he ever escape.

Knowing that vengeance could consume and destroy Dantès, the Abbe Faria teaches him a final lesson before he dies—to not deny the

Lord's justice: "Do not commit the crime for which you now serve the sentence. God said, vengeance is mine."

Edmond Dantès replied, "I don't believe in God."

Abbe Faria responded, "It doesn't matter. He believes in you."

Dantès remained unconvinced.

Upon the death of Faria, Dantès devises a clever plan to hide himself in Faria's death shroud and finally escape his fourteen years of torment at the Chateau d'if. After so many years of suffering, he is finally free; and having found the treasure, he is extremely wealthy. During the next few years he assumes a new identity as the Count of Monte Cristo and devises an elaborate plan of revenge.

Before implementing his plan he bestows gifts upon those who have been kind to him. He then bids "farewell to kindness, humanity and gratitude. I have substituted myself for Providence in rewarding the good; may the God of vengeance now yield me His place to punish the wicked."

For the evil men who colluded against him, he plans a painful and prolonged punishment, a just recompense for the fourteen years he barely endured subsisting in the dungeon to which they sent him.

With precision, Dantès sets in motion his plan of revenge, and his enemies suffer the punishment he has carefully devised for each of them.

When we read *The Count of Monte Cristo,* there is something in us that wants to see justice served against those evil men who inflicted such injustice upon an innocent man. There is a sense of fairness and desire in each of us that good must prevail over evil, that things lost must be restored, and that broken hearts must be mended. Until these things happen there is an injustice gap that is hard to reconcile in our minds, and even more so in our hearts, leaving us troubled and unable to move on.

People try to reconcile this injustice gap in many ways: through revenge, sometimes justifying or excusing it, or seeking redress and imposed consequences. We ultimately discover that the Lord's way is the only way for true and complete reconciliation.

The scriptures contain scores of examples of self-defense. Righteous societies have always created laws to maintain justice and peace and to protect the innocent. And it is entirely appropriate for the innocent to seek protection according to those laws.

The error of Dantès was not seeking redress according to the law and bringing devious facts to light, but letting his desire for justice turn to bitterness, hatred, and anger that consumed him. In his duplicity, he descended to his enemies' level of impiety and used deception, lies, and fraud to entrap them, all outside the lawful process, just as they had done to him and just as the Abbe Faria had prophesied.

Those who rely on the law of Moses—an eye for an eye and a tooth for a tooth—rather than on the law of the gospel, including forgiving and praying for one's enemies, condemn themselves to a sentence of torment and unrest equal in length to the duration of their bitterness.

In *denying the Lord's justice,* they choose to serve the sentence that Christ has already served in their behalf. It robs them of a life of greater happiness that could have been theirs but for the want of revenge.

Trusting in the Atonement of Jesus Christ is to trust that He will correct all injustices, restore all things lost, and mend all things broken, including hearts. He will make all things right, not leaving any detail unattended. Therefore, "Ye ought to say in your hearts—let

God judge between me and thee, and reward thee according to thy deeds" (D&C 64:11).

FORGIVENESS AND 100% RESPONSIBILITY

A paradox is a statement or situation that seems to be absurd or contradictory but in fact is true.[23] The Savior often phrased His teachings in the form of a paradox: "The last shall be first, and the first last" (Matt. 20:16); "He that loses his life shall find it" (Matt. 10:39); "Let him . . . that is chief, [be] as he that doth serve" (Luke 22:26).

Some of the most perplexing paradoxes taught by the Savior are commandments concerning love, which are difficult even for the valiant: "Love your enemies, bless them that curse you, do good to them that hate you, and pray for them who despitefully use you and persecute you" (3 Ne. 12:44). Like Edmond Dantès, many victims have been so cruelly injured, with no apparent forthcoming justice, that they felt like the Lord was asking the impossible.

The Lord has said, "I, the Lord, will forgive whom I will forgive, but of you it is required to forgive all men" (D&C 64:10). I don't believe the Lord would have used the word *all* unless He meant it. The word *all* is yet another insight into 100% responsibility.

Anger, blaming, and self-pity are all elements of not forgiving. And just like these disabling taboos from the anti-responsibility list, not forgiving comes with the same negative consequences, such as being acted upon rather than acting and losing control over future positive outcomes. By using people's anger against them, Satan begins to exercise a measure of control over their lives and can transform loving marriages and families into dysfunctional or destroyed ones.

Forgiving involves taking responsibility for how we act and even how we feel and respond to an injustice or offense. There is wisdom in being able to control our response, or to be response-able.

Of course, it is easier to forgive minor offenses that have no lasting negative consequences. However, as injustices and consequences escalate, forgiveness becomes increasingly difficult. Consider these three scenarios and the increasing difficulty in forgiving:

- A husband accidentally breaks his wife's favorite vase. (Offenses like this are unintentional and the result of carelessness, forgetfulness, or a lack of judgment.)
- A wife neglects her family in favor of spending too much time watching TV, browsing the internet, and on social media. Many important priorities go unfulfilled. (Offenses like this are the result of unwise, inconsiderate, and irresponsible behavior.)
- A husband commits many horrible offenses against his wife including making cruel remarks, committing adultery, spending money on himself and making it difficult for her to even buy groceries, and physically abusing her. (In this category offenses are intentional and evil.)

Of the three scenarios, the last case is the most troubling, because it is a breach of the most sacred trust—the one person in all the world who should have loved her most has betrayed her and caused unimaginable suffering. This hurt goes deep. Is asking her to forgive asking too much?

RESPONDING TO ABUSE

In my Church service I have reviewed hundreds of cases of struggling marriages. With marital discord it is rarely a one-sided story, but there are many situations where one spouse has betrayed their marital vows and is unwilling to repent. In many of these cases you find a husband (or sometimes the wife) living a sinful life and "breaking the heart of his tender wife" (Jacob 2:35). In some of these cases the woman is a victim of cruel and unthinkable abuse—verbal, emotional, physical, or sexual (and often a combination of all).

There is a common pattern with abuse cases—the abuser nearly always blames the victim, just as Laman and Lemuel blamed Nephi for the abuse they inflicted upon him. To protect himself and his family, Nephi followed the counsel of the Lord and separated his family and loved ones from his brothers and their wicked intentions (see 2 Ne. 5:1–7).

Let's assume that the abused woman mentioned above finds herself in a Nephi-like situation. Like Nephi, she has prayed and hoped for reconciliation and that her husband's heart would be softened. However, after agonizing months of painstaking decision-making and seeking answers through humble prayer and counsel, she receives a similar direction to separate herself and the children from a cruel and wicked man. She finds the strength to act on that revelation and separates.[24]

She is now free from the abusive environment, but she is finding it hard to forgive her husband for the sustained and escalating cruelty. Are there extreme situations like this one when offenses against someone are so hurtful and wicked that 100% responsibility should not apply, and when anger, blaming, and self-pity may be justified? It seems unjust to ask the abused woman to forgive her cruel husband when he is unrepentant. It just doesn't seem fair for her, the innocent one, to be suffering; while he, the guilty one, gets off scot-free with no apparent justice forthcoming. Is there peace to be found without justice?

GOD'S JUSTICE—THE ABUSED SPOUSE

Some injustices are so cruel and painful that as with deep wounds, it will take time and the Savior's grace for the pain to finally begin subsiding. Even then, there will undoubtedly be emotional scars reminding us of the pain endured. Forgiveness is a spiritual balm that can hasten the healing process.

Though forgiveness may take time, it is helpful for any victim of an injustice to understand that the forgiving process will be advanced by better understanding and trusting in the justice of God.

The Guide to the Scriptures gives the following definition for justice:

"Justice is an eternal law that requires a penalty each time a law of God is broken (Alma 42:13–24). The sinner *must pay the penalty* if he does not repent (Mosiah 2:38–39; D&C 19:17). If the former husband does not repent, he will suffer the penalty, 'how sore you know not, how *exquisite* you know not, yea, how hard to bear you know not' (D&C 19:15)" (emphasis added).

If he does repent, the Savior will pay the penalty, invoking mercy. The former wife will know if he truly repents, because his restitution will include humbly and sincerely asking for her forgiveness and striving to make amends. One way or another, justice will be served—she can be assured.

Elder Neal A. Maxwell wisely taught that "faith in God includes faith in His purposes as well as in His timing. We cannot fully accept Him while rejecting His schedule."[25] "The Gospel guarantees ultimate, not proximate, justice."[26] The Lord made this truth clear in a revelation to Joseph Smith in the midst of his suffering in jail:

"Behold, mine eyes see and know all their works, and I have in reserve a swift judgment in the season thereof, for them all" (D&C 121:24).

Those who have experienced permanent damage or prolonged suffering or loss from an offense face a more difficult challenge in forgiving and turning justice over to the Lord. There is comfort to be found in something the Prophet Joseph Smith taught: "What can [these disasters] do? Nothing. All your losses will be made up to you in the resurrection, provided you continue faithful."[27]

As we learn in *Preach My Gospel,* "All that is unfair about life can be made right through the Atonement of Jesus Christ."[28] Those patient in affliction have a "firm hope that [they] shall one day rest from all [their] afflictions" (Alma 34:41). Furthermore, "He that is faithful in tribulation, *the reward of the same is greater* in the kingdom of heaven" (D&C 58:2; emphasis added).

Elder D. Todd Christofferson shared this additional perspective on how the law of justice restores losses to the victim: "The Atonement also satisfies the debt justice owes to us by healing and compensating us for any suffering we innocently endure."[29]

The tragedy and pain of abuse are often multiplied by haunting memories of the abuse. Without forgiveness, the nightmares will likely continue. Forgiving the abuser doesn't set him free, but it begins to set the victim free. Forgiving an abusive husband does not excuse or condone his cruelty. It doesn't erase the injury he has caused. It doesn't mean forgetting his brutality—you can't un-remember or erase a memory so traumatic. It doesn't mean trusting him and giving him yet another chance to abuse his wife and children. Trust is something that has to be earned and evidenced by good behavior over time, which the abuser clearly has not demonstrated. And forgiving the abuser doesn't mean granting forgiveness of his sins; only the Lord can do that.

What forgiving the abuser *does* do is begin to put the abused victim back in control of her life, allowing her to refocus her energy on her future with hope rather than reliving the pain of the past. It is a way of taking back responsibility for her life and control over her happiness. She learns that forgiveness is part of being 100% responsible for her own happiness. She learns that any desire for justice or to "get even" is a form of self-pity, which is disabling to her. Most importantly, she learns that no matter how wise her judgment is, it will always fall short of the Lord's perfect judgment. The degree to which she forgives the offenses of her abuser is one indicator of her increasing faith in the Lord, His timing, and His ability to wisely judge.

As in other cases we have discussed, *even if she is right,* it does not help her to use any of the disabling devices on the anti-responsibility list, as they are counterproductive and self-destructive.

EMPATHY—A KEY TO FORGIVING

With her life back in her own control, the abused woman may even find it in her heart to pray for the one who has despitefully abused her. The prayer will benefit her as much, and probably more, than him. It will help transform her inward feelings of pain and anger into outward feelings of empathy for the offender and his pitiful and miserable life. In the act of dying, the Savior showed this pure love, empathy, and compassion toward the Roman soldiers who scourged Him and were now crucifying Him.

While in excruciating agony, His thoughts turned outward. He pitied His persecutors and then prayed for them, "Father, forgive them; for they know not what they do" (Luke 23:34). Perhaps the Savior meant not so much "they know not what they do" (to me), but rather "they know not what they do" (to themselves).

Regarding empathy for the abuser, Elder Richard G. Scott has shared this helpful insight: "As impossible as it may seem to you now, in time the healing you can receive from the Savior will allow you to truly forgive the abuser and *even have feelings of sorrow for him or her.*"[30]

DENYING MERCY

Perhaps the hardest forgiveness of all is forgiving oneself. Not forgiving others is to deny the Savior's justice, as discussed above. To not forgive oneself is to deny the Savior's mercy. "But it is mockery before God, denying the mercies of Christ, and the power of his Holy Spirit" (Moro. 8:23). While this scripture refers to those who deny the Lord's mercy toward little children, it applies equally to those who have truly repented but cannot forgive themselves. They are not trusting in His word, which says, "Come now, and let us reason together [another way of saying 'please internalize this'], saith the Lord: though your sins be as scarlet, they shall be as white as snow; though they be red like crimson, they shall be as wool." (Isa. 1:18). Modern scripture confirms the Lord's mercy for the truly penitent: "Behold, he who has repented of his sins, the same is forgiven, and I, the Lord, *remember them no more*" (D&C 58:42; emphasis added).

In the case of Alma and the sons of Mosiah, who had fought against the Church, their expectation was to be dealt with *justly*. What a surprise it was to them when instead of justice, they received mercy from the Lord. "Behold, he did not exercise his justice upon us, but in

72

his great mercy hath brought us over that everlasting gulf of death and misery, even to the salvation of our souls" (Alma 26:20).

THE LORD'S GRACE

According to the Bible Dictionary, the Lord's grace is a "divine means of help or strength, given through the bounteous mercy and love of Jesus Christ."

In the case of the abused wife, we have two parties—the abusive husband and the victim wife, both of whom need divine help. The scriptures teach us that the Savior suffered for both of them—for the sins of the man and for the anguish and pain of the woman.

For the abuser—"Now the Spirit knoweth all things; nevertheless the Son of God suffereth according to the flesh that he might take upon him the sins of his people, that he might blot out their transgressions according to the power of his deliverance" (Alma 7:13).

For the abused—"And he shall go forth, suffering pains and afflictions and temptations of every kind; and this that the word might be fulfilled which saith he will take upon him the pains and the sicknesses of his people . . . and he will take upon him their infirmities, that his bowels may be filled with mercy, according to the flesh, that he may know according to the flesh how to succor his people according to their infirmities" (Alma 7:11–12). "He hath sent me to heal the broken hearted . . . to set at liberty them that are bruised" (Luke 4:18).

To access the Savior's grace and the healing power of the Atonement, the Savior requires something from both of them.

The husband's key to access the Lord's grace is *repentance.* If he doesn't repent, he cannot be forgiven by the Lord (see D&C 19:15–17).

The wife's key to access the Lord's grace and allow Him to heal her is *forgiveness*. Without forgiving, she will suffer the anguish which the Lord has already suffered in her behalf. Not forgiving denies His mercy to her. In a sense, she fulfills the scripture, "I, God, have suffered these things . . . that they might not suffer. . . . But if they would not repent [or forgive] they must suffer even as I" (D&C 19:16–17).

As she begins to forgive her abuser, the Lord's grace begins to ease and lift her anguish and pain, and she is finally able to experience the healing she so desperately wants and deserves. The Savior knows exactly how to heal her because He precisely knows her pain, having lived it vicariously.

"Have faith that with effort His perfect, eternal, infinite Atonement can heal your suffering from the consequences of abuse," Elder Richard G. Scott taught. "When you can forgive the offense, you will be relieved of the pain and heartache that Satan wants in your life by encouraging you to hate the abuser. As a result, you will enjoy greater peace. While an important part of healing, if the thought of forgiveness causes you yet more pain, set that step aside until you have more experience with the Savior's healing power in your own life. . . .

"I pray that you, as one abused or one who has caused it, will act now to avail yourself of the healing power of the Atonement of Jesus Christ. I testify that your faith and obedience will assure that He will help you."[31]

LITTLE OFFENSES

Major offenses can certainly destroy a marriage, but Satan destroys far more families through minor and even trivial offenses, which over time manage to erode patience and love to the breaking point.

Spouses can irritate each other in countless ways—perhaps leaving socks on the floor, piling dishes in the sink, being a backseat driver, nagging, not listening, being critical and sarcastic, making the other wait, or something as trivial as not replacing the toilet paper roll. Petty things seem to be magnified a thousand times bigger than they are when repeated over and over. It is like picking at a scab—the irritation continues to fester and only gets worse.

A happy and successful marriage depends on two good forgivers, or as President Gordon B. Hinckley pointed out, "a high degree of mutual toleration."[32] That implies using the phrases "I am sorry" and "please forgive me" with much greater frequency than we may be used to.

Even little things that cause contention can drive away the Spirit. At age 76, David Whitmer was asked, regarding the Prophet Joseph Smith, "What kind of man was he when you knew him personally?"

Whitmer answered, "He was a religious and straightforward man. He had to be; for he was illiterate and he could do nothing of himself. He had to trust in God. He could not translate unless he was humble and possessed the right feelings towards every one.

"To illustrate, so you can see. One morning when he was getting ready to continue the translation, something went wrong about the house and he was put out about it. Something that Emma, his wife, had done. Oliver and I went upstairs, and Joseph came up soon after to continue the translation, but he could not do anything. He could not translate a single syllable. He went down stairs, out into the orchard and made supplication to the Lord. He was gone about an hour—came back to the house, asked Emma's forgiveness and then came up stairs where we were and the translation went on all right. He could do nothing save he was humble and faithful."[33]

FORGIVENESS AND THE SACRAMENT

It is through faith in Jesus Christ, repentance, and the ordinances of baptism and the sacrament that we are forgiven of sin and granted the healing blessings of the Atonement. It is in the ordinances of the gospel that the "power of godliness is manifest [in this case, that power is forgiveness]. And without the ordinances thereof, and the authority of the priesthood, the power of godliness is not manifest unto men in the flesh" (D&C 84:20–21).

Those who have been endowed in the temple know that if we have unkind feelings toward others, we are not invited to participate in some ordinances. That admonition applies to all ordinances, including the sacrament:

President Spencer W. Kimball taught, "When we have angers and hatreds and bitterness, we should consider seriously if we should take the sacrament. Yesterday I saw a mother-in-law and a daughter-in-law both take the bread and water, yet there was confessed irreconcilable animosity between them. . . . The sacrament is so sacred, and yet we find very few people who refrain from taking it—I guess because it is embarrassing not to do so."[34]

A major offense can certainly canker a soul, but often it's the little things that embitter a person. Sometimes these actions are not even intended as offenses—forgetting a person's name, not acknowledging someone with a handshake, or an irksome personality quirk. You can almost tell the measure of a person's character by what it takes to offend them. The Savior simply never took offense—His patience and long-suffering, His understanding and compassion, His mercy and forgiveness were all perfect.

In partaking of the sacrament, we become hypocrites if we seek mercy and hope to be forgiven of our sins yet in our minds still demand justice and are unwilling to forgive others for their sins. For that reason the Savior gives this counsel: "Therefore, if ye shall come unto me, or shall desire to come unto me, and rememberest that thy brother hath aught against thee—Go thy way unto thy brother, and first be reconciled to thy brother, and then come unto me with full purpose of heart, and I will receive you (3 Ne. 12:23–24). There is a doctrinal disconnect if we demand justice for others while seeking mercy for ourselves. In not forgiving others, we cannot *feel* forgiven ourselves, because the Spirit cannot grant mercy's peace and comfort contrary to the will of the Lord. As the scriptures say, "If ye forgive not men their trespasses neither will your Father forgive your trespasses" (3 Ne.13:15).

An invitation: If you are having a hard time letting go of angry feelings toward someone, try praying for him or her and see what impact it has on you. Two blessings will come to pass: anger's corroding toxins will begin to be cleansed from your heart, and you will finally begin to experience the peace of forgiveness of your own sins. This invitation came directly from the Lord when He taught, "But behold I say unto you, love your enemies, bless them that curse you, do good to them that hate you, and pray for them who despitefully use you and persecute you; That ye may be the children of your Father who is in heaven" (3 Ne. 12:44–45).

BY HIS GRACE—BECOMING SPOTLESS

It is awe-inspiring, almost beyond comprehension, to ponder the concept that the Savior achieved 100% purity in His life. For the rest of us, the law of justice demands 100% responsibility for all of our choices, including our sins. After all, it is due to our sins that "man became fallen [and was] cut off from the presence of the Lord" (2 Ne. 9:6).

Therefore, if we want to be 100% responsible for all of our choices, we must follow the command to "come unto Christ, and be *perfected in him,* and deny yourselves of all ungodliness; and if ye shall deny yourselves of all ungodliness, and love God with all your might, mind and strength, then is his grace sufficient for you, that by his grace ye may be perfect in Christ; and if by the grace of God ye are perfect in Christ, ye can in nowise deny the power of God.

"And again, if ye by the grace of God are perfect in Christ, and deny not his power, then are ye sanctified in Christ by the grace of God, through the shedding of the blood of Christ, which is in the covenant of the Father unto the remission of your sins, that ye become holy, *without spot*" (Moroni 10:32–33; emphasis added).

SUMMARY

- Agency and responsibility are inseparable. With 100% agency we are also 100% responsible.
- Trying to separate agency and responsibility is one of Satan's most cunning strategies.
- We have all used the anti-responsibility list and will continually be tempted to use the devices on it.
- When we avoid being responsible, we limit our own agency.
- Responsibility is as much a gift as agency, with increased blessings given to those who are responsible for their choices.
- The anti-responsibility list is self-deceptive and self-destructive and damages relationships with others.
- When we are not responsible before God, Satan begins to take control.

- The law of justice demands 100% responsibility for sin.
- Not being responsible is to deny the Lord's justice and mercy.
- Not confessing serious sins is not being responsible.
- Not forgiving is self-defeating and self-destructive.
- Forgiving is a requirement to partake of the sacrament worthily.
- We must forgive even if the offender is unrepentant, and until we do so, we will not access the Lord's grace and find healing and peace.

NOTES

1. John Medina, *Brain Rules* (Seattle: Pear Press, 2008), 223.
2. "Confirmation Bias," *Wikipedia*, last modified January 7, 2015, http://en .wikipedia.org/wiki/Confirmation_bias.
3. "Demosthenes," *Quoteworld.org*, http://www.quoteworld.org/quotes/3580.
4. See Doctrine and Covenants 101:78.
5. There are three exceptions to this principle: 1) Children younger than the age of accountability (see Mosiah 3:16–18; Mosiah 15:25; Moroni 8:8; Doctrine and Covenants 29:46–47; 68:27; 137:10); 2) The intellectually disabled (see Moroni 8:10; *Handbook 1: Stake Presidents and Bishops* [2010], 16.3.5); and 3) Those who have not received the law or gospel (see 2 Nephi 9:26; Mosiah 3:11; Mosiah 15:24; Alma 42:21).
6. Dallin H. Oaks, "Be Not Deceived," *Ensign*, Nov. 2004, 44.
7. Thomas S. Monson, "Crisis at the Crossroads," *New Era*, Nov. 1983, 4.
8. John 8:32.
9. David B. Hart, "Freedom and Decency," *First Things: A Monthly Journal of Religion and Public Life*, no. 144 (June 2004): 40.
10. Quoted in Jon Huntsman, *Winners Never Cheat* (Upper Saddle River, New Jersey: Wharton School Publishing, 2005), 58.
11. General Authority Training, April 1993.
12. Ralph Parlette, *The University of Hard Knocks* (2012).
13. Adapted from Irene Eubanks, "Putting My Marriage before My Pride," *Ensign*, Jan. 2008, 33.
14. See Matthew 7:3.
15. See Luke 9:56.
16. Boyd K. Packer, "The Candle of the Lord," *Ensign*, Jan. 1983, 55.

17. See Job 38:4–7.
18. Thomas Carlyle, quoted in Spencer W. Kimball, *The Miracle of Forgiveness* (1969), 31.
19. Benson, "Beware of Pride," 4.
20. Ibid., 5.
21. *Merriam-Webster's Collegiate Dictionary*, 11th ed., s.v. "chasten."
22. The Guide to the Scriptures is a study aid found in the online scriptures produced by The Church of Jesus Christ of Latter-day Saints © 2001–2005 Intellectual Reserve, Inc. All rights reserved.
23. Encarta Dictionary, "paradox."
24. It is important to note that while divorce may be a wise decision in cases of abuse and cruelty, couples should carefully consider the long-term consequences before taking this action. Increased expenses results in *all* cases, as two households are more expensive than one, along with a host of other negative consequences—perhaps the most serious being the impact on any children. As hard as the marriage may have been, the divorce is harder. Though there are exceptions, a marriage worth entering is nearly always a marriage worth saving and nurturing.
25. *The Neal A. Maxwell Quote Book*, ed. by Cory H. Maxwell (Salt Lake City: Deseret Book, 2009), 133; emphasis added.
26. Ibid., 213.
27. *Teachings of Presidents of the Church: Joseph Smith* (2007), 51.
28. *Preach My Gospel: A Guide to Missionary Service* (2004), 52.
29. *Church News,* Jan. 12, 2014, 16.
30. Richard G. Scott, "To Heal the Shattering Consequences of Abuse," *Ensign,* May 2008, 42–43; emphasis added.
31. Ibid.
32. Hinckley, "A Conversation with Single Adults," 60.
33. *David Whitmer Interviews: A Restoration Witness,* ed. by Lyndon W. Cook (United States of America: Grandin Book Company, 1991), 84–88; see also Willam Kelley and George A. Blakeslee, "David Whitmer Interview—Sept. 15, 1881, *Saints' Herald,* March 1, 1882, 82.
34. *Teachings of Spencer W. Kimball,* 225.

CHAPTER 3

AGENCY AND VIRTUE

Have you ever imagined what it would be like to go back in time and follow alongside the Savior for just one day to be "eyewitnesses of his majesty" (2 Pet. 1:16); to have "our heart burn within us, while he talked with us by the way" (Luke 24:32); to feel of and observe firsthand His ennobling virtues? Such a thought is not uncommon: "Many prophets and righteous men have desired to see those things which ye see, and have not seen them; and to hear those things which ye hear, and have not heard them" (Matt. 13:17).

It would be glorious to spend one day or even one hour witnessing His character and behavior. It would be awe-inspiring to hear Him teach, to be sure, but what a treasure it would be to observe the little things that aren't always recorded in the scriptures. Nothing about Him could be considered little or trivial, yet some simple, daily routines might have been considered inconsequential or insignificant to historians or even to the writers of the Gospels.

If you were to walk with Him, you would surely witness Christ's divine character multiple times a day. But it would be enlightening to also observe His tenderness mixed with His candor; His humor mixed with His nobility; His diligence mixed with taking time to smell the roses. There are hundreds of things that could be gleaned by such a firsthand experience.

It would be inspiring to observe the Savior's facial expressions and body language throughout the day. Beyond learning from the doctrine He taught, what could be learned by observing His demeanor, His countenance, and His warmth as He spoke?

THE SAVIOR'S GREATEST TEACHING

We could argue that the Savior's greatest teaching was not in a synagogue, nor at the temple, nor from a mount, but in the hundreds of little ways in which He lived His life. His life was His greatest sermon. We are in awe as we contemplate His perfect life and His attributes. Likewise, one of the most important ways for us to worship Him may not be in a church pew, or by our bedside, or at the temple—as important as those places are—but in the way we live our lives. Elder Neal A. Maxwell said, "Emulation is the greatest form of adoration."[1] Therefore, it could be argued that the most important invitation the Savior ever extended to us was, "What manner of men [and women] ought ye to be? Verily I say unto you, even as I am" (3 Ne. 27:27).

The word *virtue* originates from the Latin *virtus,* meaning strength and manliness, and from *vir,* Latin for man.[2] A virtuous man or woman is strong in spirit and striving to become as He is. Because the family is central to the plan of our Father in Heaven, the best laboratory and testing grounds to learn, develop, and refine Christlike virtues is in the home with our loved ones. As we learn how to develop these virtues, we will naturally strengthen our marriages, homes, and families.

Studying the Savior's virtues may not be the same as traveling back in time and observing Him in person, but if one has a desire to become as He is, then a study of His divine character can lead to a better understanding of "the mind of Christ" (1 Cor. 2:16). When we begin to think as He did, then "virtue will garnish [our] thoughts unceasingly" (D&C 121:45). The mind of Christ begins to inspire each thought, influence each act, and shape each virtue. Line upon line and day by day, His image is slowly engraven upon our countenance, divine characters are forged, and families experience greater and greater happiness until they eventually achieve a fullness of joy.

HOW WOULD JESUS BE?

People often ask, "What would Jesus do?" The real power in this question is to help us act upon the underlying, weightier question—"How would Jesus be?" In fact, why would we even ask ourselves what Jesus would do unless our true motivation was to *be* like Him?

The question "What would Jesus do?" is usually asked when people find themselves at a moral fork in the road or in a spontaneous situation calling for a decision of character. It is a very good question, but we don't need to wait for the spontaneous situation to ask it. It can and should be part of our daily planning.

Our *to-dos* (actions) help forge our *to-bes,* or our character. The more we become as He is, the less necessary the question "What would Jesus do?" will be, because our actions will over time become more and more instinctively and instantaneously like His. For example, if a person has a forgiving heart (a to-be), the act of forgiving is accomplished in advance, long before an offense actually occurs. The act of forgiving will be a spiritual reflex—a habit.

RIGHTEOUS HABITS

Developing scores of virtues may seem overwhelming. Understanding that, Benjamin Franklin devised a program to convert virtues into *habits:*

"My intention being to acquire the habitude of all these virtues, I judged it would be well not to distract my attention by attempting the whole at once, but to fix it on one of them at a time, and, when I should be master of that, then to proceed to another, and so on, . . . the acquisition of some might facilitate the acquisition of certain others, I arranged them with that view. . . .

"Temperance first, as it tends to procure that coolness and clearness of head which is so necessary where constant vigilance was to be kept up, and guard maintained against the unremitting attraction of ancient habits and the force of perpetual temptations. This being acquired and established, [the others] would be more easy."[3]

While Franklin thought it best to begin with *temperance,* the gospel teaches us to begin with *faith* in Jesus Christ. Faith has to be the foundation of a Christlike character. Temperance is certainly a kingly virtue, and there are many others that have been referred to as cardinal virtues, such as those highlighted in chapter 6 of *Preach My Gospel.* We should try to make each virtue become a habit.

You turn a virtue into a habit by continually placing action items on your to-do list that strengthen that virtue. Take charity, for example—what kind deeds are on your daily to-do list? If we claim that we have charity but we aren't *doing* our home teaching or visiting teaching, then like faith without works, our charity is also dead. "Therefore to him that knoweth to do good, and doeth it not, to him it is sin" (James 4:17). Home and visiting teaching, temple work, personal and family scripture study and prayer, family home evening, and other to-dos that the Lord has asked of us should be the first things calendared at the beginning of each month.

If motivation is lacking, this counsel from Brigham Young may be helpful: "If my heart is not fully given up to this work, I will give my time, my talents, my hands, and my possessions to it, until my heart consents to be subject. . . . I will make my hands labour in the cause of God until my heart bows in submission to it."[4]

If we continually accomplish our to-dos, over time they become habit. They become ingrained as something we want to do, and we become more charitable.

A common refrain puts it beautifully:

> *Sow a thought; reap an action* [do].
> *Sow an action; reap a habit.*
> *Sow a habit; reap a character* [be].
> *Sow a character; reap a destiny.*

The Book of Mormon also clearly outlines this principle: "For I remember the word of God which saith by their works ye shall know them; for if their works [habits] be good, then they are good also" (Moro. 7:5).

AGENCY, VIRTUES, AND EMOTIONS

How far-reaching is our agency—the inalienable right to choose and control our own life? In earlier chapters we learned that agency plays a far greater role in matters of love, patience, and forgiveness than people generally assume.

But there are other emotions and experiences that, at least initially, seem impossible to control. Are children's nighttime fears, for example, a choice? Does an inexperienced speaker choose to be nervous when addressing a large group? When people feel worried or embarrassed or lonely, did they choose those emotions, or are they normal and expected reactions to unexpected and adverse events? Are there some virtues, such as being naturally happy, or brave, or optimistic, that you are either born with or without? If virtues are gifts of the Spirit, doesn't that imply that they are given, not chosen? Just how much of our life is really in our control? What role does agency play in the development of Christlike attributes?

Lehi taught that some adverse emotions and conditions are a necessary part of the mortal learning experience (see 2 Ne. 2). It is the bitter that helps us understand and appreciate the sweet. It is only through sadness or sorrow that joy is understood; and it is an occasional absence that makes the heart grow fonder, as the adage goes. Even the Savior "learned . . . obedience by the things which he suffered" (Heb. 5:8).

There are many emotions and experiences that qualify as adverse but are not necessarily sins. Emotions like anxiety, embarrassment, fear, loneliness, worry, doubt, discouragement, frustration, despair, hurt, stress, and so on are often unavoidable and may actually be a necessary part of our mortal probation, as mentioned above. They may also help motivate us to respond to or correct the unwanted situation that brought them about.

"Who among us can say that he or she has not felt fear?" asked President Gordon B. Hinckley. "I know of no one who has been entirely spared." He also said, "Let us recognize that fear comes not of God, but rather that this gnawing, destructive element comes from the adversary of truth and righteousness. Fear is the antithesis of faith. It is corrosive in its effects, even deadly."[5] Because Satan can use these kinds of emotions against us, they can be minimized or eliminated as Christlike virtues are developed, such as faith, hope, and charity to replace fear, doubt, and despair.

A second class of emotions fit into a category that is sinful, and these emotions should be eliminated from our lives. The scriptures indicate that much of Satan's stratagem and success is in stirring up these negative emotions, such as hatred, anger, pride, vanity, jealousy, and so on. The world calls seven of these the "deadly sins"—wrath, greed, sloth, pride, lust, envy, and gluttony.[6] They are sometimes called "capital sins" because they usually lead to other sins. These kinds of emotions stunt spiritual growth and are weapons used by Satan to destroy individuals and families. For each of these vices, though, there is a contrasting positive virtue to replace and elimi-nate it; love to replace fear and hatred; forgiveness to replace anger; humility, meekness, and gratitude to replace vanity, envy, and greed; compassion and contentedness to replace jealousy and covetousness.

As mentioned earlier, a sinful emotion is often an inappropriate reaction to pride and fear. When you are angry, envious, or jealous, what are you afraid of? "For God hath not given us the spirit of fear; but of power, and of love, and of a sound mind" (2 Tim. 1:7). If we are to act and not be acted upon, we must develop Christlike attri-butes that will help overcome adverse emotions and eliminate sinful emotions. Only then can we become stripped of sinful passions in all their ugly expressions and minimize adverse emotions in all their disabling manifestations.

"True doctrine understood not only changes attitudes and behav-ior,"[7] but can also change feelings and emotions—things that much of the world believes to be spontaneous and outside of our own con-trol or agency.

HOW DO I DEVELOP CHRISTLIKE ATTRIBUTES?

Chapter 6 of *Preach My Gospel* teaches that "Christlike attributes are gifts from God," but "they come as you use your agency righteously. Ask your Heavenly Father to bless you with these attributes; you cannot develop them without His help."[8]

The development of spiritual strength is not unlike strengthening the body. A prayer for good health would be in vain if we weren't striving to achieve it through healthy eating, exercise, and sleeping habits. We would not expect to reap where we have not sown. Similarly, we would not expect virtue without effort. Prayer by itself is insufficient. The Lord's love for us and His desire to bless us is always balanced with the principle of self-reliance and His respect for our agency. To access His grace, or divine help, He expects us to do everything in our power, or to pray and act in faith (see D&C 123:17). Faith is a principle of action. I like the imagery in the adage, "The Lord cannot steer a parked car."

VISION, GOALS, PLANS, AND VIRTUE

When you do an internet search of "New Year's resolutions," you discover that most are to-do items, such as lose weight, reduce debt, quit a bad habit, finish a project, spend more time on a worthwhile goal, etc. While commendable, the power behind all to-dos (the *what*) is an inspiring vision, or a *to-be,* (the *why*). For example, why would a person want to lose weight? That is the weightier question. Possible answers might include a combination of any of the following to-bes:

- To be more healthy
- To be more obedient to the spirit of the Word of Wisdom (see D&C 89)

- To be in control, having the virtue of self-mastery
- To be more attractive and confident

It is in the *why,* or the underlying reason for a goal, where we find the power and motivation to accomplish the *what.* The *what* then inspires the *how, where, who,* and *when,* or in other words, the plan. In the weight loss example, the plan might consist of a diet and exercise regimen. But it all begins with the *why* at the foundation.

To illustrate the motivating power of a vision combined with supporting goals and plans, consider a scenario. Picture yourself in a rowboat lost in the middle of a vast ocean, with no land anywhere in sight. You have no idea where you are and no map or other instruments to orient yourself. You have no idea where land is. Under these circumstances, how much motivation would you have to row? Most likely none—what would be the purpose? Perhaps rowing would take you even farther from land, thus wasting precious energy and hastening death. You are at the mercy of the wind and currents, destined to aimlessly drift. The situation is dire and seemingly hopeless.

Now change the scenario. As you scan the horizon, an island appears in the distance. Now how much motivation do you have to row? You will not only begin rowing, but you will do it tirelessly and with enthusiasm. The sight of the island has had a miraculous, adrenaline-producing impact on you. Prior to seeing the island, the wind was an adversary. Now it serves you as you set your sails to take advantage of its power. The currents may at times be against you, but they won't deter you. In this scenario, the vision, or *why,* is survival; the goal, or *what,* is the island; and the plan, or *how,* is rowing or setting your sails.

Chapter 8 of *Preach My Gospel* uses this model: "*Goals* reflect the desires of our hearts and our *vision.* . . . Through goals and *plans,* our hopes are transformed into action. Goal setting and planning are acts of faith. Prayerfully set goals."[9]

One of the most quoted verses in the scriptures is Moses 1:39: "For behold, this is my work and my glory—to bring to pass the immortality and eternal life of man." This is our Father in Heaven's goal—His *what* or His to-do. His motivation comes from His *why*, which is that He is our Father. We are His children—His family. He loves us. His plan to accomplish His goal is called the plan of salvation or the plan of happiness and includes His ordinances and commandments.

Captain Moroni gives us a great example. When the Nephites' freedom was threatened by the wicked Amalickiah, who was leading the Lamanites, the goal (the *what*) was self-defense. Captain Moroni's plans (the *how*) consisted of battle strategies, fortifying cities, war councils, etc., but Moroni knew their success depended on a shared vision, or an inspiring *why*. "And it came to pass that he rent his coat; and he took a piece thereof, and wrote upon it—In memory of our God, our religion, and freedom, and our peace, our wives, and our children—and he fastened it upon the end of a pole . . . and he called it the title of liberty" (Alma 46:12–13). These were some very important and inspiring *whys*. It is from the vision, or the *why*, that all inspiration comes.

When our goals are based upon a worthy vision, then through obedience, prayer, and inspiration, our plans will be acts of faith inspired and supported by a loving Father in Heaven.

BECOMING LIKE JESUS CHRIST—THE VISION

Why should you pray for the gift of charity with all the energy of your heart? Why do you want to be more loving, patient, diligent, and obedient? In short, why do you want to be like Jesus Christ? As stated earlier, it could be argued that the most important invitation the Savior ever gave to us was, "What manner of men [and women] ought ye to be? Verily I say unto you, even as I am" (3 Ne. 27:27). There are some pretty incredible, glorious, and inspiring *whys* underlying this vision:

- **To be truly great**—"Christ . . . possesses every virtue in its perfection. Therefore, the only measure of true greatness is how close a man [or woman] can become like Jesus. That man is greatest who is most like Christ, and those who love him most will be most like him."[10]

- **To be worthy of heaven's power**—"And the whole multitude sought to touch him: for there went virtue out of him, and healed them all" (Luke 6:19). We know "that the rights of the priesthood are inseparably connected with the powers of heaven, and that the powers of heaven cannot be controlled nor handled only upon the principles of righteousness" (D&C 121:36).

- **To grow in light**—As we become more like the Savior, and more fully keep our covenants, we grow in light and truth, worthy of an increased portion of the Spirit, and "that which is of God is light; and he that receiveth light, and continueth in God, receiveth more light; and that light groweth brighter and brighter until the perfect day" (D&C 50:24).

- **To receive promised blessings**—Incredible blessings are promised to those who become like Him, such as, "Blessed are all they who do hunger and thirst after righteousness, for they shall be filled with the Holy Ghost" (3 Ne. 12:6). Throughout the scriptures there are blessings mentioned in association with

Christlike virtues, such as, "And inasmuch as they were humble they might be made strong, and blessed from on high, and receive knowledge from time to time" (D&C 1:28).

- **To be happy**—Virtue's reward is joy and happiness. Virtue and truth make us free from the negative consequences of misery and pain. "And moreover, I would desire that ye should consider on the blessed and happy state of those that keep the commandments of God. For behold, they are blessed in all things, both temporal and spiritual; and if they hold out faithful to the end they are received into heaven, that thereby they may dwell with God in a state of never-ending happiness" (Mosiah 2:41).

- **To make good decisions**—Who we are is who we are becoming. Who we are drives all our decisions. The more like Jesus Christ we become, the wiser our decisions will be at the many forks in the road of life. Wiser use of our agency leads to better and happier results.

- **To become worthy to return to the presence of God**—To enter into the presence of the Lord, we must be like Him. The instruction to become like Christ is more than a suggestion—it is the formula for exaltation. From the *Lectures on Faith* we learn that to "exercise faith in God unto life and salvation" one must have a "correct idea of his character, perfections, and attributes. . . . No being can enjoy his glory without possessing his perfections and holiness."[11]

BECOMING LIKE JESUS CHRIST—THE GOAL

The goal is to become like Jesus Christ. "Therefore I would that ye should *be* perfect even as I, or your Father who is in heaven is perfect" (3 Ne. 12:48; emphasis added). "It isn't enough to be just as good today as we were yesterday," taught Elder Richard L. Evans. "We should be better. The Lord doesn't deal in theories. When he says perfection is possible, we'd better be improving."[12]

Because our spiritual growth happens "in process of time" (Moses 7:21), it may be difficult to perceive our progress from day to day. With physical growth, it takes time-lapse photography to be aware of the change in one's stature. That is a good reminder to help us be patient with ourselves in the process of our spiritual development. "Do not expect to become perfect at once," President Lorenzo Snow counseled. "If you do, you will be disappointed."[13]

Elder Bruce R. McConkie taught that "nobody becomes perfect in this life. Only the Lord Jesus attained that state, and he had an advantage that none of us has. He was the Son of God. . . . Becoming perfect in Christ is a process. . . . We attain perfection a little at a time, with the Lord's help. We begin to keep the commandments today and we keep more of them tomorrow, and we go from grace to grace, up the steps of the ladder, and thus we improve and perfect our souls."[14]

We can't become perfect on our own. We need the Savior's help. "Yea, come unto Christ, and be perfected in him, and deny yourselves of all ungodliness; and if ye shall deny yourselves of all ungodliness, and love God with all your might, mind and strength, then is his grace sufficient for you, that by his grace ye may be perfect in Christ; and if by the grace of God ye are perfect in Christ, ye can in nowise deny the power of God" (Moro. 10:32).

You already have many years of experience in learning and striving to become more like the Savior. To help in your continued quest, identify an attribute you most need or want to develop (for ideas, see the list of attributes in the Appendix, "Christlike Virtues").

BECOMING LIKE JESUS CHRIST—THE PLAN

Once you identify the to-be, or the Christlike attribute you want to develop, be mindful of behaviors that would help you grow in that attribute, including action items on your to-do list.

For example, let's say that you want to be more patient. Here are some to-dos you could glean from scriptures on patience:

- I resist the temptation to get angry when my children misbehave (see 3 Ne. 11:29–30; Col. 3:19, 21; D&C 121:41, 42).
- I resist the temptation to lash out at my spouse when I feel criticized (see Prov. 15:1)
- I wait patiently for the blessings and promises of the Lord to be fulfilled (see 2 Ne. 10:17).
- I am able to wait for things without getting upset or frustrated (see Rom. 8:25).
- I am patient and long-suffering in challenges (see Alma 17:11).
- I am patient with the faults and weaknesses of others (see Rom. 15:1).
- I am patient with myself and rely on the Lord as I work to overcome my weaknesses (see Ether 12:27).
- I face adversity and afflictions calmly and hopefully (see 1 Ne. 19:9; Alma 34:40–41).

A VIRTUE CARRIED TO EXCESS

If a virtue is not balanced by complementary virtues, it can become compromised or corrupted. What once was a strength can become a weakness.

Elder Dallin H. Oaks gave a marvelous talk explaining how our strengths can become our downfall. He taught that Satan not only exploits a person's weaknesses but also attacks and attempts to corrupt strengths. Here are three of the many examples that Elder Oaks cited:

"The person who has a strong desire to be led by the Spirit of the Lord but unwisely extends that strength to the point of desiring to be led in all things. . . . Our Heavenly Father leaves many decisions for our personal choices. . . .

"A willingness to sacrifice all we possess in the work of the Lord is surely a strength. In fact, it is a covenant we make in sacred places. But even this strength can bring us down if we fail to confine our sacrifices to those things the Lord [has] asked of us at this time. . . .

"Carried to excess, a love of and commitment to work can also become an excuse to neglect family and church responsibilities."[15]

We could say that the virtue of temperance, "being temperate in all things" (D&C 12:8), also applies to other virtues. In Alma 38:12, Alma counsels his son Shiblon to "use boldness, but not overbearance." If enthusiasm is not bridled, it could become obsessive and fanatical. "And every man that striveth for the mastery is *temperate* in all things," including virtues.[16]

The Savior's invitation to us is to be as He is, which requires using our agency to develop Christlike virtues. May His invitation become a consuming desire in each of our minds and hearts.

SUMMARY

- Be mindful of the question "How would Jesus be?," which is the precursor to the question "What would Jesus do?"
- With constant effort, a virtue will eventually become a habit, a spiritual reflex.
- Developing Christlike virtues helps us control adverse emotions

(such as stress or nervousness) and overcome sinful emotions (such as envy or anger).

- Developing a Christlike character is the work of a lifetime.
- Developing a virtue begins with the vision, or *why,* followed by the goal, or *what,* and finally the plan, or *how.*
- Remembering that virtues are gifts of the Spirit, a virtue cannot be developed without the Lord's help and much pondering and prayer.
- A virtue is no longer a virtue when carried to excess.

NOTES

1. Neal A. Maxwell, "From the Beginning," *Ensign,* Nov. 1993, 20.
2. *Merriam-Webster's Collegiate Dictionary,* 11th ed., s.v. "virtue."
3. *The Autobiography of Benjamin Franklin,* ed. by Frank Woodworth Pine (New York: Henry Holt and Company, 1916).
4. Brigham Young, *Journal of Discourses* 1:202.
5. Gordon B. Hinckley, "God Hath Not Given Us the Spirit of Fear," *Ensign,* Oct. 1984, 2–5.
6. "Seven Deadly Sins," *Wikipedia,* last modified January 15, 2015, Wikipedia .org/wiki/Seven_deadly_sins.
7. Boyd K. Packer, "Little Children," *Ensign,* Nov. 1986, 17.
8. *Preach My Gospel,* 115.
9. *Preach My Gospel,* 146.
10. Ezra Taft Benson, in Conference Report, Oct. 1972, 53.
11. *Lectures on Faith,* 3.4; 7.10.
12. Richard L. Evans, in Conference Report, October 1969, 68.
13. *Teachings of the Presidents of the Church: Lorenzo Snow* (2012), 103.
14. 1976 Devotional Speeches of the Year, Provo: Brigham Young University Press, 1977, 399–400.
15. Dallin H. Oaks, "Our Strengths Can Become Our Downfall" (Brigham Young University devotional, June 7, 1992), 3–4; speeches.byu.edu.
16. 1 Corinthians 9:25; emphasis added.

CHAPTER 4

"Even as I Am"

*T*o be, or not to be" is actually a very good question.[1] As discussed in the previous chapter, the Savior posed the question in a far more profound way, making it a vital doctrinal question for each of us: "What manner of men [and women] ought ye *to be?* Verily I say unto you, even as *I am*" (3 Ne. 27:27; emphasis added). The first-person present tense of the verb *be* is *I am.* As "the Great I am" (D&C 29:1), Christ invites us to take upon us His name and His nature.

To become as He *is,* we must also *do* the things He *did:* "Verily, verily, I say unto you, this is my gospel; and ye know the things that ye must *do* in my church; for the works which ye have seen me *do* that shall ye also *do*" (3 Ne. 27:21; emphasis added).

To *be* and to *do* are inseparable. As interdependent doctrines they reinforce and promote each other. Faith inspires one to pray, for example, and prayer in turn strengthens one's faith. And charity in a family inspires us to serve one another, and as we serve each other we grow in love as a family.

The Savior often denounced those who *did* without *being*—calling them hypocrites: "This people honoureth me with their lips, but their heart is far from me" (Mark 7:6). *To do* without *to be* is hypocrisy, or feigning to be what one is not—a pretender or phony.

Conversely, *to be* without *to do* is void, as in "faith, if it hath not works, *is dead,* being alone" (James 2:17; emphasis added). *Be* without *do* really isn't *being*—it is, in the words of James, "deceiving your own selves" (James 1:22), or believing oneself to be good merely because one's intentions are good.

Do without *be*—hypocrisy—portrays a false image to others, while *be* without *do* portrays a false image to oneself.

The Savior chastised the scribes and Pharisees for their hypocrisy: "Woe unto you, scribes and Pharisees, hypocrites! for ye pay tithe"—something they *did*—"of mint and anise and cummin, and have omitted the weightier matters of the law, judgment, mercy, and faith" (Matthew 23:23). Or in other words, they failed *to be* what they should *have been.*

While He recognized the importance of *do,* the Savior identified *be* as a "weightier matter." The greater importance of *being* is illustrated in the following examples:

- Entering the waters of baptism is something we *do.* The *be* that must precede it is faith in Jesus Christ and a mighty change of heart.

- Partaking of the sacrament is something we *do. Being* worthy to partake of the sacrament is a weightier and much more important matter.

- Ordination to the priesthood is an act, or *do.* The weightier matter, however, is power in the priesthood, which is based "upon the principles of righteousness" (D&C 121:36), or *be.*

THE WISDOM OF TEACHING BE

Many of us create *to do* lists to remind us of things we want to accomplish. But people rarely have *to be* lists. Why? *To dos* are activities or events that can be checked off the list when *done*. *To be,* however, is never done. You can't earn checkmarks with *to bes*. I can take my wife out for a lovely evening this Friday, which is a *to do*. But *being* a good husband is not an event; it needs *to be* part of my nature—my character, or who I am.

Or as a parent, when can I check a child off my list as *done?* We are never done *being* good parents. And to be good parents, one of the most important things we can teach our children is how *to be* more like the Savior. What greater thing could we teach to strengthen our families?

Christlike *to bes* cannot be seen, but they are the motivating force behind what we *do,* which can be seen. When parents help a child learn to walk, for example, we see parents *doing* things like steadying and praising their child. These *dos* reveal the unseen love in their hearts and the unseen faith and hope in their child's potential. Day after day their efforts continue—evidence of the unseen *bes* of patience and diligence.

Because *be* begets *do* and is the inspiration behind *do,* teaching *be* will improve behavior more effectively than focusing on *do* will improve behavior.

When children misbehave, let's say when they quarrel with each other, we often misdirect our discipline on what they *did,* or the quarreling we observed. But the *do*—their behavior—is only a symptom of the unseen motive in their hearts. Rather than try to correct behavior from the outside-in, which only produces temporary results, it would be wiser to work from the inside-out, which over time, achieves permanent results. We might ask ourselves, "What attributes, if understood by the child, would correct this behavior in the future? Being patient and forgiving when annoyed? Loving and being a peacemaker? Taking personal responsibility for one's actions and not blaming?"

HELPING OUR CHILDREN BECOME AS HE IS

How do parents teach these attributes to their children? We will never have a greater opportunity to teach and show Christlike attributes to our children than in the way we discipline them. *Discipline* comes from the same root word as *disciple or discipleship* and implies patience and teaching on our part. It should be done "when moved upon by the Holy Ghost" (D&C 121:43), and not when moved upon by anger which comes from Satan. "He that hath the spirit of contention is not of me, but is of the devil, who is the father of contention, and he stirreth up the hearts of men to contend with anger" (3 Ne. 11:29). We can and should discipline the way that Doctrine and Covenants 121 teaches us: "by persuasion, by long-suffering, by gentleness and meekness, and by love unfeigned; by kindness and pure knowledge" (verses 41–42). These are all Christlike *bes* that should be a part of who we, as parents and *disciples* of Christ, *are.*

Through discipline the child learns of consequences and to be responsible for their own behavior. In such moments it is helpful to turn negatives into positives, such as praising the courage and honesty it took to confess and calling attention to the child's true and innate character and potential: "That is not like you—you are a kind and loving boy."

Ask the child what he or she learned from the mistake or misdeed, which gives you, and more importantly, the Spirit an opportunity to touch and teach the child. When we teach children doctrine by the Spirit, that doctrine has the power to change their very nature—*be*—over time.

Alma discovered this same principle, that "the preaching of the word had a great tendency to lead the people *to do* that which was just—yea, it had had more powerful effect upon the minds of the people than the sword [or spanking]" (Alma 31:5; emphasis added). Why? Because the sword focused only on symptoms (working from the outside in), by punishing behavior—or *do*, while preaching the word changed people's very nature (working from the inside out)—who they *were* or could *become*.

A sweet and obedient child will enroll a father or mother only in Parenting 101. If you are blessed with a child who tests your patience to the nth degree, you will be enrolled in Parenting 505. Rather than wonder what you might have done wrong in the premortal life to be so deserving, you might consider the more challenging child a blessing and an opportunity to become more godlike yourself. With which child will your patience, long-suffering, and other Christlike virtues most likely be tested, developed, and refined? Could it be possible that you need this child as much as this child needs you?

OUR CHILDREN'S TRUE IDENTITY

During Christ's visit to the Americas, the Savior did something extraordinary with the children: "And it came to pass that he did teach and minister unto the children of the multitude . . . and he did loose their tongues, and they did speak unto their fathers great and marvelous things, even greater than he had revealed unto the people; and he loosed their tongues that they could utter. . . . And they both saw and heard these children; yea, even babes did open their mouths and utter marvelous things" (3 Ne. 26:14, 16).

I don't believe the Lord was opening the mouths of babes as much as He was *opening the eyes and ears* of their parents. The Lord revealed what the parents could not even imagine—their children's true identity and potential. It was as if He had given the parents a preview of coming attractions. Would that not change forever after the way the parents saw their children? With the eye of faith a wise parent would see that potential in each child, and as a spiritual mirror would reflect back to the child the image of who they really are or are becoming. Can you imagine the impact on the child and the difference such an attitude would make in the father's or mother's parenting?

The phenomenon of children internalizing the positive image their parents see in them, along with the positive change that ensues, is sometimes referred to as the Pygmalion effect. This effect was brought to life in the famous play in which the gutter snipe, Eliza Doolittle, becomes the refined "My Fair Lady." The dormant beauty was always there; Eliza only needed help from others to discover and develop it.

We have all heard the advice to condemn the sin and not the sinner. Likewise, when our children misbehave, a loving parent must be careful not to say things that would cause them to believe that what they *did* wrong is who they *are*. "Never let failure progress from an action to an identity," with its attendant labels like "stupid," "slow," "lazy," or "clumsy."[2] Our children are God's children. That is their true identity and potential as noted above. His very plan is to help His children overcome mistakes and misdeeds and to progress to become as He *is*. Disappointing behavior, therefore, should be considered as something temporary, not permanent—an act, not an identity.

A loving parent needs to be careful, therefore, about using permanent phrases such as "You always . . ." or "You never . . ." or "You are . . ." when disciplining. Take care with phrases such as "You never consider my feelings" or "You are so inconsiderate" or "Why do you always make us wait?" Phrases like these make actions appear as an identity and can adversely influence the child's self-perception and self-worth. A positive way to communicate the same messages might be, "What you *did* was inconsiderate, which surprises me, because you are not an inconsiderate person," or "Because you are a considerate person, I am surprised you kept us waiting—it makes me so happy when you are on time."

Identity confusion can also occur when we ask children what they want to *be* when they grow up, as if what a person *does* for a living is who he or she *is*. Neither professions nor possessions should define identity or self-worth. "For a man's life consisteth not in the abundance of the things which he possesseth" (Luke 12:15). The Savior was a humble carpenter, but that hardly defined His life.

DEALING WITH PROBLEMS

President Thomas S. Monson has taught, "Never let a problem to be solved become more important than a person to be loved."[3] The most important application of this principle is how we interact with our children.

A family and parenting website shared this insight: "When problems arise with our children, many parents confront them: 'You spilled the milk.' 'You left the door open.' 'You didn't feed the dog.' When we use such 'you' statements, children can feel attacked and become defensive. When they are trying to defend themselves, they have a hard time focusing on the problem at hand. More helpful responses would be: 'The milk spilled. We need something to clean it up.' 'The door is open. It needs to be closed.' 'The dog doesn't have any food. We need to feed him.' When we simply state the problem, our children will be able to focus on the issue instead of being distracted by an 'accusation.'"4

In their book *How to Talk So Kids Will Listen and Listen So Kids Will Talk,* Adele Faber and Elaine Mazlish say, "When we describe the event, (instead of talking about what 'you did'), we make it easier for the child to hear what the problem is and deal with it."5 Using statements like these are better than accusations because they help the child avoid confusing what they *did* with who they *are.*

PRAISING THE BE

In helping children discover who they are and helping strengthen their self-worth, we can appropriately compliment their achievement or behavior—the *do.* But it would be even wiser to focus our primary praise on their character and beliefs—who they *are.* There are many contexts in which we can practice this as parents.

Character development programs (such as Duty to God, Personal Progress, and Boy or Girl Scouts)—These programs are focused on character development, or *be* based. It would be helpful for you as a parent to keep the Christlike attributes in mind as you help them with any *do-based* achievement steps and praise them accordingly.

While these programs are comprised of a lot of *do* achievements—merit badges, medallions, and so on—the more important goals to praise are those *be* goals that form the foundation, the character development, such as a Scout becoming "trustworthy, loyal, helpful, friendly, courteous, kind, obedient, cheerful, thrifty, brave, clean, and reverent."

Sports—In a game of sports, a wise way to compliment our children's performance—*do*—would be through the point of view of *be*—like their energy, perseverance, poise in the face of adversity, etc.—thus complimenting both *be* and *do*.

Chores—When we ask children to *do* chores, we can also look for ways to compliment them on *being,* such as, "It makes me so happy when you do your chores with a willing heart." Or rather than simply saying "It's your turn to do the dishes," you could add, "Thank you for always being so helpful with the dishes."

In his book *The Game of Work,* Charles A. Coonradt teaches that when assigning chores to children it is wiser to focus on attributes—*be*—rather than activities—*do*. "Sweep the floor," for example, doesn't necessarily mean "a clean floor." "Sweep" focuses on the verb *do,* not so much on the attributes of thoroughness or cleanliness. It would be wiser to say, "What we want is a clean floor." Or rather than telling a child to "mow the lawn," it is more effective to focus on the joys of "a beautiful yard." The vision and motivation are quite different. When the child is finished with the chore, make sure to praise any one of a score of attributes.

Schoolwork—When children receive test scores or a report card from school, we can praise them for their good grades, but it may be of greater lasting benefit to praise them for their *diligence*: "You turned in every assignment. You are one who knows how to tackle and finish difficult things. I am proud of you."

Scripture study—Another time to teach and instill Christlike attributes is during family scripture time. Look for and discuss examples of attributes discovered in your reading that day. "Because Christlike attributes are gifts from God and cannot be developed without His help,"[6] pray for those gifts in family and personal prayers.

Dinnertime—At the dinner table, occasionally talk about attributes, especially those you discovered in the scriptures earlier that morning. "In what way were you a good friend today? In what way did you show compassion? How did faith help you face today's challenges? In what way were you dependable? honest? generous? humble?" There are scores of attributes in the scriptures that need to be taught and learned. It may be helpful to choose one attribute each week or month for the family to focus on and pay extra attention to (see Appendix, "Christlike Virtues").

Bedtime—Another marvelous and very effective way to teach positive attributes is through a story at bedtime, as the children are far more attentive then (especially if they get a back rub during the story—I never met a child who didn't love getting their back rubbed). There are many wonderful children's books that teach and illustrate Christlike virtues. Even better than a book is a story from your own childhood that illustrates a virtue. My children and grandchildren loved to hear stories of when I was a boy, just as I loved to hear stories of when my mom and dad were children.

When my father visited my family's home he would often ask permission to tuck the grandchildren into bed. He would ask the grandchildren if he could kneel with them and if they would permit him to say the prayer at the side of their bed. He would then thank Heavenly Father for the grandchildren and pray for them and praise them in the prayer. These many years later they fondly remember and cherish his stories, his back rubs, and his prayers. They love and adore him because of his love for them.

When they do something praiseworthy—The most effective

be praise is given when associated with something the child *did,* so that the child can connect the be-do dots. It is when children understand the be-do connection that they are most likely to repeat the *do* in the future. This in turn will help them further develop the *be.* If a *be* compliment is given without the *do* connection, there can be a disconnect in the children's mind. It becomes an elusive compliment, possibly leaving them wondering what they *did* to deserve such praise or what they can do to truly deserve it in the future.

FOCUSING ON BE IS WISER ENCOURAGEMENT THAN FOCUSING ON DO

Once when one of my sons was a young boy, he wanted a peanut butter sandwich. He asked me to help him spread the peanut butter on his bread. Wanting him to learn self-reliance, I told him that I believed that he could do it all by himself. He insisted that he couldn't. I insisted that he could, that he was very capable. He adamantly insisted that he could not do it. I restated my belief in him and asked him to just try, to not give up before he even tried. Our "yes-you-can—no-I-can't" conversation went back and forth a few more times until he was in tears. My mistake was that I focused exclusively on *do.*

If I could relive that little episode, I would focus more on *be.* In trying to reassure my son by focusing on *do,* I was communicating an unintended negative message, such as "you're just too lazy." In the mind of my son, spreading peanut butter on the bread did seem impossible.

A wiser response on my part would have been, "I can see that spreading the peanut butter is hard for someone who has never done it. I am pleased that you are willing to try—that shows you are one who can face difficult tasks with courage and diligence." My words would have been focused on his effort and his "stick-to-itiveness." I might have even held his hand and helped him begin the task to bolster his faith in himself. When children realize that we appreciate their efforts in the face of challenges, they will be more likely to try and master difficult tasks in the future.

PRAISING DOESN'T COME NATURALLY

Praise is a powerful motivator in reinforcing the development of Christlike attributes and good behavior. On at least three separate occasions the Father openly praised the Savior: "This is my beloved Son, in whom I am well pleased" (Matt. 3:17; Matt. 17:5; 3 Ne. 11:7).

Many years ago I learned an insightful business principle that good customer service is transparent. Put another way, we tend not to notice normal service or behavior because that's what we expect—we take it for granted.

This is why wives and mothers are seldom thanked—their service to the family is transparent. We forget to thank them for, cleaning the house, fixing the meals, teaching the children, etc., because that's what mothers have traditionally done—their good service is "transparent," and they often feel unappreciated. In just the same way, parents that work outside the home are seldom thanked for going to work each day to provide for their family.

This is a tendency between spouses, as well as between parents and children. We tend to take our spouse's good character traits for granted and instead focus on their faults, with very harmful results. And when children are well-behaved, we tend not to notice. It is when they misbehave that we notice and react. The result is that we are continually catching them doing things wrong and seldom catching them doing things right, which over time has a tremendous negative impact on their self-worth and identity.

CATCHING OUR LOVED ONES BEING GOOD AND DOING RIGHT

In 1982 Ken Blanchard authored a book titled *The One Minute Manager.* He introduced the concept of "catching people doing things right." Because good behavior is transparent, it takes effort to catch them doing things right.

I remember talking to my wife, Jan, about this principle many years ago. We were driving down the freeway with our seven children in the back of our van. So often when driving long distances, I became frustrated with the children when they misbehaved in the back of the car. More than once I was known to have said, "If you kids don't settle down right now we are turning this car around and going straight home." On this particular occasion, I noticed that the children were behaving wonderfully. All was quiet and peaceful as they gazed out the windows enjoying the scenery. I said, "Kids, thank you for being so well behaved, I really appreciate it."

Andy, who was then about seven years old said, "You're welcome, Dad!"

I would have completely missed this opportunity to compliment them if I hadn't been talking to Jan about the principle of catching the children doing things right. Good or normal behavior is transparent and requires concerted effort to notice and compliment. A loving parent will catch their children doing things right and follow the example of the Father, who declared that He was well pleased in His Son.

SEEING AND PRAISING THE GOOD
LEADS TO HAPPIER PEOPLE

Much of the 1960 Walt Disney movie *Pollyanna* is based upon this same premise of how easy it is to see the bad in people while being blind to the good. It is a weakness of the human character so common that the Savior taught a parable about it using motes and beams (see Matt. 7:3–4). In one scene in the movie, Pollyanna approaches the Reverend Paul Ford, who is in an open field practicing his sermon for the following Sunday. Because he has always seen the bad in people in order to call them to repentance, he is rehearsing a hellfire-and-damnation speech with a lot of emotion. When he is interrupted by Pollyanna, the two begin a conversation in which Pollyanna talks about her deceased father, who, as a preacher himself, had changed his sermons to focus on the "glad" passages in the Bible. It is a life-changing moment for the reverend. Pollyanna then opens her locket necklace, a gift given to her by her father, and Reverend Ford reads the inscription inside, a quotation by Abraham Lincoln: "If you look for the bad in people expecting to find it, you surely will."

The reverend repents, vowing to never look for the bad in his parishioners anymore. The following Sunday he preaches a "glad" sermon for the first time. The entire congregation of the town of Harrington is *gladly* amazed, almost dumbstruck. The reverend tells the congregation that there will be no more hellfire-and-damnation speeches, but that he is going to begin looking for the good in people and basing his sermons on the hundreds of glad verses in the Bible. As Pollyanna's contagious optimism spreads, the whole town becomes a happier place.

THE IMPORTANCE OF A PARENT'S EXAMPLE

The most important way to teach *to be* is *to be* the kind of parents to our children that our Father in Heaven is to us. We must believe in them the way he believes in us. We must see their divine potential just as he does. He is the one perfect parent, and He has shared with us His parenting manual—the scriptures.[7]

How well we follow that "manual" and become as He is will be the measure of our success as spouses and parents. "Your character will be the yardstick that God will use to determine how well you have used your mortal life."[8]

If you have no children of your own, then these principles might be applied with nieces and nephews, or children in a class that you teach, or with friends and other loved ones. What greater way to love those around you than to help them become more like Jesus Christ?

May your efforts to develop Christlike attributes be successful so that His image may be engraven in your countenance and His attributes manifest in your behavior. Then, when your children or others feel of your love and see your behavior, it will remind them of the Savior and inspire them to be like Him.

SUMMARY

- The verbs *be* and *do* are inseparable and mutually strengthen each other.
- Of the two, *to-be* constitutes the "weightier matter."
- Teaching *be* will improve behavior over time better than teaching *do*.
- Discipline begins with the *be*, as the *do* is only the outward manifestation of the *be*.

- Children provide parents with an opportunity to develop virtues that help them become more Christlike.
- Our children are God's children. That is their true identity and potential.
- Inappropriate behavior should not define a child's character—treat the behavior as temporary, as an act and not an identity.
- Avoid using labels that cause a child to confuse behavior with identity.
- Take advantage of opportunities to praise children for *being* good, along with *doing* good.
- Praising the good doesn't come naturally, and it takes effort to catch loved ones being good and doing right.
- Seeing the good in others leads to happier people and families.

NOTES

1. William Shakespeare, *Hamlet,* act 3, scene 1, line 56.
2. Carol Dweck, quoted in Joe Kita, "Bounce Back Chronicles," *Reader's Digest,* May 2009, 95.
3. Thomas S. Monson, "Finding Joy in the Journey," *Ensign,* Nov. 2008, 86.
4. *Navigating Life's Journey* Facebook page, December 6, 2013.
5. Adele Faber and Elaine Mazlish, *How to Talk so Kids Will Listen and Listen so Kids Will Talk* (New York: Avon Books, Inc.: 1980), 79.
6. *Preach My Gospel: A Guide to Missionary Service* (2004), 115.
7. Portions of this chapter taken from "What Manner of Men and Women Ought Ye to Be?," *Ensign,* May 2011, 103–5.
8. Richard G. Scott, "Living a Life of Peace, Joy, and Purpose," *Ensign,* Feb. 2014, 36.

CHAPTER 5

LOVE AND SELF-RELIANCE

Like the pieces of a jigsaw puzzle, the doctrines and principles of the gospel are difficult to understand when isolated out of context. You need all pieces of the puzzle to see the whole picture. Knowing this, when the Savior taught the Nephites, He "expounded all the scriptures in one" (3 Ne. 23:14). You not only need to have all of the pieces for a complete image and for better understanding, but you generally need to piece them together in just the right way. Most doctrines have a companion doctrine, or an adjacent piece with which it fits. They are counterpart doctrines—they interconnect.

For example, Christ's Atonement could not be fully understood without a simultaneous grasp of its counterpart doctrine—the Fall. "For as in Adam all die, even so in Christ shall all be made alive" (1 Cor. 15:22). The Fall explains the need for a Savior. Here is a sampling of additional doctrinal pairs:

- Agency and accountability
- Faith and works

- Ordinances and covenants
- The Apostasy and the Restoration

Some doctrinal pairs have an inverse or complementary relationship with one another. It is essential to understand the give-and-take nature of these relationships if we are to choose wisely. Finding the right balance requires the help of the Spirit. Here is a sampling of doctrines that fit in this category:

- Justice balanced with mercy (chastisement vs. leniency)
- Boldness and meekness
- The spirit of the law and the letter of the law
- Contentedness and progress
- Diligence and not running faster than you are able
- Avoiding pride balanced with not burying talents
- Desires, passions, and appetites balanced with temperance or moderation

Another kind of complementary doctrine is a *doctrinal exception.* One example is righteous indignation as the doctrinal exception to patience, such as was displayed when the Savior cast out the money changers from the temple. Doctrinal exceptions occur when the Spirit, in what we refer to as the spirit of the law, reveals a common sense exception to the letter of the law, like the "ox in the pit . . . on the Sabbath day" (Luke 14:5). There are many scriptural examples of doctrinal exceptions. Here is a sampling of a few doctrinal exceptions:

- "Come ye out from the wicked" (Alma 5:57) versus "This man receiveth sinners and eateth with them" (Luke 15:2).
- "That the church may stand independent above all other creatures" (D&C 78:14) versus "This is wisdom, make unto

yourselves friends with the mammon of unrighteousness, and they will not destroy you." (D&C 82:22).

- The Savior is the Prince of Peace but is also "the Lord of Hosts" meaning a man of war, a God of battles (Exodus 15:3).

CHARITY AND SELF-RELIANCE

Charity and self-reliance fit into the second category of doctrinal counterparts, forming a complementary and counterbalancing continuum. Theirs is an inverse relationship. The following are examples of love not balanced by self-reliance or love unwisely applied by a parent, resulting in unbridled agency in the child:

- Indulge/overindulge—to treat with excessive leniency, to show undue favor, to appease to an excessive degree.
- Spoil—to harm the character of somebody, especially a child, by repeated overindulgence.
- Coddle—to excessively protect and pamper.
- Enable—to help another persist in self-destructive behavior by providing excuses or making it possible to avoid the consequences of such behavior.

We recognize the above behaviors as excessive and dangerous. Each is a form of "parental over-involvement and leads to entitlements."[1] Parents exercising pure and wise love would never do those things. *Over*protection can result in the *under*development of children by depriving them of opportunities to solve their own problems. The one perfect parent (and teacher) allows His children to face the consequences of poor choices, that they may learn from their own experience to distinguish good from evil, right from wrong, and wise from foolish. Only in this way will they grow in wisdom and learn the relationship between choice and accountability. It is according to the Father's plan that they "learn obedience . . . by the things which they suffer" (D&C 105:6).

Just as mercy and justice are complementary principles on the same doctrinal continuum, charity and self-reliance counterbalance each other in a similar way. And just as mercy cannot rob justice (see Alma 42:25), neither can charity rob self-reliance, or the result is dependence rather than independence, a hand-out instead of a hand-up. In areas where welfare programs are not counterbalanced by self-reliance, you find indolence, entitlements, and welfare abuse—good intentions run amok. "What more could I have done?" is sometimes the desperate lament of a parent who hasn't done too little, but too much.

We could call charity without self-reliance *Santa Claus* and self-reliance without charity *Scrooge.* Like a doctrinal teeter-totter, either one by itself is incomplete and imbalanced and will usually lead to painful consequences. When considering the two, our image of Santa Claus is positive, while we tend to hold Scrooge in contempt. But my experience has taught me that Santa Claus, by himself, can be as dangerous, if not more so, than Scrooge.

A classic adventure story that illustrates this is *Captains Courageous,* by Rudyard Kipling. It is the story of Harvey Cheyne Jr., a very spoiled fifteen-year-old and the only son of very wealthy parents. After smoking a cigar, Harvey becomes sick, leans too far over the rail of an ocean liner, and falls overboard into the North Atlantic, unbeknownst to anyone. After being rescued by a fishing schooner he arrogantly demands to be taken ashore. When his demands are not met he stubbornly refuses to help with even the simplest of chores and insists that the fishing crew wait upon him in his accustomed manner. Captain Disko Troop administers a dose of "Scrooge" (sometimes called tough love) to the spoiled brat, who soon learns that if he doesn't work, he doesn't eat. Stranded on the boat, he must adapt to the ways of the fishermen. In time he learns self-reliance and self-respect. After a few months at sea, the boy is returned to his distraught and grateful father, who sees the remarkable transformation that has occurred in his now responsible and mature son.

EXCEPTIONS WHEN CHARITY IS NEEDED WITHOUT SELF-RELIANCE

Unlike the previous story, there are certain situations in which needy people, such as some disabled people or small children, aren't capable of self-reliance. In such cases, charity is administered without any thought to self-reliance, just as mercy saves such without any thought to justice (see Moro. 8:19–20). I have heard President Monson teach on more than one occasion, "No bishop should knowingly allow any child in his ward to go to bed hungry."

In life-threatening situations, such as after an earthquake, hurricane, or tsunami, there is often a need to respond with immediate help with little thought to self-reliance—a time when Santa is needed. But, as assistance continues, self-reliance must be expected to preserve a work ethic, self-worth, and a healthy society. Otherwise, charity is unbalanced and the damage of the disaster is compounded. Third- and fourth-generation welfare recipients are a good case in point.

And so it is with spiritual needs. Some success is achieved by teaching a child *what to think*. But the greater success and only lasting hope in raising spiritually self-reliant children is to teach them *how to think*. It is in guiding them in the wise use of their agency and in teaching them how to recognize the whisperings of the Spirit and choose wisely on their own. One day they will leave the nest, and if they do not know how to fly spiritually, they will fall or flounder spiritually.

With those who haven't yet received the gospel, we may begin with a *spiritual fish* by sharing the doctrines and principles, but our ultimate goal is to invite and help others learn *the art of spiritual fishing* through faith in Jesus Christ and His Atonement, repentance, baptism, receiving the gift of the Holy Ghost, and enduring to the end. With the Spirit as their private tutor, they are on the road to spiritual self-reliance.

The scriptures record that "our father Adam taught these things" (Moses 7:1). Earth's first mortal father set an example for all parents in teaching their children self-reliance, or helping them transition from childhood to responsible adulthood. "And again, inasmuch as parents have children in Zion, or in any of her stakes which are organized, that teach them not to understand the doctrine of repentance, faith in Christ the Son of the living God, and of baptism and the gift of the Holy Ghost by the laying on of the hands, when eight years old, the sin be upon the heads of the parents" (D&C 68:25). Choosing to teach children is a decision that must be made anew every day. Doing so yields the greatest dividends in life—success in the home.

PARENTING WITH CHARITY AND SELF-RELIANCE

In our desire to be good parents we are often tempted to hold our children's hand too tightly and drag them, if necessary, along the strait and narrow path. Tight-grip dragging is almost always unwise and is usually charity misapplied and unbalanced. The reason we often hold too tightly is because the thought of losing a child in the mists of darkness is so frightening that we find it difficult to relax our grip. The handholding that was comforting to a child, however, may feel constraining to a teenager. Even small children, when dragged, will generally resist and exert their agency and self-reliance to go in any other direction than the one in which they are being forced. For our children to successfully navigate and complete life's journey, we must ease our grip on them as we help them tighten their own grip on the iron rod.

In Lehi's dream there was no handholding between parent and child, only beckoning on Lehi's part. Beckoning is the Lord's way: "Come unto me and ye shall partake of the fruit of the tree of life; yea, ye shall eat and drink of the bread and the waters of life freely" (Alma 5:34). "Therefore . . . whosoever will come may come and partake of the waters of life freely; and whosoever will not come the same is *not compelled* to come" (Alma 42:27; emphasis added). The iron rod is the Lord's way of reaching out to us while at the same time fostering our self-reliance. He provides the rod, but He doesn't force the grasp. What a powerful doctrinal symbol of the Father's love for His children balanced with spiritual self-reliance!

Easing our grip and letting go of our child's hand may feel counterintuitive to our grasping impulse, especially as we see the approaching mists. But easing our grip doesn't mean standing idly by doing nothing. We are close at hand when our children slip or stumble or fall (as all do) to love and help them back on their feet again, just as the Savior does with us.

His grace is a "divine means of help or strength . . . an enabling power that allows men and women to lay hold on eternal life and exaltation after they have expended their own best efforts."[2] The word *after* in this Bible Dictionary definition of grace should not be misinterpreted to mean only at the journey's end. With faith in every

footstep, His grace is with us and His loving eye is upon us throughout our entire journey.

His grace and love help us not only to "lay hold on eternal life"
but to "lay hold on the iron rod" while getting there. That "divine
means of help or strength" is manifested hundreds of times in the
Book of Mormon as the Lord inspires, lightens burdens, strengthens,
delivers, protects, heals, and otherwise "succors his people" as they
tread the strait and narrow path (Alma 7:12). We rely "wholly upon
the merits of him who is mighty to save" (2 Ne. 31:19) during and
after the journey.

In the parable of the ten virgins (see Matt. 25), the five foolish
virgins were unwise in depending too much on the five who were
wise. We could say that the Savior had the five wise virgins respond to
the request of the five foolish in a Scrooge-like way: "Go get your own
oil." One of the fundamental doctrines taught by this parable is spiritual self-reliance—that no one can live or depend on borrowed light.
The five foolish virgins needed and were given a dose of self-reliance,
or a spoonful of "Scrooge." Like the iron rod, the lamp and the oil are
also compelling symbols in teaching spiritual self-reliance.

SELF-RELIANCE AND CHILDREN

In raising children there is a constant need for parents to discern the wise balance between charity and self-reliance. For example,
in teaching a one-year-old how to be self-reliant with the use of a
spoon, a loving parent is patiently tolerant of the messes made in the
highchair. The parent helps only to the extent that help is needed.
Likewise, a loving mother allows a young child to make the bed,
even though she could make it so much better herself. As her charity
gives way to the child's self-reliance, her tolerance for mistakes and

her patience and long-suffering become manifestations of her love, patterned after the even greater patience and long-suffering the Lord feels toward each of us with our mistakes and sins. The loving mother guides her child in decision-making and is careful not to make decisions for him or her. She teaches correct principles relating to the decisions at hand and allows the child to govern him or herself. Mistakes that are made become opportunities to reteach principles, or to *discipline*—a word whose etymology is the same as that of *disciple,* which implies *teaching* the child.

Finances can be a very effective tool for parents in teaching their children self-reliance. Let's use clothing as an example. For the four-year-old, self-reliance may focus mostly on simple decisions—choices like, "What color of shirt would you like to wear today?" Older children, however, can become more involved in the whole process. Rather than buying older children's clothing for them, it would be wise to provide them with a clothing fund based upon family chores and responsibilities and empower them to buy their own clothes (with guidance) using the very same money the parent would have spent. The process helps them learn several virtues beginning with agency and including responsibility, industry, frugality, and self-reliance, to name a few. For the teenager, the virtue of self-reliance can be taken to a new level as part-time employment begins to supplement their income and have a direct impact on their finances.

When the Church welfare program was first introduced in 1936, the First Presidency said, "The aim of the Church is to help people to help themselves."[3] Should it be any different for parents raising a child? Isn't that what our Father in Heaven is doing with us—raising us to become like Him, to become self-reliant in the absolute and ultimate sense, to become celestial adults?

PRAYER AND SELF-RELIANCE

Nearly synonymous to the complementary doctrines of charity and self-reliance is the pairing of prayer and self-reliance. In several scriptures the Lord says, "Ask and ye shall receive." Yet, the Lord taught Oliver Cowdery, "You have not understood; you have supposed that I would give it unto you, when you took no thought save it was to ask me" (D&C 9:7).

If we had a child that came to us and asked, "Mom/Dad, will you help me with my math assignment?" we would be happy to help, but we would not do the assignment for them. We might respond, "What is it that you don't understand about your assignment?" We would give them some tutoring and then say, "Now you work on it, and when you solve the problem come to me and I'll tell you if you have the correct answer." Why do we do that? Because our children won't learn unless they do it themselves. That is precisely what the Lord did with Oliver. It's as if the Lord responded to Oliver, "Did you think all you had to do was ask?" Rather, He counseled, "Behold, I say unto you that you must study it out in your mind; then you must ask me if it be right, and if it is right I will cause that your bosom shall burn within you, therefore, you shall feel that it is right" (D&C 9:8). This is an excellent example of the Lord balancing charity (help in request to a prayer) with self-reliance.

The Lord applied the same two doctrines of prayer and self-reliance with the brother of Jared in the building of the Jaredite barges. One reason the Lord gave the brother of Jared *incomplete* boat plans (not solving the air and light challenges) was to teach him to be *reliant on the Lord.* The Lord had earlier chastised the brother of Jared for not relying on the Lord: "And for the space of three hours did the

Lord talk with the brother of Jared, and chastened him because he remembered not to call upon the name of the Lord" (Ether 2:14).

Another reason for the incomplete boat plans was to teach the brother of Jared *self-reliance,* or to cause him to use his brain and to develop his ability to think, ponder, and reason. The Lord helped the brother of Jared with part of his homework by providing him with a solution to the air problem, but the Lord then forced him to use his own reasoning on the light problem. The task not only required the brother of Jared to think, but to think outside the box by eliminating the only two sources of light known to man at that time—the sun (the boats couldn't have windows) and fire (see Ether 2:23). The only other option for the brother of Jared was the Light of the World. He would need to rely on the Lord for both physical and spiritual light. So the Lord responded, "Therefore what will ye that *I should prepare* for you that ye may have light when ye are swallowed up in the depths of the sea?" (Ether 2:25; emphasis added).

You know the rest of the story—how the brother of Jared acted in faith and performed a lot of work to help the prayer come to pass. It is one of many wonderful stories from the scriptures in which the Lord balances charity and prayer with self-reliance.

The Lord maintains a very wise balance with His involvement in our lives. To strengthen our faith, He gives us enough "evidence" of His love and unseen presence, but not so much as to invalidate the test of faith. This balance is critical in His desire for us to be spiritually self-reliant as we nurture the seed of faith and tend to its growth.

THE GIFT OF SELF-RELIANCE

In many countries there are poor families who cannot afford to support their children who desire to serve missions. In such cases there is a Financial Assistance Request form, which is filled out as part of the missionary recommendation packet. The form asks what the missionary, the missionary's family, and the ward are willing to contribute toward this young person's mission. To comply with the doctrine of self-reliance, the bishop certifies that the amount committed represents a *maximum* sacrifice that the family is able to pay on their own. When the combined total falls short of the necessary amount, the General Missionary Fund helps make up the balance.

While serving in the Central American Area presidency many years ago, I learned of a poor widow from Honduras whose monthly income was just $48.00, a hundred times less than what many North American families make, and well below the poverty level in Honduras. When her son submitted his missionary recommendation packet, the Financial Assistance Request showed a commitment of $6.00 per month by the widow and her son, far short of the amount needed to finance a mission. For this family, $6.00 represented a maximum sacrifice.

In this touching story our heart goes out to the widow, and we may have a charitable urge to say, "She can't afford to pay one dime! Let the General Missionary Fund pay for that boy's mission entirely!" Whether it is with missionary support, tithing, or fast offerings, all God's children are expected to learn and live the doctrines of sacrifice and self-reliance. Our charitable and compassionate impulses should not rob them of the vital learning experiences that come with sacrifice and self-reliance, or else we would also rob them of the blessings associated with these doctrines (see Mark 12:41–44; Luke 21:1–4).

COMPLEMENTARY PRINCIPLES:
ADMINISTERING VS. MINISTERING

Because each situation is unique, the only way for a priesthood or auxiliary leader or parent to discern the correct balance between the complementary doctrines of charity and self-reliance is by the Spirit. In a welfare case, for example, the bishop or those delegated with the responsibility to help the needy individual will have to do some *ministering* by following the principles of self-reliance found in the booklet *Providing in the Lord's Way* (2009). "Too many bishops," I have heard President Thomas S. Monson state on more than one occasion, "try to solve welfare cases with the checkbook rather than the Handbook."

An *administrative* solution by itself, or playing Santa Claus with the checkbook, is always the easy way, but not the *Lord's way.* Inspiration will only come through prayer after a leader balances administering with ministering and charity with self-reliance. The leader will spend the least amount of time necessary on *administrative* tasks in order to spend the greatest amount of time possible on *ministering* opportunities (which is also a wise guideline for conducting ward councils).

And so it is with the parent-child relationship. A parent's heart should carry a constant prayer to be blessed with the spiritual gifts of revelation, discernment, love, and wisdom to know the correct balance between love and self-reliance in raising their children.

SUMMARY

- Most doctrines have complementary doctrines that are counterpoints, counterbalancing, or exceptions.
- Charity's complementary doctrine is self-reliance.

- Charity without self-reliance is like Santa Claus; self-reliance without charity is like Scrooge. Either one by itself is incomplete and dangerous.
- There are times when charity is appropriately administered without self-reliance, such as in an emergency or with those incapable of self-reliance.
- The iron rod and the oil in the lamp are examples and symbols of the Lord's charity balanced with self-reliance.
- Prayer is the means to access the Lord's grace and charity. But prayer, as an act of faith, requires work or self-reliance on our part before the Lord can bless us with His part.
- In welfare cases, for a bishop to achieve a wise and inspired solution, he must learn to balance his administrative duties with his ministering responsibility by balancing charity with self-reliance. Not balancing these complementary doctrines will lead to an uninspired solution.

Notes

1. Elizabeth Svoboda, "Art of Living," *Psychology Today*, quoted in *Reader's Digest*, February 2014, 41.
2. Bible Dictionary, "Grace"; emphasis added.
3. Conference Report, Oct. 1936, 3.

CHAPTER 6

AGENCY AND LOVE IN THE FAMILY

B elow is a picture of a happy family. They were all smiles when they posed for this picture. Looking at the family, it would appear as if dad and mom are happily in love and probably great parents—always kind and loving.

It would be easy to always be kind and loving parents if the kids were always well behaved, but because they aren't, they "occasionally" do things to irk their parents. When that happens, "we have learned by sad experience that it is the nature and disposition of almost all [parents] . . . [to] immediately begin to exercise unrighteous dominion" (D&C 121:39), as depicted in this candid shot of them taken with a "hidden camera."

"It is [our] *nature* and disposition . . . to exercise unrighteous dominion" because of the "*natural* man" and woman in each of us (Mosiah 3:19; emphasis added), "who is carnal, sensual, and devilish, by *nature*" (Alma 42:10; emphasis added). When something upsets us, Satan will tempt us to become angry, as he did with this couple.

Our parenting skills are not tested so much when the children are pleasant and obedient—that would be a piece of cake, and would enroll us only in Parenting 101. The real test is how we respond to behavior when it is defiant, irritating, and even maddening—the kind of behavior that enrolls us in Parenting 505.

OUR FATHER IN HEAVEN IS THE ONE PERFECT PARENT

The scriptures contain many principles that display how the one perfect parent is raising His children, all of whom have been disobedient, except for One. The closer we follow our Father's example and apply His parenting principles, the greater success we will have as parents. This chapter explores some of those principles.

As discussed in earlier chapters, the more we *become* like our Father in Heaven and Savior, the more instinctively correct will be our response in any given situation, but especially in the greatest work we will ever do—within the walls of our home.

To repeat a question from chapter 2, how often does the one perfect parent *force* His children at the crossroads of life? Never. But He doesn't leave us helpless, either. He has given all His children the Light of Christ to help them discern between good and evil (see Moro. 7:16). And through His prophets and scriptures He teaches us the blessings of choosing the right road and the negative consequences of choosing the wrong road. He may even command us to take the right road and avoid the wrong road, "nevertheless, thou mayest choose for thyself, for it is given unto thee" (Moses 3:17).

If His children choose the correct road, "if their works were good in this life, and the desires of their hearts were good, that they should also, at the last day, be restored unto that which is good" (Alma 41:3). But, "if their works are evil they shall be restored unto them for evil. Therefore, all things shall be restored to the proper order, everything to its natural frame" (Alma 41:4). "And thus they stand or fall; for behold, they are their *own judges,* whether to do good or do evil" (Alma 41:7, emphasis added). In other words, the one perfect parent teaches thoroughly enough that when His children knowingly choose evil, the consequences become the discipline and are essentially self-administered—meaning the child becomes his or her own judge.

THE GREATEST WORK WE WILL EVER DO

Consider combining the following two principles taught by two of our latter-day prophets into one "blended" principle. I believe the result will be insightful. The first is from President Gordon B. Hinckley: "Effective teaching is the very essence of leadership."[1] The second is from President Harold B. Lee: "The most important of the

Lord's work you will ever do will be within the walls of your own homes."[2] Now, try your hand at combining them.

Here are a couple of possibilities in blending or combining these two principles:

- "Effective teaching is the very essence of parenting."
- "The most important work you will ever do is to effectively teach your children."

It is interesting that the Book of Mormon begins with this principle: "I, Nephi, having been born of goodly parents, therefore I was taught" (1 Ne. 1:1).

However, the greatest example of effectively teaching children comes from our own Father in Heaven. If we have a desire to improve our own teaching skills and more effectively raise our posterity, it would be wise to follow the principles of effective teaching as exemplified by the one perfect parent.

LEADING BY EXAMPLE

The Savior always showed the way. He never established expectations nor asked His disciples to do something without first giving them an example so that He could invite them with conviction and power: "Follow me." Whether it was an attribute or a behavior, He always showed the way (see 3 Ne. 27:21, 27).

When He taught the Nephites about prayer, for example, He knelt and prayed with them. Then He said, "And as I have prayed among you even so shall ye pray in my church, among my people who do repent and are baptized in my name. Behold I am the light; I have set an example for you" (3 Ne. 18:16). His life was His greatest sermon. I hope that can be said of us as well.

DOCTRINES, PRINCIPLES, AND RULES

One helpful insight is to consider the Lord's teaching method through the lens of doctrines, principles, and rules.

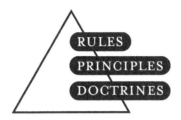

Doctrines: The doctrines of the gospel form the foundation of our faith and beliefs. They are eternal truths *not* subject to "the conditions of the children of men" (D&C 46:15). In his inspiring book *Act in Doctrine,* Elder David A. Bednar teaches us that "a gospel doctrine is a truth of salvation revealed by a loving Heavenly Father . . . [they] are eternal, do not change, and pertain to the eternal progression and exaltation of Heavenly Father's sons and daughters. Doctrines such as the nature of the Godhead, the plan of happiness, and the Atonement of Jesus Christ are foundational, fundamental, and comprehensive. Gospel doctrines answer the question of 'why?'"[3]

It is in the doctrines of the gospel where we find the power and inspiration for everything we do because they answer the deep "why?" questions of life. That is why President Boyd K. Packer has taught, "True doctrine, understood, changes attitudes and behavior. The study of the doctrines of the gospel will improve behavior quicker than a study of behavior will improve behavior."[4]

Principles: When the Prophet Joseph was asked how he governed so many people, he replied, "I teach them correct principles, and they govern themselves."[5] Elder Bednar explains that "A gospel *principle* is a doctrinally based guideline for the righteous exercise of moral agency. Principles provide direction. Correct principles always are based upon and arise from doctrines, do not change, and answer the question of 'what?' . . . A principle is not a behavior or a specific action. Rather, principles provide basic guidelines for behavior and action."[6] Principles are guiding standards that help one think clearly and wisely when facing a decision. The wisdom of a decision depends upon correctly applying the principle in any given situation.

Rules: The one perfect parent rarely gives rules to His children: "For behold, it is not meet that I should command in all things; for he that is compelled in all things, the same is a slothful and not a wise servant; wherefore he receiveth no reward" (D&C 58:26). As taught in the last chapter, our Father in Heaven balances love with self-reliance, and if He were to tell us every little thing to do, it would cripple and stunt our spiritual growth by taking away the need to think for ourselves.

By contrast, the governments of the world are inclined to govern by rules—lots of them. The Internal Revenue Code, for example, is around 5,000 pages of rules. When you add regulations, federal and tax court cases, and private letter rulings to that number, it grows to a staggering number of pages—all to help us calculate taxes.

Conversely, how many pages has the Lord given to help us calculate tithing? Because the Lord governs with principles rather than rules, he doesn't even need one page. The principle in this case is, "Those who have thus been tithed shall pay one-tenth of all their interest annually" (D&C 119:4). Interest "is understood to mean income. No one is justified in making any other statement than this."[7] No additional pages are needed.

When people aren't faithful in paying their tithing, it is because they either don't understand the "why?" (the underlying doctrines) or they are choosing to willfully disobey. The *why* doctrines in this case would include a love of God and our fellowmen, the trial of one's faith, obedience, sacrifice, gratitude, kingdom building, and so on.

One reason rules often become the default approach by unwise parents is because they are easily enforced on the spot, with immediate results. Conversely, teaching doctrine and principles requires repeated training with patience and long-suffering, with results coming "in process of time" (Moses 7:21). Rules, without the support of underlying doctrines and principles, however, may change behavior in the short run, but usually with resentment, because there is no understanding in the one whose behavior is being corrected. Rules focus on symptoms, or outward signs, rather than on the root cause, which is the belief and understanding in the mind and heart. Rules try to change a person from the outside in, while doctrines go to the heart of the matter and change a person from the inside out by answering the *why*, thus changing understanding, beliefs, and desire to repent. This principle clarifies why the Lord said, "I will put my law in their inward parts, and write it in their hearts; and will be their God, and they shall be my people."[8]

RULES AND THE LETTER OF THE LAW

Perhaps the most serious consequence of trying to govern with rules is that too many rules cause one to depend entirely on "the letter of the law" to the utter exclusion of the whisperings of the Spirit. Too many rules stifle the flexibility needed in applying a principle, "as given by the Holy Ghost . . . according to the conditions of the children of men" (D&C 46:15). This was the exact trap into which the

Pharisees fell. Even centuries later we use the adjective *pharisaical* to describe someone who advocates "strict observance of external forms and ceremonies of religion or conduct without regard to the spirit."⁹ According to the Bible Dictionary, the Pharisees, "reduced religion to the observance of a multiplicity of ceremonial rules."

There were so many pharisaical rules that governed Sabbath-day behavior, for example, that the people lost all common sense concerning how to keep it holy. Such extremism is unbalanced, fanatical, and can even become militant. When the Savior failed to observe some of their traditional rules regarding Sabbath day behavior, "they were filled with madness; and communed one with another what they might do to Jesus" (Luke 6:1–11).

Too many rules had caused the Pharisees to rely so totally on the letter of the law that they forgot the reason for the law. They essentially ceased to rely on the Holy Ghost and lost the common sense that comes from the Light of Christ. Like the damaging impact of too many rules on the Pharisees, a parent can likewise unwittingly cripple a child mentally and spiritually by trying to govern the pharisaical way.

We know that it is wiser to teach a man the art of fishing than it is to give him a fish. Likewise, it is far more important for a parent to help children learn the art of wise decision-making than it is to try to make their decisions for them, or to try to control their children's lives with too many rules. Children will need years of practice and thousands of experiences making wise decisions to master the use of their agency.

With the Word of Wisdom the Lord did give us a few rules—to avoid coffee, tea, tobacco, and alcohol. But, if we were to include every harmful substance known to man in section 89 of Doctrine and

Covenants, the section would be as voluminous as the tax code. The Lord knows that it is wiser to allow His children to be agents unto themselves (see 2 Ne. 2:26) and to follow the principles in section 89, which are in turn based upon the doctrine that "your body is the temple of the Holy Ghost which is in you" (1 Cor. 6:19).

Heavenly Father's way of raising His children is to respect their agency while helping them to be wise agents by teaching them doctrines and principles and only rarely giving them rules. Only when His children are rebellious does He begin adding more rules, as "to the house of Israel, as a replacement of the higher law that they had failed to obey."[10] The next time you hear yourself saying "no" to a child, make sure you explain to them *why* you are telling them "no"— otherwise it may be an indication that you are basing your parenting skills on rules more than on doctrine and principles.

LETTING OUR CHILDREN EXERCISE AGENCY

When my oldest daughter was ten years old she came to me one Sunday morning and asked me if she could watch a scary movie on television that Sabbath afternoon. From our family home evenings and family scripture time I knew that she had been taught the doctrine of keeping the Sabbath day holy to remember and worship our Father in Heaven and Savior. I also knew that she had been taught principles of Sabbath day observance such as those found in *For The Strength of Youth:* "Sunday is not a day for shopping, recreation, or athletic events. Do not seek entertainment or make purchases on this day" (31).

I thought this was a good teaching moment to let her "wrestle" with the whisperings of the Holy Ghost, so I responded, "This is your choice. You can make this decision on your own." This was not the answer she was seeking. She was hoping for a permission, which would have allowed her to watch the movie guilt-free, having passed the accountability for the decision to me. The person who desires rules is, in essence, uncomfortable with the responsibility that comes with choice in the absence of rules. Rules tend to shift responsibility for choice to the rule-giver, and they remove the need to think on the part of the governed. When choice is stifled by rules, it essentially eliminates the need for agency in favor of blind and strict obedience. Does that remind you of someone's plot in the premortal life?

My daughter left my office for about five minutes and then returned and asked emphatically, "PLEASE can I watch it?" Well, I hadn't denied her first request, but here she was again trying to make me the accountable one.

I responded, "I'm not going to tell you that you can or can't; this is your decision to make." Frustrated that she didn't get the answer she wanted, she left my office a second time. I was pleased to see her wrestling with the decision, trusting that the Spirit was guiding her.

She returned after another five minutes and said, "Dad, I've made my decision—I'm going to watch it."

There is risk in honoring the agency of our children and leaving them at the forks in the road, trusting in the Holy Ghost to guide them. But, didn't our Father in Heaven take that same risk in the premortal life with one-third of the host of heaven—so important was the doctrine of agency? We can trust the Holy Ghost in helping our children because "there is no witness so terrible or no accuser so powerful as the conscience."[11] "The worst punishment of all is that in the court of his own conscience no guilty man is acquitted."[12]

I am not espousing permissiveness, nor a lack of boundaries, and I have subsequently thought I should have retaught my daughter the doctrines and principles of Sabbath day observance at that very moment so they would be fresh in her mind. But, in this particular case, I had told my daughter twice that she could make her own decision. I had respected her agency twice and decided that I would not exert force at this point.

In raising children, consider this slight addition to what the Prophet Joseph taught: "We teach them correct principles, because whether we like it or not, they will govern themselves." The day will come when my daughter will be living on her own. The only hope my wife and I have is to guide her in the wise use of her agency, teaching correct principles and helping her to recognize the whisperings of the Spirit. Of all the things we could teach her throughout her life, this one is perhaps the single most important. If my wife and I have not taught her how to make wise decisions in this, the Lord's way, there is a chance we could lose her.

I decided to leave her at the crossroads with the Holy Ghost, trusting that the Holy Ghost would bother her conscience sufficiently to help her choose the right and not go forward with her decision to watch the movie. The hour came, and she turned on the television. I thought, "She'll change her mind and will soon turn it off." However, my hope was in vain—she watched the whole thing. But having watched this scary and suspenseful movie, especially as a ten-year-old girl, that night she had a nightmare. The following morning she came to me and said, "Dad, I'm feeling bad about the decision I made yesterday to watch that movie. I should not have watched it."

I thought to myself, "My daughter is learning from her own experience to distinguish right from wrong." If I had denied her request I would have deprived her of an experience with the whisperings of the Spirit. It is experiences like this one that have helped her become the wonderful wife and mother and valiant daughter of our Father in Heaven that she is today.

In telling this story I am not making a statement on whether we should or shouldn't watch television on Sunday. We are certainly grateful that *Music and the Spoken Word* and general conference are broadcast on Sunday and that BYU Television "sees the good in the world" every day, including Sunday.

The iron rod is the word of God[13] and is the rod we should use in disciplining, rather than using a literal rod or sword. Alma discovered that "the preaching of the word had a great tendency to lead the people to do that which was just—yea, it had had more powerful effect upon the minds of the people than the sword, or anything else, which had happened unto them—therefore Alma thought it was expedient that they should try the virtue of the word of God."[14]

It was this righteous strategy that time and again in the Book of Mormon produced the greatest results or positive outcomes. "And it came to pass that the Lamanites did hunt the band of robbers of Gadianton; and they did preach the word of God among the more wicked part of them, insomuch that this band of robbers was utterly destroyed from among the Lamanites."[15]

The sword, or punishment, only focuses on symptoms and doesn't change beliefs or behavior long-term. Punishment is usually carried out in anger and contempt. It is something you do *to* another person, and it is taken with resentment. Discipline, conversely, is carried out with love and is something you do *for* another person. Discipline is teaching the word of God—the iron rod, rather than the other rod.

DISCIPLINING CHILDREN

Because teaching is the very essence of parenting, disciplining is one of the most important teaching moments for a parent.

Regarding disciplining children, President Joseph F. Smith taught, "If children are defiant and difficult to control, be patient with them until you can conquer by love, and you will have gained their souls, and you can then mold their characters as you please."[16] "You can't force your boys, nor your girls into heaven. You may force them to hell, by using harsh means in the efforts to make them good, when you yourselves are not as good as you should be. The man that will be *angry* at his boy, and try to correct him while he is in *anger,* is in the greatest fault; he is more to be pitied and more to be condemned than the child who has done wrong. You can only correct your children by love, in kindness, by love unfeigned, by persuasion, and reason."[17]

It is noteworthy that in teaching how to discipline children, the prophets seem to always refer to Christlike attributes. President James E. Faust adds these insights:

"Parents should administer discipline through love and righteousness. Children cannot be forced into obedience. As President Hinckley has said, 'There is need for discipline with families. But discipline with cruelty, inevitably leads not to correction, but rather to resentment and bitterness. It cures nothing and only aggravates the problem. It is self-defeating.'[18] Our best method for correcting children when they have done wrong is by firmness, love, patience, kindness, persuasion, and reason."[19]

A revelation in Doctrine and Covenants gives us this well-known advice: "No power or influence can or ought to be maintained by virtue of the priesthood, only by persuasion, by long-suffering, by gentleness and meekness, and by love unfeigned; By kindness, and pure knowledge, which shall greatly enlarge the soul without hypocrisy, and without guile—Reproving betimes with sharpness, when moved upon by the Holy Ghost; and then showing forth afterwards an increase of love toward him whom thou hast reproved, lest he esteem thee to be his enemy" (D&C 121:41–43).

This scripture teaches us to reprove, or discipline, "when moved upon by the Holy Ghost," *not* when moved upon by anger. The Holy Ghost and anger are incongruent and mutually exclusive. George Albert Smith taught that "unkind things are not usually said under the inspiration of the Lord. The Spirit of the Lord is a spirit of kindness; it is a spirit of patience; it is a spirit of charity and love and forbearance and long suffering. . . . But if we have the spirit of fault finding, of pointing out the weaknesses and failings of others in a destructive manner, that never comes as a result of the companionship of the Spirit of our Heavenly Father and is always harmful. . . . Kindness is the power that God has given us to unlock hard hearts and subdue stubborn souls . . . [with] our children . . . so love them and earn their love that they will be glad to listen to our advice and counsel."[20]

Ultimately, we are to "bridle all [our] passions, that [we] may be filled with love" (Alma 38:12).

ELIMINATING ANGER HELPS MAKE YOUR HOUSE A LOVING HOME

In April 1998 I gave my first general conference address, titled "Agency and Anger." At that time I was serving on a committee that required me to review hundreds of letters from couples who had filed for divorce. Anger was such a common element in these cases that I was inspired to address the topic in general conference. I include here much of what I said then.[21]

We learn in the proclamation on the family that "husband and wife have a solemn responsibility to love and care for each other" and a "sacred duty to rear their children in love and righteousness."[22]

One of Satan's key strategies is to stir up anger between family members. Satan is the "father of contention," and he "stirreth up the hearts of men to contend with anger, one with another" (3 Ne. 11:29). The verb "stir" sounds like a recipe for disaster: put tempers on medium heat, stir in a few choice words, and bring to a boil; continue stirring until thick; remove from heat and let cool; let feelings chill overnight; serve cold; lots of leftovers.

A cunning part of Satan's strategy is to dissociate anger from agency, making us believe that we are victims of an emotion that we cannot control. We hear the phrase "I lost my temper." Losing one's temper is an interesting choice of words that has become a widely used idiom. To "lose something" implies "not meaning to," "accidental," "involuntary," "not responsible"—careless perhaps, but "not responsible."

"He made me mad." This is another phrase we hear, also implying lack of control or agency. This is a cunning myth that must be debunked. No one makes us mad. Others don't make us angry. There is no force involved. Becoming angry is a conscious choice or decision. Therefore, we can make the choice not to become angry. We choose!

To those who say, "But I can't help myself," author William Wilbanks responds, "Nonsense." "Aggression . . . suppressing anger, talking about it, screaming and yelling, are all learned strategies in dealing with anger. We choose the one that has proved effective for us in the past. Ever notice how seldom we lose control when frustrated by our boss, but how often we do when annoyed by friends or family?"[23]

In his sophomore year Wilbanks tried out for the high school basketball team and made it. On the first day of practice his coach had him play one-on-one while the team observed. When he missed an easy shot, he became angry and stomped and whined. The coach walked over to him and said, "You pull a stunt like that again and you'll never play for my team." For the next three years he never lost control again. Years later, as he reflected back on this incident, he realized that the coach had taught him a life-changing principle that day: anger can be controlled.[24]

In the Joseph Smith Translation of Ephesians 4:26, Paul asks the question, "Can ye be angry, and not sin?" The Lord is very clear on this issue. "He that hath the spirit of contention is not of me, but is of the devil, who is the father of contention, and he stirreth up the hearts of men to contend with anger, one with another. Behold, this is not my doctrine, to stir up the hearts of men with anger, one against another; but this is my doctrine, that such things should be done away" (3 Ne. 11:29–30). This doctrine or command from the Lord presupposes agency and is an appeal to the conscious mind to make a decision. He expects us to make the choice not to become angry.

The Lord does not justify anger. In Matthew 5, verse 22, the Lord says: "But I say unto you, That whosoever is angry with his brother *without a cause* shall be in danger of the judgment" (emphasis added). How interesting that the phrase "without a cause" is not found in the inspired Joseph Smith Translation (see Matt. 5:24), nor in the 3 Nephi 12:22 version. When the Lord eliminates the phrase "without a cause," He leaves us without an excuse. "But this is my doctrine, that such things should be done away" (3 Ne. 11:30). We can "do away" with anger, for He has so taught and commanded us.

Anger is a yielding to Satan's influence by surrendering our self-control. Anger can spark hostile feelings or behavior. It is the detonator of road-rage on the freeway, flare-ups in the sports arena, and domestic violence in homes.

Unchecked, anger can quickly trigger an explosion of cruel words and other forms of emotional abuse that can scar a tender heart. It is "that which cometh out of the mouth," the Savior said, "this defileth a man" (Matt. 15:11). David O. McKay said, "Let husband and wife never speak in loud tones to each other, unless the house is on fire."[25]

Physical abuse is anger gone berserk and is never justified and always unrighteous.

Anger is an uncivil attempt to make another feel guilty or a cruel way of trying to correct them. It is often mislabeled as discipline, but is almost always counterproductive. Therefore the scriptural warning: "Husbands love your wives, and be not bitter against them," and "Fathers provoke not your children to anger, lest they be discouraged" (Col. 3:19, 21).

Understanding the connection between agency and anger is the first step in eliminating anger from our lives. We can choose not to become angry. I invite you to make the choice today to eliminate anger from your life."[26]

MY OWN EXPERIENCE WITH ANGER

Reading the Savior's words—"This is not my doctrine, to stir up the hearts of men with anger . . . but this is my doctrine, that such things should be done away"—changed my life. As a young father I had been in elders quorum meetings where more seasoned fathers emphasized the Old Testament phrase "spare the rod and spoil the child" and endorsed anger and spanking.

When I read the insights shared above by William Wilbanks—that anger is a decision—it impacted me profoundly. I decided I would no longer discipline that way.

My oldest son was the brunt of much of my anger. When he was a teenager and doing things that caused me great concern, I would get angry. The angrier I got, the more counterproductive it became. Rather than helping him I was driving him away. The day I learned that anger is a decision, I took him aside and shared this new insight with him. I sincerely apologized for the many occasions on which I had become angry with him. I asked him if he would please forgive me, with the promise that I would never get angry with him ever again. He forgave me, and I kept my promise. It changed his life and it changed mine. He also dramatically reduced his own anger. He served a wonderful mission, married in the temple, has a beautiful family, and is valiant in the gospel. But I think about how close I came to possibly losing him because of my foolishness in not following the example of the one perfect parent.

SAINT VS. NATURAL MAN AND WOMAN

Let's do some comparisons between the parent that "putteth off the natural man and becometh a saint through the atonement of Christ the Lord" and the parent that is a natural man or woman and "an enemy to God" (Mosiah 3:19). The Christlike attributes on the left are not comprehensive, but I hope will be insightful.

SAINT	NATURAL MAN OR WOMAN
The home is a safe and peaceful environment; non-threatening	**The house** is a place of fear, anxiety, and enmity
Teacher—the very essence of parenting	**Tyrant**
Agency—guides child in decision-making	**Force, compulsion**—decisions made by controlling parent
Teaches doctrine and principles	**Dictates** with rules and demands; stifles agency
Disciplines with love, focuses on "be" or character, remains calm	**Punishes**—withdraws love, shows anger, attacks "do" or behavior
Praises—"In whom I am well pleased"	**Shames, ridicules, condemns**
Teaches by example	**Hypocrite**
Love—inspires trust, is a friend and confidant	**Enmity**—creates fear, causing child to hide and avoid pain
Shares pure knowledge—	**Makes little or no effort to teach**
Why was the Savior a great teacher?	**Loses temper, shows contempt, threatens, alienates**
His teachings were great	**Cruel and unjust**
Long-suffering, patient	**Lazy**—Lets TV do the teaching
Merciful and just	**Unclear standards**—leads to injustice with no clear standards for wise decisions
Diligent—invests time	
Firm—with clear and consistent standards	**Harsh, unsympathetic, insensitive, inconsiderate**
Calm, gentle, and meek	**Abusive, cruel, punitive**
Shows kindness	**Full of duplicity, hypocrisy**
Without guile	**Reproving with anger**
Reproving with the Holy Ghost	**Pride**—seeks the honor of men
Humility—seeks to honor God	

When disciplining a child, we might not always have a smile on our face, as depicted above. We might discipline with a look of concern and disappointment, but we definitely don't want to use hostile body language that shows anger, which alienates and creates fear.

DISCIPLINE, LOVE, AND SACRIFICE

"Verily, thus saith the Lord unto you whom I love, and whom I love I also chasten that their sins may be forgiven, for with the chastisement I prepare a way for their deliverance in all things out of temptation, and I have loved you" (D&C 95:1). How many times does the Lord use the word *love* in the above statement on chastisement or discipline? *Chasten* comes from the Latin *castus*, or to be morally pure. It also implied some kind of sacrifice.

In cases of Church discipline, members often default to the world's way of thinking rather than the Lord's. For example, when we think of courts, judges, attorneys, plaintiffs, defendants, guilty verdicts, and prison sentences, *mercy* means commuting the sentence. In the Lord's kingdom, however, it is not the disciplinary council that puts a sinner in prison. Sin puts the sinner in spiritual prison, and the disciplinary council holds the keys to unlock the prison doors. Look at the verse above again(D&C 95:1) and see what it says about chastisement: "preparing a way for their *deliverance*." The Lord used the word *love* three times in the above verse. Mercy usually means going forward with *loving* discipline or teaching.

When Joseph Smith lost the 116 pages, he recognized his sin and was truly remorseful, but the Lord still went forward with the discipline and withdrew all of Joseph's privileges for a season. Did the Lord love Joseph? Yes: "The angel was rejoiced when he gave me back the Urim and Thummim and said that God was pleased with my faithfulness and humility, and *loved* me for my penitence and diligence in prayer."[27] It was a lesson Joseph never forgot, and it teaches us that the withdrawal of privileges for a time is appropriate discipline.

In ancient Israel, those who sinned also had to offer up a sin sacrifice in memory or in similitude of the greater sacrifice that the Savior would endure for that same sin.[28] The Lord has promised us that when we truly repent, "I, the Lord, remember [sins] no more" (D&C 58:42). He may remember them no more, but we often have a hard time forgetting. Many continue to mentally flog themselves. In part, the sin sacrifice was a merciful gift to help the penitent person to forgive themselves. That is why discipline in the Lord's way is as much about mercy as it is about justice and why it requires a sacrifice on the part of the one being disciplined.

I like the metaphor that President Kimball taught—that the bandage ought to fit the wound. It would not be merciful or kind to give only a Band-Aid to a cancer victim, for example. If they needed an operation to remove a tumor, a Band-Aid would actually be cruel and totally ineffective. By the same token, some transgressions may need more than informal probation for proper healing to occur.

DISCIPLINING, PERSUASION, AND CONSEQUENCES

What does a parent do when a child is about to make a serious mistake that will have lifelong consequences? These are perhaps the most challenging situations in life for a parent. I hope the following stories will give some insight.

Missionaries often become discouraged when they first arrive in the mission field and find that the work can be extremely trying at times and is not very fun when you are rejected and despised several times a day. Many want to give up and go home, which would be a huge mistake and would cause great concern for a parent. It happens to even the best of missionaries. It happened to Ammon: "When our hearts were depressed, and we were about to turn back, behold the Lord comforted us" (Alma 26:27).

It happened to Gordon B. Hinckley when he was serving a mission in London in 1933. "A pivotal spiritual experience soon followed. President Hinckley would refer to it again and again as 'my day of decision. . . . Everything good that has happened to me since then I can trace back to [it].'"[29] Discouraged over preaching to uninterested audiences and knocking on unopened doors, Gordon wrote to his father that his being there was a waste of time and money and that he didn't see any point in staying.

"Bryant Hinckley, ever the educator and wise disciplinarian, replied: 'Dear Gordon. I have your letter. . . . I have only one suggestion. Forget yourself and go to work. With love, Your Father.' Letter in hand, Gordon returned to his apartment contemplating a scripture he had studied just that morning: "For whosoever will save his life shall lose it; but whosoever shall lose his life for my sake and the gospel's, the same shall save it" (Mark 8:35).

"I got on my knees," he recalled, "and made a covenant with the Lord that I would try to forget myself and go to work."[30] While President Hinckley's father reproved with sharpness (see D&C 121:43), he did so with love—not anger.

When I was serving as Area President in Argentina, there was an elder in the Argentina Resistencia Mission who told his mission president that he was going home. The president was not successful in talking him out of it. If a missionary decides to go home of his or her own insistence, the family is expected to pay all travel expenses.

Knowing this policy, the mother of this missionary told her son how disappointed she would be if he made the decision to abandon his mission. She then told him, "If you quit your mission early you will need to stay in Argentina and find a job to earn your own airfare home, because we are not going to pay for it." Well, the boy stayed and served an honorable mission. He just needed a mother with firmness, persuasion, and knowledge, or the virtues of discipline found in Doctrine and Covenants 121.

Alma's son Corianton abandoned his mission: "Thou didst do that which was grievous unto me; for thou didst forsake the ministry, and did go over into the land of Siron among the borders of the Lamanites, after the harlot Isabel" (Alma 39:3). Alma disciplined, or *effectively taught* Corianton by teaching him doctrine and principles that comprise four of the most insightful chapters in the Book of Mormon, Alma 39 through 42. Teaching his son doctrine, or the *why*, changed Corianton's life. Corianton returned and completed his mission, and his name became listed among the faithful missionaries (see Alma 49:30).

SETTING STANDARDS AND BOUNDARIES

Holding a person responsible for his or her behavior is one of the most charitable acts of kindness we can offer—it is the opposite of enabling. There is an interesting verse in 4 Nephi that relates to this principle: "And it came to pass that when two hundred and ten years had passed away there were many churches in the land; yea, there were many churches which professed to know the Christ, and yet they did deny the more parts of his gospel, insomuch that they did receive all manner of wickedness, and did administer that which was sacred unto him to whom it had been forbidden because of unworthiness" (4 Ne. 1:27).

In this verse we learn that rather than holding people responsible to live up to the Lord's standards, the standards were lowered (administered) down to the level of the peoples' unworthy behavior—not to please God, but to please men. Elder Neal A. Maxwell stated that such a lowering of standards leads to self-contentment, not self-improvement."[31] It ultimately hurts a person, not helps them. Lowering standards is synonymous with, and a good definition of, apostasy.

Priesthood leaders are called to boldly defend the Lord's standards and to remember which way they face. Too many priesthood leaders have compromised the Lord's standards by giving ecclesiastical endorsements to youth to attend a church university, knowing they weren't fully worthy; or giving a temple recommend to someone unworthy because the recipient begged for leniency hoping to be present when a child was married in the temple, etc. It is not fair to a bishop for members to make such requests, and it is not wise for a bishop to grant them.

President Henry B. Eyring has taught, "The Lord sets His standards so that He can bless us. . . . His standards . . . **are high and they are unchangeable. We have no right to alter them or to ignore** them. . . . You begin by holding up the Lord's standards clearly and without apology. And the more the world drifts from them and mocks them, the bolder we must be in doing that."[32]

BOUNDARIES IN THE HOME

Standards begin in the home, "for if a man know not how to rule his own house, how shall he take care of the church of God?" (1 Tim. 3:5). This was the case of Eli, who did not discipline his sons who "lay with the women that assembled at the door of the tabernacle of the congregation" (1 Sam. 2:22). As a result, Eli was disciplined: "I will judge his house for ever for the iniquity which he knoweth; because his sons made themselves vile, and he restrained them not" (1 Sam. 3:13).

It is wiser to establish boundaries for our children in the form of doctrine and principles than through rules. For example, we expect our children to keep their bedrooms clean. In disciplining children with messy rooms, you may want to consider teaching some of the following:

- Expectation and agreed-upon consequences
- Agency and self-judging
- Doctrine and principles:
    - "And the Lord God took the man, and put him into the Garden of Eden to *dress it and to keep it.*"[33]
    - "Behold, mine house is a house of order, saith the Lord God."[34]
    - "Organize yourselves; prepare every needful thing; and establish . . . a house of order."[35]
    - "Let all things be done in cleanliness before me."[36]
    - Keeping our home clean and orderly is a sign of wise stewardship and shows gratitude and respect to the Lord.
    - Be considerate: always leave a room cleaner than you found it.
    - Our home is a sacred place; we keep it clean and orderly to be a more inviting place for the Spirit, like the temple.
    - There is a feeling of happiness and contentment when we take care of our things and live in a clean and orderly environment.
    - Identify a place for everything and keep everything in it its place.

Let's take another example, establishing a curfew:

- "Cease to sleep longer than is needful; retire to thy bed early, that ye may not be weary; arise early, that your bodies and your minds may be invigorated" (D&C 88:124).
- The more tired we become, the less invigorated are the body and mind, and the less resistant to temptation.
- While we don't want to sleep longer than is needful, we also don't want to sleep shorter than is necessary, so that our minds and bodies will be invigorated during the day.
- A "rise-early" principle that has been repeated several times by prophets and apostles is that revelation comes early: "And in the morning, rising up a great while before day, he went out, and departed into a solitary place, and there prayed" (Mark 1:35).

HOPE THROUGH LOVE

Because a parent has "no greater joy than to hear that my children walk in truth" (3 John 1:4), the corollary is also true—the greatest anguish a parent endures is when a child wanders spiritually.

In his wonderful and insightful talk "Enduring Well," Elder Neal A. Maxwell taught that the love of children is often unreciprocated. "This is part of coming to know, on our small scale, what Jesus experienced." Elder Maxwell quoted this insightful observation by Edith Hamilton: "'When love meets no return the result is suffering, and the greater the love the greater the suffering.' There can be no greater suffering than to love purely and perfectly one who is bent upon evil and self-destruction. That was what God endured at the hands of men.'"[37]

In following the pattern of the one perfect parent, our love makes us vulnerable to the same suffering endured by the Savior, whose love was so often scorned. A parent's love, freely given to a child, may also be spurned and cause long-suffering, and yet it is the greatest way, and ultimately the only way, to conquer a stubborn soul. "If children are defiant and difficult to control, be patient with them until you can conquer by love, and you will have gained their souls, and you can then mold their characters as you please."[38] Charity truly is "the greatest of all," and there really is beauty all around when there is love at home.

SUMMARY

- It is the nature and disposition of almost all parents to exercise unrighteous dominion.
- The scriptures contain many principles of how the one perfect parent is raising His children.
- The greatest work you will ever do is to effectively teach your children.
- Our Father in Heaven and the Savior lead by example. They show the way.
- Our Father in Heaven never forces His children. He guides His children in the wise use of their agency by teaching them doctrine and principles and providing them with the Light of Christ and the Holy Ghost. Seldom would He govern with rules.
- Doctrines explain why we do things. A correct understanding of doctrine can create righteous motivation to act.
- Forcing appropriate behavior only focuses on the outward symptoms, while the word of God changes beliefs and long-term behavior from within.

- Knowing good from evil, God's children become their own judges—hence discipline is essentially self-administered in the form of consequences that follow their choices.
- Discipline comes from the same root word as *disciple*, which means to teach, and is one of the most powerful teaching moments.
- Discipline should be done with love and all of its component virtues.
- Discipline should be administered when moved upon by the Holy Ghost, not anger. Anger should be eliminated from our lives and homes.
- Discipline is a merciful act and requires a sacrifice on the part of the one being disciplined.
- In disciplining, one of the most important things a parent can teach is the consequences of choice.
- God does not lower His standards. Standards are evidence of His love to raise His children to the level of His character and nature.
- Standards or boundaries in the home should be doctrinally based and wisely administered in the Lord's way.

NOTES

1. *Teaching, No Greater Call: A Resource Guide for Gospel Teaching* (1999), 150.
2. *Teachings of Presidents of the Church: Harold B. Lee* (2000), 134.
3. David A. Bednar, *Act in Doctrine* (Salt Lake City: Deseret Book, 2012), xiv.
4. Packer, "Little Children," 17.
5. *Teachings of Presidents of the Church: Joseph Smith* (2007), 284.
6. Bednar, *Act in Doctrine*, xiv.
7. *Handbook 1: Stake Presidents and Bishops* [2010], 125.
8. Jeremiah 31:33.
9. *Dictionary.com*, "pharisaic," http://dictionary.reference.com/browse/pharisaical?s=t.
10. Bible Dictionary, "Law of Moses."

11. Sophocles, quoted in Huntsman, *Winners Never Cheat,* 26.
12. Juvenal (60–140), Roman satirical poet, quoted in Richard L. Evans "The Spoken Word: Beauty and Morality," *Ensign,* May 1971, 12.
13. 1 Nephi 11:25.
14. Alma 31:5.
15. Helaman 6:37; see also Helaman 5:17.
16. Joseph F. Smith, *Gospel Doctrine* (Salt Lake City: Deseret Book, 1986), 295.
17. Ibid., 317; emphasis added.
18. *Teachings of Gordon B. Hinckley* (1997), 418.
19. "Strengthening the Family: Happiness in Family Life," *Liahona,* Sept. 2005.
20. *Teachings of Presidents of the Church: George Albert Smith* (2011), 225–6, 228.
21. Lynn G. Robbins, "Agency and Anger," *Ensign,* May 1998, 80–81.
22. "The Family: A Proclamation to the World," *Ensign,* November 2010, 129.
23. William Lee Wilbanks, "The New Obscenity," quoted *in Reader's Digest,* December 1988, 24.
24. Ibid, 23.
25. David O. McKay, *Stepping Stones to an Abundant Life,* comp. Llewelyn R. McKay (1971), 294.
26. Robbins, "Agency and Anger," 80.
27. *Teachings of Presidents of the Church: Joseph Smith* (2007), 71; emphasis added.
28. Bible Dictionary, "Sacrifices."
29. Sheri L. Dew, *Go Forward with Faith: The Biography of Gordon B. Hinckley* (1996), 64.
30. Jeffrey R. Holland, "President Gordon B. Hinckley: Stalwart and Brave He Stands," *Ensign,* June 1995, 8.
31. Neal A. Maxwell, "Repentance*," Ensign,* Oct. 1991.
32. Henry B. Eyring, "Standards of Worthiness*," First Worldwide Leadership Training Meeting,* Jan. 2003, 10–11.
33. Genesis 2:15; see also Moses 3:15; Abraham 5:11.
34. Doctrine and Covenants 132:8.
35. Doctrine and Covenants 88:119; see also 109:8.
36. Doctrine and Covenants 42:41.
37. Edith Hamilton, *Spokesman for God* (1936), 112, quoted in Neal A. Maxwell, "Enduring Well," *Ensign,* April 1997, 8.
38. Joseph F. Smith, *Gospel Doctrine,* 295.

CHAPTER 7

CHOOSING HAPPILY
EVER AFTER

The more one learns and lives the gospel, the more it becomes the gospel of common sense. We learn from our own experiences that the fruit of the gospel, like the fruit of the tree of life, is indeed precious and "most sweet, above all that [we] ever before tasted" and that it "[fills our souls] with exceedingly great joy" (1 Ne. 8:11, 12). We grow to love it because of the blessings, the control, and the power it gives us over positive outcomes in our lives.

In this book you have learned about the power of choice. You have learned that love is a choice; that anger is a choice; that Christlike virtues are choices, and so on. You have learned the power and blessings of being more responsible for choices you make. You have learned that you have far greater control over your life than you ever imagined. You have learned through the rearview mirror of mortality why agency was worth defending in the premortal life and why it is such a precious gift in this life. In this final chapter of Part I, I want to conclude with one more choice—how to choose happily-ever-after.

IS HAPPINESS A CHOICE?

The Book of Mormon teaches us that man is that he might have joy. It also teaches us that we are to act for ourselves and not to be acted upon. The fact that these two highly quoted verses are sequential (see 1 Ne. 2:25–26) is not a coincidence.

They are the same tandem principles over which the war in heaven was fought—the Father's plan of happiness and the agency of mankind. We already *chose* the plan of happiness once, and these two interconnected verses invite us to *choose* it anew in this life.

One of the pivotal revelations in life is to discover that we have far more control over our happiness than we sometimes think we do. How we see life's glass—half-full or half-empty—is primarily a choice. It is a matter of attitude more than of circumstance, as we discover in the story of Nephi, Laman, and Lemuel in the Book of Mormon. This account is an interesting and insightful case study illustrating that happiness is to be found by expecting it and looking for it, even when living in less than desirable circumstances.

Laman and Lemuel seemed to always see their glass as half empty (or mostly empty!). They constantly murmured. Their incessant complaining was a vocalization of their self-pity, one of the crippling taboos from the anti-responsibility list. Their cynical nature blinded them to the portion of their glass that was half full. Consequently, misery was the harvest they reaped from the seeds of pessimism they continually sowed. Their misery became a self-fulfilling prophecy.

Nephi, by contrast, always saw the *very same glass* as half full, and happiness was his reward, even though he had to endure the very same burdens and trials. Said he, "And so great were the blessings of the Lord upon us, that while we did live upon raw meat in the wilderness, our women did give plenty of suck for their children, and were strong, yea, even like unto the men; and they began to bear their journeyings *without murmurings*" (1 Ne. 17:2; emphasis added).

As Johann Wolfgang von Goethe put it, "A man sees in the world what he carries in his heart." I like the poetic version of this principle by the poet Richard Chenevix Trench:

> *Some murmur when the sky is clear*
> *And wholly bright to view,*
> *If one small speck of dark appear*
> *In their great heaven of blue:*
> *And some with thankful love are filled,*
> *If but one streak of light,*
> *One ray of God's good mercy, gild*
> *The darkness of their night.*
>
> *In palaces are hearts that ask,*
> *In discontent and pride,*
> *Why life is such a dreary task,*
> *And all good things denied;*
> *And hearts in poorest huts admire*
> *How Love has in their aid*
> *(Love that not ever seems to tire)*
> *Such rich provision made.*

Our world becomes a creation after our own image, a reflection of our own faith or lack thereof, and of our understanding of key doctrines and principles.

So if happiness is something we can choose, we would truly be fools if we did not make that choice. You will be "as happy as [you] make [your mind] up to be," said Abraham Lincoln.

HAPPINESS THROUGH OPPOSITION

We learn in 2 Nephi that opposition is a prerequisite in our search for happiness: "For it must needs be, that there is an opposition in all things. If not so . . . righteousness could not be brought to pass, neither wickedness, neither holiness nor misery, neither good nor bad. Wherefore, all things must needs be a compound in one; wherefore, if it should be one body it must needs remain as dead, having no life neither death, nor corruption nor incorruption, happiness nor misery, neither sense nor insensibility" (2 Ne. 2:11).

Opposition is an essential part of our earthly and eternal education and reveals the truth, power, and happiness available to us. Having been sick, for example, health becomes more precious to us. Having seen devastation through dishonesty and deceit, we come to treasure integrity in those around us. Having seen or experienced the injustices and pains of cruelty, we gain a testimony of the power and healing influence of love and kindness. We only learn "line upon line and precept upon precept" through opposition in all things. Obedience to God's commands promises ultimate happiness *through* opposition, not *around* it.

Opposition is no respecter of persons. However, when trials come, the wise choose happiness. They are lovely people to be around, as opposed to the unpleasantness of a complainer or pessimist. "But what if that is the way I am?" someone might ask. Or, "What if I don't feel like smiling?" Benjamin Franklin referred to pessimism as a "bad habit" to be broken and advised avoiding people so "infected."[1] Overcoming the bad habit of pessimism begins with an understanding that no one forces us into the "saloon of self-pity."[2] Paraphrasing Elder Marion D. Hanks, "Pain is inevitable, but misery is optional." And from Elder Jeffrey R. Holland: "No misfortune is so bad that whining about it won't make it worse."[3]

Of course, there are times in everyone's life when it is difficult to smile, times of trial and tragedy, times of distress and misfortune, of poor health and death. But even in such difficult times it is helpful and wise to look to the future with hope and optimism, just as Nephi did. And with our Father in Heaven's help, our faith, hope, and optimism can grow. "For I do know that whosoever shall put their trust in God shall be supported in their trials, and their troubles, and their afflictions, and shall be lifted up at the last day" (Alma 36:3).

President Dieter F. Uchtdorf gives us this insight on happiness: "The gospel of Jesus Christ has the answers to all of our problems. The gospel is not a secret. It is not complicated or hidden. . . . It is not someone's theory or proposition. It does not come from man at all. It springs from the pure and everlasting waters of the Creator of the universe, who knows truths we cannot even begin to comprehend. And with that knowledge, He has given us the gospel—a divine gift, the ultimate formula for happiness and success."[4]

"In this world your joy is not full," the Savior taught, "but in me your joy is full" (D&C 101:36). David O. McKay was a happy man. Said he, "Happiness is the purpose and design of existence. 'Men are, that they might have joy.' Virtue, uprightness, faithfulness, holiness, and keeping the commandments of God lead to a happy life; those who follow that path are not long-faced and sanctimonious, depriving themselves of the joys of existence."[5]

THE PLAN OF HAPPINESS

There is only one plan of happiness (see Alma 42:8). In the words of Elder Neal A. Maxwell, all other options are "multiple-choice misery."[6] In the premortal life there was only one plan of happiness presented, and that was the Father's plan. Satan's proposal wasn't a plan at all, but a plot. All options other than the Father's plan, are "contrary to the nature of happiness" (Alma 41:11).

The Lord's plan is known by many names: the plan of salvation (see Alma 24:14); the plan of mercy (see Alma 42:15, 31); the plan of redemption (see Jacob 6:8); the plan of deliverance (see 2 Ne. 11:5); and the plan of happiness (Alma 42:8).

The plan of happiness seldom makes sense to the natural man because he is "carnal, sensual and devilish" (Moses 6:49) and seeks "for happiness in doing iniquity, which thing is contrary to the nature of that righteousness which is in our great and Eternal Head" (Hel. 13:38). Sooner or later the natural man discovers for himself that "wickedness never was happiness" (Alma 41:10).

This is true from two perspectives. First, as Elbert Hubbard insightfully phrased it, "Men are punished by their sins, not for them," meaning they eventually find out that the fruit of their labors is bitter. Secondly, blessings are denied them because blessings come "by obedience to that law upon which [they] are predicated" (D&C 130:20, 21) and in no other way.

Abraham found "there was greater happiness and peace and rest . . . [in seeking] for the blessings of the fathers . . . [and being] a follower of righteousness" (Abr. 1:2). And finally, the proclamation on the family succinctly teaches us that "happiness in marriage and family life is most likely to be achieved when founded upon the teachings of the Lord Jesus Christ."

THE VIRTUE OF HAPPINESS—TO BE OR NOT TO BE

In chapter 3, "Agency and Virtue," and chapter 4, "Even as I Am," we learned that virtues, our *to-be* list, depend on supporting items from our *to-do* list, since these two principles form a doctrinal pair. To *be* happy, we must *choose* to *do* things that will increase our joy. Because there are numberless items that could go on a to-do list to increase happiness, I am going to focus only on general principles and categories rather than on specifics.

To-Do List—Meet Needs

There are many models proposed by philosophers, psychologists, and others to represent the spectrum of human needs necessary for happiness. This is my list of "six L's," which may not be a perfect list, nor is it meant to be prioritized or hierarchal, but I know that without them none of us can be as happy as we would like to be.

- **Live**—to survive, not die. This one is self-evident.
- **Life**—to live well, to seize the day and enjoy life; to minimize sickness and suffering; to experience variety; to "smell the roses" along the way and have sensory experiences with beautiful sights, sounds, tastes, smells, and feelings.
- **Love of self**—to have self-worth and self-respect; to have a purpose; to learn and progress; to work, to feel accomplished; to achieve and create. The innate need and joy of creating begins early in life with crayon art, building snowmen, and making cardboard forts. The creation that leads to ultimate joy

162

and rejoicing is to become co-creators by having children and creating a family and home.

- **Love of others**—to help others or experience the joy in serving and kind acts. There is no lasting happiness if our life is self-centered and selfish. We find ourselves (or experience happiness) by losing ourselves (see Matt. 16:25).
- **Love of family**—sharing life with and providing for loved ones.
- **Love of God**—having peace of conscience, living after the manner of happiness by following the Savior's example and His gospel; being worthy of the Spirit's guidance.

If we don't fulfill this final need, a love of God, and live without the Spirit's guidance, we become easy targets for Satan to trick us with his counterfeit options for fulfilling needs. Take the above need of "love of self," or self-worth and self-respect, for example:

- A man might come to believe that his self-worth is based upon his job, his income, and his possessions. This could tempt him to "keep up with the Joneses" and lead to excessive and unnecessary debt and flaunting. Other men may base their self-worth upon position and authority. If they are not careful, Satan can turn that into arrogance and unrighteous dominion (D&C 121:39).
- If a woman's self-worth is based upon the praise of the world, she may be tempted to spend excessive and unnecessary time outside the home and start neglecting her family (not to be confused with necessary time in a career for a single mom and other exceptional circumstances).

- If a young woman's self-worth is based upon popularity and physical appearance, it could lead to inappropriate behavior such as anorexia, bulimia, or immodest dress, or she can become an easy target for Satan, who will turn her natural beauty into a reason for vanity.
- If a young man's self-worth is based upon physical strength, prowess, and dominance, Satan may tempt him to use that strength unrighteously, such as in bullying others.

Regarding filling needs, Spencer W. Kimball taught that all "sin [springs] from deep and unmet needs on the part of the sinner."[7] They either knowingly or unwittingly try to fill their unmet needs in inappropriate ways, as cited in the above examples. Satan can't sell misery to fulfill needs, so his common approach is to focus on the immediacy of the need, without any thought of consequences, like selling a birthright for a mess of pottage (see Gen. 25:28–34). The subtlety in Satan's menu is that he makes his offerings appear mouthwatering, even without any nutritional value, and "the effect thereof is poison" (Mosiah 7:30). Like the unwise child who opts for the more colorful cotton candy over vegetables, Satan's fare cankers over time. "But if not built upon my gospel . . . [but] upon the works of the devil, verily I say unto you they have joy in their works *for a season*, and by and by the end cometh, and they are hewn down and cast into the fire, from whence there is no return" (3 Ne. 27:11; emphasis added).

To-Do List—Smile More

"A 30-year study by psychologists LeeAnne Harker and Dacher Keltner at the University of California at Berkley studied 141 high school senior-class photos from the 1960 yearbook of Mills

College. . . . Women with natural smiles were more likely to be married and stay married and also more likely to experience a greater sense of personal well-being. These results were found to be consistent in a 30-year followup. . . . The conclusion was that a habit of genuine smiling may contribute to happiness and better adjustment in life."[8] An equally interesting study by British researchers stated that "smiling stimulates our brain reward mechanism" in ways similar to chocolate, a well-known "pleasure inducer."[9]

So, "if you chance to meet a frown do not let it stay. Quickly turn it upside down and smile that frown away."[10] Since a smile is a decision, why not make the choice? Why not put on a happy face and experience the benefits? Let your smile become a self-fulfilling prophecy in your life. Our Father in Heaven expects it, and He can help us: "If thou art sorrowful, call on the Lord thy God with supplication, that your souls may be joyful" (D&C 136:29).

To-Do List—Count Your Daily Blessings

President Henry B. Eyring shared with us that he keeps a gratitude journal. "As I kept at it, something began to happen. As I would cast my mind over the day, I would see evidence of what God had done for one of us that I had not recognized in the busy moments of the day. As that happened, and it happened often, I realized that trying to remember had allowed God to show me what He had done. . . . You remember that song we sometimes sing: 'Count your many blessings; name them one by one, And it will surprise you what the Lord has done' ("Count Your Blessings," *Hymns,* no. 241)."[11]

If we aren't grateful for our daily blessings then we risk not recognizing the happiness to be found in little everyday things and missing out on many of life's joys by thinking our happiness depends on future events or accomplishments. "The fool, with all his other faults, was this also: he is always getting ready to live."[12]

Andy Rooney shares this helpful insight: "For most of life, nothing wonderful happens. If you don't enjoy getting up and working and finishing your work and sitting down to a meal with family or friends, then the chances are that you're not going to be very happy. If someone bases his happiness or unhappiness on major events like a great new job, huge amounts of money, a flawlessly happy marriage or a trip to Paris, that person isn't going to be happy much of the time. If on the other hand, happiness depends on a good breakfast, flowers in the yard, a drink or a nap, then we are more likely to live with quite a bit of happiness."[13]

Thinking of Christmas as a metaphor, there is as much enjoyment to be experienced from December 1st through the 24th— the anticipation of Christmas—as there is on Christmas Day itself. Joy is to be found in the journey, not just in the destination.

Those who have a lingering feeling that everyday things aren't sufficiently spectacular or thrilling enough can make the same mistake as the prodigal son who sought greener pastures only to painfully discover the happiness he had abandoned back home. Thank goodness for second chances!

Being grateful can help us cultivate "the little happiness" as writer Ardis Whitman puts it. "Look forward to the beauty of the next moment, the next hour, the promise of a good meal, sleep, a book, a movie, the likelihood that tonight the stars will shine and tomorrow the sun will shine."[14] As the Psalm happily reminds us, "This is the day which the Lord hath made; we will rejoice and be glad in it."[15] As our days go, so goes our lives.

THE ATONEMENT AND HAPPINESS

The Savior's Atonement is a gift of hope in eternal happiness. It is also a gift of hope and happiness for this life: "I am come that they might have life, and that they might have it more abundantly" (John 10:10). "Learn that he who doeth the works of righteousness shall receive his reward, even peace in this world, and eternal life in the world to come" (D&C 59:23).

"The Atonement gives rise to gospel gladness," observed Elder Neal A. Maxwell, "permitting us to be of good cheer even in the midst of tactical tribulation." Indeed, the Savior Himself reminded us, "In the world ye shall have tribulation: but be of good cheer; I have overcome the world" (John 16:33).

Elder Maxwell continues, "Jesus refused to be one of 'woeful countenance.' Not only did He refuse to let the establishment of the time tell Him with whom he might dine; He also refused to insist that people look mournful when they were fasting. Though He was called 'man of sorrows,' that description refers to His bearing of *our* sorrows—not His; it does not describe His day-to-day bearing!"[16]

I love this happy insight from Heber C. Kimball: "I am perfectly satisfied that my Father and my God is a cheerful, pleasant, lively, and good-natured Being. Why? Because I am cheerful, pleasant, lively, and good-natured when I have His Spirit. That is one reason why I know; and another is-the Lord said, through Joseph Smith, 'I delight in a glad heart and a cheerful countenance.' That arises from the perfection of His attributes; He is a jovial, lively person, and a beautiful man."[17]

Because the Savior was a happy person it is disconcerting to see so many Christian artists depict Him without a smile and often as "weak, pale, austere, and somehow inhuman and otherworldly . . . anything but warm and human."[18] That isn't being true to His genuine happy nature as recorded in the Book of Mormon: "And he did smile upon them again" (3 Ne. 19:30).

Because happiness is a choice, the phrase "men are, that they might have joy" (2 Ne. 2:25) should be considered more an expectation than an axiom, more a commandment than a suggestion. Why is joy a commandment? Because the Savior has borne our sorrows that we might have joy. Not choosing joy would be a sign of ingratitude for the greatest gift of joy ever given. We have every reason to rejoice and to count our many blessings. As one of the Christlike virtues, happiness is one of the blessings of following Him and striving to become like Him.

"Consider on the *blessed and happy state* of those that keep the commandments of God. For behold, they are blessed in all things, both temporal and spiritual; and if they hold out faithful to the end they are received into heaven, that thereby they may dwell with God in a state of *never-ending happiness*" (Mosiah 2:41, emphasis added).

CHOOSING THE TEMPLE FOR A HAPPILY-EVER-AFTER ENDING

The temple is a great symbol that represents our ability to one day be "received into heaven, [and] dwell with God in the state of never-ending happiness." President Howard W. Hunter identified the temple as the great symbol of our membership.[19] As the house of the Lord, entering the temple is symbolic of entering into His presence. Being worthy to enter His presence on earth is the greatest evidence we have of one day being able to enter His presence in heaven, the one being symbolic of the other.

The corollary, and common sense, should warn us that if we are not worthy to enter His house here, what makes us think we will be able to enter His presence there, where "no unclean thing can dwell with God" (1 Ne. 10:21)? The temple becomes our hope of having a happily-ever-after love story and never-ending happiness.

In three separate standard works, when speaking of His Second Coming, the Lord has said, "I will suddenly come to my temple."[20] This should be considered a one-sentence sermon. Because He will come to His temple, He is telling us how to prepare. When He appeared to the Nephites, He came to the temple in Bountiful, and only the worthy were able to meet Him there (see 3 Ne. 9:13; 11:1).

Is being temple-worthy one of the Lord's messages in the parables of the ten virgins (see Matt. 25:1–13) and the marriage of the king's son (see Matt. 22:2–14)? These are parables with more than one possible interpretation. However, the parallels between these parables and the need for a temple marriage to qualify for exaltation are compelling. Let us examine some of these parallels.

The kingdom of heaven. The Savior opens His parable of the ten virgins by saying, "And then, at that day, before the Son of Man comes, shall the *kingdom of heaven* be likened unto ten virgins" (JST, Matt. 25:1; emphasis added).

The Bible Dictionary illuminates this symbol for us: "Generally speaking, the *kingdom of God* on the earth is the Church. It is a preparation for the greater kingdom—the celestial or *kingdom of heaven*."[21] The purpose of these parables is to prepare disciples for the celestial kingdom, not an inferior kingdom. As a parallel, the celestial room in the temple represents entering into the presence of God.

A marriage. In both parables, the kingdom of heaven was likened unto a marriage. As a parallel, "In the celestial glory there are three heavens or degrees; "And in order to obtain the highest, a man must enter into this order of the priesthood [meaning the new and everlasting covenant of marriage]" (D&C 131:1–2).

A bridegroom. The Savior uses the title *Bridegroom* when He refers to His Second Coming, as He did in both of these parables. Speaking of the marriage of the king's son, the Prophet Joseph Smith said, "That this son was the Messiah will not be disputed, since it was the kingdom of heaven that was represented in the parable."[22] The parallel to the temple is obvious—a worthy bridegroom coming to the temple for his marriage.

A bride. "That thy church may come forth out of wilderness . . . and be adorned as a bride for that day when thou shalt unveil the heavens" (D&C 109:73–74). The Prophet Joseph Smith expounded on the parallel of a worthy bride: "The Saints, or those who are found faithful to the Lord, are the individuals who will be found worthy to inherit a seat at the marriage supper . . . [or receive] a crown of righteousness from the hand of the Lord, with the Church of the Firstborn."[23]

Virgins, five foolish and five wise. The ten virgins, according to Elder Bruce R. McConkie, "represent those church members who are looking for the Bridegroom to come."[24] In parallel to our day, Elder McConkie explains that this parable is not about "good and bad, not righteous and wicked, but *wise* and *foolish*. That is, all of them have accepted the invitation to meet the Bridegroom; all are members of the Church . . . but only five are valiant therein."[25] They may be good and morally clean, as the term *virgin* implies, but they are not all valiant (see D&C 76:79; 58:27).

Marriage in the house of the bridegroom. "They that were ready went in with him to the marriage: and the door was shut" (Matt. 25:10). In Biblical times, "On the marriage day, the bride was escorted to her husband's [bridegroom's] home by a procession consisting of her own companions and the 'friends of the bridegroom,' or 'children of the bride-chamber.' . . . When she reached the house, words such as 'Take her according to the law of Moses' . . . were spoken, . . . and a marriage deed was signed. After the prescribed washing of hands and benediction, the marriage supper was held."[26] In parallel to our day, a marriage ceremony in the house of the Lord (the Bridegroom's house) is the qualifying ordinance for family life in the celestial kingdom (see D&C 131:1–3).

Lamps (a flame or light). "Then all those virgins arose, and trimmed their lamps" (Matt. 25:7). According to one commentary, "the oil-filled lamps are symbolic of the Holy Spirit which lights the way before the saints."[27] The ten virgins all thought they were ready. Outwardly, they all appeared prepared. A parallel light, The Holy Ghost is that same light that guides us to the Lord's house or His presence today. Wilford Woodruff taught that "there is but one right road."[28] There is only one right destination, which is the celestial kingdom, represented by the house of the Bridegroom.

Oil. "They that were foolish took their lamps, and took no oil with them; But the wise took oil in their vessels with their lamps" (Matt. 25:3–4). In the parable, only those with oil in their lamps were able to enter the house of the bridegroom. Anciently, "pure olive oil

[was] beaten for the light, to cause the lamps to burn continually"
(Lev. 24:2) The entry on oil in the Guide to the Scriptures teaches us
that "olive oil is a symbol of purity and of the presence and influence
of the Holy Ghost." The parallel today is a temple recommend, which
is also symbolic of a person's purity or worthiness. In modern times,
only those worthy of a temple recommend may enter the house of
the Bridegroom. And like oil, which has to be replenished, a temple
recommend has to be renewed.

In an additional parallel, the foolish virgins "said unto the wise,
Give us of your oil; for our lamps are gone out" (Matt. 25:8), but the
wise could not give of their own oil. Similarly, a temple recommend
cannot be loaned to those who do not have them. How can one loan
personal purity? Each person must go to his or her own bishop and
qualify for one.

A wedding garment. In the parable of the marriage of the king's
son, only those wearing the wedding garment were allowed to participate. Worthy members of the Church are those invited to the marriage supper spoken of in Revelation 19:7–8: "For the marriage of
the Lamb is come, and his wife hath made herself ready . . . arrayed
in fine linen, *clean and white*: for the fine linen is the *righteousness*
of saints" (emphasis added). In parallel, the recommend isn't just a
record, nor is the temple garment just an emblem of past behavior.
They are reminders of covenants made concerning future behavior—a
promise to stay on the path and endure to the end, to be temple
worthy. The final verse of the parable of the marriage of the king's
son states, "For many are called, but few are chosen" (Matt. 22:14).
Joseph Smith added a key phrase: "For many are called, but few are

chosen: wherefore all do not have on the *wedding garment*" (JST, Matt. 22:14; emphasis added).

A door. "And while they went to buy, the bridegroom came; and they that were ready went in with him to the marriage: and the door was shut. . . . Afterward came also the other virgins, saying, Lord, Lord, open to us" (Matt. 25:10–11). The fact that the five foolish virgins knocked expecting to enter the marriage supper indicates one of two things: either they had deceived themselves, believing they were worthy to participate without oil, or they knew they weren't prepared to enter but were hoping for mercy. Either way, the door was shut— oil was indispensable. Verse 12 continues, "But he answered and said, Verily I say unto you, I know you not."

This is not an accurate translation, for He knows each one of us, including the thoughts and intents of our heart (see Alma 18:32). The Joseph Smith Translation places responsibility for being prepared right where it belongs: "Ye know me not" (JST, Matt. 25:11).

In this parable it was the Bridegroom Himself who answered the door, for the "keeper of the gate is the Holy One of Israel; and he employeth no servant there; . . . for he cannot be deceived" (2 Ne. 9:41). He is the one who will symbolically be "checking recommends" at the door to the kingdom of heaven.

In parallel to our own lives, the shut door is a poignant reminder that "this life is the day for men to perform their labors" (Alma 34:32). It would be foolish to procrastinate the day of our repentance until the midnight hour. Just as oil is not purchased at midnight, neither is righteousness developed in an instant in order to qualify for a recommend. Without a recommend, we too will be turned away at the door to the temple.

"While the bridegroom tarried, they all slumbered and slept. And at midnight there was a cry made, Behold, the bridegroom cometh; go ye out to meet him" (Matt. 25:5–6).

Elder McConkie explains that "from evening to midnight there was no direct word from the bridal party. At midnight, the most unlikely of all hours for a joyous celebration to begin, the cry goes forth to a sleeping world."

Midnight is a dark hour. The Lord will come again in a "dark hour," when the world is ripe in iniquity, when for the "elect's sake those days shall be shortened" (Matt. 24:22). In such a dark time, what a truly stunning moment it will be when the Light of the World appears and darkness is banished!

WHY PARABLES?

According to the Bible Dictionary, the Savior used parables "to veil the meaning. . . . To the dull and uninspired a parable is a mere story, 'seeing they see not,' while to the instructed and spiritual it reveals the mysteries . . . of the kingdom of heaven."

The Church has no official interpretation of the parables discussed above. However, just as the righteous will recognize the signs of His coming, the righteous will also know how to prepare. "Wherefore, be faithful, praying always, having your lamps trimmed and burning, and oil with you, that you may be ready at the coming of the Bridegroom" (D&C 33:17). We must continually watch and prepare, for we "know neither the day nor the hour wherein the Son of man cometh" (Matt. 25:13).

A sealing between husband and wife is the Lord's way of making it a happily-ever-after marriage. There is no other way. The temple is the great symbol of a husband and wife *being one* with Him. His desire is to "seal you his, that you may be brought to heaven, that ye may have everlasting salvation and eternal life" (Mosiah 5:15). A current temple recommend is the great symbol of a husband and wife *being one* with Him. What greater symbol of being united in love than being sealed in the temple, not just to each other, but to Him—being "'at-one'—not only with Him but also 'at-one' like Him?"[29] For a husband and wife, the sealing is a covenant relationship with each other and with the Lord. A current temple recommend, like the virgins' oil, is the evidence of keeping that covenant.

Only with a temple sealing can a love be made complete. "If we love one another, God dwelleth in us . . . and he that dwelleth in love dwelleth in God, and God in him. Herein is our *love made perfect*" (1 John 4:12, 16–17, emphasis added).

THE END

"The End" is a fitting conclusion for dime novels and Hollywood love stories, but not for *true* love, made perfect in Christ. This pure love is *endless* and is genuinely *happily-ever-after*.

The doctrines of the Savior are wise and powerful. This book has attempted to demonstrate the power and common sense of His principles and the control and happiness that come by following them. I have shared many insights into the Savior's teachings that affect the choices that make a marriage great and a family happy. May you choose His plan of happiness, that your marriage may become great and that *your joy shall be full forever!*[30]

NOTES

1. "The Handsome and the Deformed Leg." *Writings of Benjamin Franklin.*
2. Neal A. Maxwell, "Jesus Christ, the Perfect Mentor," *Ensign,* Feb. 2001, 16.

3. Jeffrey R. Holland, "The Tongue of Angels," *Ensign,* Apr. 2007, 18.
4. Dieter F. Uchtdorf, "The Way of the Disciple," *Ensign,* May 2009, 75.
5. David O. McKay, *Pathways to Happiness,* ed. by Llewelyn R. McKay (Bookcraft: Salt Lake City, 1968), xi.
6. Neal A. Maxwell, "The Net Gathers of Every Kind," *Ensign,* Nov. 1980, 15.
7. Spencer W. Kimball, "Jesus: The Perfect Leader," *Ensign,* Aug. 1979, 5.
8. "Viewpoint: The Power of a Smile," *Church News,* November 23, 2014, 16.
9. Abby Stevens,"Key to happiness: simple act makes you happier than 2,000 bars of chocolate can" *Deseret News,* September 30, 2013.
10. "Smiles," *Children's Songbook,* 267.
11. Henry B. Eyring, "O Remember, Remember," *Ensign,* Nov. 2007, 67.
12. Epicurus, quoted in Richard Evans, *Richard Evans' Quote Book* (Publishers Press, 1971), 218.
13. Andy Rooney, "Quotes," *Goodreads,* www.goodreads.com/quotes/490569.
14. Ardis Whitman, quoted in "The Little Happiness," *Dare To Be Happier,* April 12, 2011.
15. Psalm 118:24.
16. Neal A. Maxwell, *Even as I Am* (Deseret Book: Salt Lake City, 1982), 103.
17. *Journal of Discourses by Brigham Young* (1967), 4:222.
18. Bruce Porter, *The King of Kings* (Deseret Book: Salt Lake City, 2000), 77.
19. Howard W. Hunter, "The Great Symbol of Our Membership," *Ensign,* Oct. 1994, 5.
20. D&C 36:8; see also 42:36; 133:2; Malachi 3:1; 3 Nephi 24:1.
21. Bible Dictionary, "Kingdom of Heaven or Kingdom of God"; emphasis added.
22. *Teachings of the Prophet Joseph Smith,* sel. Joseph Fielding Smith (1976), 63.
23. Ibid., 63–64.
24. Bruce R. McConkie, *Doctrinal New Testament Commentary,* 3 vols. (1965–73), 1:684.
25. Ibid., 1:685.
26. Bible Dictionary, "Marriage."
27. McConkie, *Doctrinal New Testament Commentary,* 1:684.
28. *Teachings of Presidents of the Church: Wilford Woodruff,* (2004), 213.
29. Tad R. Callister, "Our Identity and Our Destiny," (Brigham Young University Campus Education Week devotional, August 14, 2012), 8.
30. See 2 Nephi 9:18.

PART II:

Resources for Practicing
Great Choices

CHAPTER 8

OF ONE HEART, MIND, AND BANK ACCOUNT

E pluribus unum is a Latin phrase meaning "out of many, one." It became the motto of the United States of America at the country's inception because survival of this new nation depended on uniting the independent colonies for the common good of all. Though *E pluribus unum* is still found on the Seal of the United States, Congress replaced it as the official motto in 1956 with one even more fundamental to lasting unity—"In God We Trust."[1]

Because the Lord was the real Founding Father who inspired the establishment of both the United States and the City of Enoch, it shouldn't surprise us that these same two mottoes could also describe that holy city. In fact, the City of Enoch fulfilled those mottoes to their utmost level: "And the Lord called his people Zion, because they were of *one heart and one mind,* and dwelt in *righteousness*" (Moses 7:18; emphasis added). The happiest and most successful marriages are built on the same principles.

However, just as the U.S. Constitution doesn't guarantee happiness, only the pursuit of it, neither did the City of Enoch grant its inhabitants happiness without requiring work on their part.

THE MATH OF UNITY IN MARRIAGE

Please indulge me for a moment while I depict unity in marriage in mathematical terms. The equation of "they twain shall be one flesh" (Mark 10:8) might look like this: $1 + 1 = 1$. What a beautiful equation for a young couple being sealed.

Because the husband and wife are not whole when they are separate, it might be more accurate to write their marriage equation as $\frac{1}{2} + \frac{1}{2} = 1$: "Neither is the man without the woman, neither the woman without the man, in the Lord" (1 Cor. 11:11). Unless they are combined, their potential lies dormant.

From an entirely different perspective, the marriage equation could also be written as $1 + 1 = 3$ because of the *multiplier* or synergistic effect produced by combining complementary parts, not to mention the extra blessings the Lord pours out upon a righteous and united couple. They complete each other in a wondrous relationship of divine symbiosis.[2] In mathematical terms, we could call it *love squared* (love^2), or love raised to the power of two, with exponential blessings.

Satan's math, conversely, focuses on *division*, with contention as the common denominator. Contention comes in many forms, such as anger, blaming, and faultfinding, among many others. Contention is very displeasing to the Lord: "For verily, verily I say unto you, he that hath the spirit of contention is not of me, but is of the devil, who is the father of contention, and he stirreth up the hearts of men to contend with anger, one with another" (3 Ne. 11:29).

DIVIDE AND CONQUER

Satan's ultimate purpose with contention is to *divide and conquer* families. Even though he is the author of this very cunning and effective military strategy, it has been linked to other warmongers, like Julius Caesar, Napoleon, and others. The concept refers to a strategy of using contention to divide and break up a strong single unit into weaker separate units.[3] It divides through distrust and enmity and pits the separated parties against each other on a course of self-destruction or mutual annihilation.

Unlike plain math, this strategy doesn't just separate, it also weakens and even destroys one or both of the individual parties, which is precisely what happened to the Nephite and Jaredite nations. When Satan influenced infighting among the Nephites, Captain Moroni sought power from the "governor of the land . . . to compel those dissenters to defend their country. . . . For it was his first care to put an end to such contentions and dissensions among the people; for behold, this had been hitherto a cause of all their destruction" (Alma 51:15–16).

In a marriage, this arithmetic often results in a divorce as the quotient, with the children as the remainder, or the collateral damage who have been critically wounded by friendly fire. Because contention is so divisive, it seems that for every positive step a couple takes forward, one contentious episode can take them back several, and that is a horrible equation to follow.

CONTENTION—"THIS IS NOT MY DOCTRINE"

The Lord taught that "if a house be divided against itself, that house cannot stand" (Mark 3:25). Concerning things that divide, He said, "Behold, this is not my doctrine, to stir up the hearts of men with anger, one against another; but this is my doctrine, that such things should be done away" (3 Ne. 11:30). Couples who are not "determined in one mind and in one heart, united in all things . . . come down into captivity" (2 Ne. 1:21) and fail to achieve the success they could have enjoyed by following the Savior's teachings.

President Spencer W. Kimball said that nothing should divide or come between a husband and wife. "And, when the Lord says with all thy heart, it allows for no sharing nor dividing nor depriving. The words 'none else' (D&C 42:22) eliminate everyone and everything. The spouse then becomes pre-eminent in the life of the husband or wife. And neither social life nor occupational life nor political life nor any other interest nor person nor thing shall ever take precedence over the companion spouse."[4]

PRINCIPLE OF UNITY—
"BY THE UNANIMOUS VOICE OF THE SAME"

In accordance with revelation, all decisions of the First Presidency and Quorum of the Twelve "must be by the unanimous voice of the same; that is, every member in each quorum must be agreed to its decisions, in order to make their decisions of the same power or validity one with the other" (D&C 107:27). The First Presidency and the Twelve simply do not go forward with a major decision until they are all united in their decision.

President Boyd K. Packer has mentioned that in over forty years as a member of the Quorum of the Twelve Apostles, he has only been a part of two decisions that were agreed upon without any delay. One was to add the subtitle "Another Testament of Jesus Christ" to the Book of Mormon, and the other was to start using the phrase *family history* in the Church rather than the word *genealogy*. All fifteen prophets, seers, and revelators agreed on these two decisions immediately. Every other key decision required further study, pondering, and prayer.

There is tremendous wisdom and safety in following this principle in our marriages and families. It helps us avoid the errors that often occur when decisions are made impulsively, carelessly, or in haste. I have heard President Gordon B. Hinckley say, "None of us is as smart as all of us."

A husband and a wife could be considered the presidency of a family. The husband presides, but he would not want to go forward on any major decision affecting the family without the complete agreement of his wife any more than the First Presidency and Twelve would go forward with a major decision without unanimity. According to "The Family: A Proclamation to the World," husband and wife should carry out their responsibilities as *equal* partners.

The First Presidency and Twelve were also given a promise in the same revelation that if their decisions were "made in all righteousness, in holiness and lowliness of heart, meekness and long suffering, and in faith, and virtue, and knowledge, temperance, patience, godliness, brotherly kindness and charity . . . they shall not be unfruitful in the knowledge of the Lord" (D&C 107:30–31). In other words, if they were of one heart and one mind and made their decisions in righteousness, they would receive revelation to guide them. And so it is with a husband and wife—"where *two* or three are gathered together in my name, as touching one thing, behold, there will I be in the midst of them" (D&C 6:32; emphasis added). Let's spend the balance of this chapter "touching on the one thing" that tends to be more divisive than any other—money.

THE ROOT OF ALL EVIL

The Bible identifies the love of money as the root of all evil (see 1 Tim. 6:10), and it appears to also be Satan's most effective artifice in triggering selfishness in marriage. President Gordon B. Hinckley once said, "I am satisfied that money is the root of more trouble in marriage than all other causes combined."[5] An internet search identifies disagreements about money as the number-one cause of divorce in many studies and one of the top reasons in almost all studies. The checkbook is one of Satan's most potent weapons to *divide and conquer* a couple, because few things can trigger acts of selfishness quite like money can. Because money constitutes such a common cause of contention and division in a marriage, I want to share some principles to help couples achieve greater unity with family finances.

ALL THINGS IN COMMON

In a righteous society, nothing divides or causes contention—not race, not gender, not economics. They have "all things in common" (Acts 2:44). This is the economic law the Lord expects of His people: "And Zion cannot be built up unless it is by the principles of the law of the celestial kingdom; otherwise I cannot receive her unto myself" (D&C 105:5).

For a couple to achieve that kind of unity they must think in terms of "our" money, no matter who is bringing home the paycheck. If a couple can't achieve oneness with their own finances, how can they ever be prepared or trusted to live this same principle or law within the broader community, which is what the Lord will require for entrance into the Celestial Kingdom?

CREATE A FINANCIAL CONSTITUTION

For a couple to experience harmony and happiness with their finances it is essential for them to agree on principles they will follow in their decisions—a financial constitution, if you will. In the absence of such an agreement, the couple is inviting misunderstandings and contention. The following are some ideas from the financial constitution my wife and I created years ago. Your family's financial constitution will be unique to you, but there may be several principles shared here that you may want to use.

- Live within our means. "He that has but four and spends five, has no need of a purse."[6]
- Spend our money according to a plan projecting monthly and periodic expenses. "Those who fail to plan, plan to fail." Or, as the scriptures put it, "For which of you, intending to build a tower, sitteth not down first, and counteth the cost, whether he have sufficient to finish it?" (Luke 14:28).
- Prioritize our spending (see Spending Matrix in this chapter).
- Pay the Lord first—a 10% tithe as well as generous offerings.
- Prepare for the day of scarcity—"At one time or another, nearly every family will face accidents, illness, unemployment, or other emergencies that will require them to depend on the resources they have stored."[7]
- Build up food storage, striving for a one-year supply (including water/filters).
- Strive for one year's worth of savings (emergency funds).
- Establish a retirement plan early and fund it consistently. "A man may, if he knows not how to save as he gets, keep his nose all his life to the grindstone, and die not worth a groat at last."[8]

- Sleep overnight on spending decisions over $_____ (choose an appropriate amount for your situation), and we both agree before going forward with the expenditure.[9]
- Be frugal. We are not wasteful with what the Lord has given us. We comparison shop and stretch our dollar.
- Take care of our things to maximize their usefulness and to foster frugality. A poster from World War II reminds us, "Use it up, wear it out, make it do, or do without.
- Strive to be debt free. We don't go into debt for consumer goods. (Some debts may be justified—a house, school loans, beginning a business, or possibly a car.) "If you would know the value of money, go and try to borrow some; for he that goes a borrowing, goes a sorrowing."[10]
- Use credit cards only for convenience, not to incur debt. We pay credit card balances monthly to avoid interest charges. "The rich ruleth over the poor, and the borrower is servant to the lender" (Prov. 22:7).
- Do not become a banking business, making or guaranteeing loans. Loans often become divisive things. If a family member has an emergency and we are in a position to help, we will advance them the resources without any expectation of repayment.
- Be content with whatever the Lord has blessed us with. We choose to be happy by being grateful for what we do have, not envious of what we do not have. "He that loveth silver shall not be satisfied with silver; nor he that loveth abundance with increase" (Eccl. 5:10). Our money belongs to God. It is a blessing from Him. We are stewards, not owners.
- In charitable giving we give anonymously, since no credit is

due us, but to God. This is in accordance with the scripture, "Let thine alms be done in secret" (Matt. 6:3). We don't flaunt for the same reason.

- Investments are always in people, not things. The foremost due diligence is focused on the people behind the investment. "The simple believeth every word: but the prudent man looketh well to his going" (Prov. 14:15).
- Invest in things we understand and avoid get-rich-quick proposals.
- Don't count your chickens before they hatch. We don't spend money until it is in the account, and we don't incur debt as an advance against future income.
- Beware of long-term spending commitments, even for small expenses. "A small leak will sink a great ship."[11]
- Don't pay in full for a service or product until the job is done.
- Be careful not to clutter life with things. Consider renting items rather than purchasing when more cost-effective.
- Be grateful and express gratitude daily in prayer. "After all, do not depend too much on your own prudence, industry and frugality, though excellent things, for they may all be blasted without the blessing of heaven, therefore pray for that blessing humbly."[12]

TEACHING OUR CHILDREN FINANCIAL WISDOM

Principles of finance are some of the most instrumental in life and yet are not widely taught in school. Therefore, we take responsibility to teach our children the following principles:

- Self-reliance (don't do for them what they can do for themselves).
- Industry and work.
- Frugality and provident living.
- Net-worth does not equal self-worth—we don't need a name brand for our self-esteem.
- Concepts of "enough" and "clutter."
- Caring for things.
- Finding the greatest joy in giving.
- Planning and saving.
- Delayed gratification.

It has been said that children don't know the value of money—that is not true. They don't know the value of *your* money, but they do know the value of their own. In our family, we used the following guidelines to teach our children the value of money and instill in them the financial principles listed above. You could follow a similar pattern in your family.

Chores and Allowances:

- **Personal chores** like making your bed, cleaning your room, etc.—the children were not paid an allowance for these chores, but they were expected to be completed.
- **Assigned family chores** like a room to vacuum or dinner cleanup—the children were paid an allowance for these chores. We created a chart showing a monthly rotation schedule. Because the children could see the equity or fairness in the rotation schedule, it essentially eliminated any bickering

or complaints like "Why do I always have to do it?" or "I did it last time!"

- **Optional family chores** like weeding the garden, cleaning windows, mowing the lawn, etc.—these chores were optional, but paid well to help the children learn and develop many virtues, as discussed in the chapter on love and self-reliance.

Purchases:

- The children were to pay for anything personal and their own clothing (to teach self-reliance, frugality, caring for things). Enough opportunities were made available to them so they could earn all they needed if they would just work.

It is important to let our children experience the natural consequences of earning, saving, and spending while they are young and not just once they grow up and get married. Don't give in to begging when the child hasn't done chores, for example, and is demanding that you pay their way, or when the child has spent foolishly and now doesn't have money for something important. These are powerful teaching moments.

Note: Several additional financial principles for families are available in a book I wrote many years ago, *Uncommon Cents.*

IT IS WISER TO SPEND BY PRIORITY THAN BY IMPULSE

The Spending Matrix below is a tool to help couples come to a consensus on their spending priorities. The more you can see your spending options in relation to your priorities, the wiser your financial decisions will be and the greater harmony you will experience as a couple.

The matrix helps you compare and rank expenditures according to present and future needs (in columns) and most important to least important items (in rows). Priorities are highest at the top left and decrease toward the bottom right. Numbers 1 through 8 indicate the order of priority. The matrix included here shows a sample spending plan for our family.

	Present—Spend	*Future—Save*
Vital	**1** Tithes and offerings Food, clothing, shelter Transportation Communication Utilities Porch railing	**2** Retirement plan Emergency fund Mission fund
Important	**3** Washer and dryer Top soil, sod Music lessons Modest vacation	**4** Piano
Nice	**5** Movies and dining out Nicer vacation New dining room set	**6** Vacation to Hawaii Cabin Boat and jet skis Entertainment system
Wasteful	**7** Late penalties and fines Interest on credit cards Brand names Speeding tickets	**8** Repairs needed due to neglect

Vital: Life-sustaining, impossible to live without (or life-sustaining in an eternal sense)

Important: Contributes significantly to the family's happiness; difficult to live without

Nice to have: Optional

Wasteful/Worthless: A detriment

HOW IT WORKS

Many financial difficulties arise in marriage when couples are unwilling (or don't know how) to fuse their individual wants and needs into shared priorities. Many years ago, not long after I had developed the idea of a priority matrix for spending, my wife and I were discussing purchases for our new home. One of the items I wanted to purchase was an entertainment system. One of her desires was topsoil and sod for the yard. We were also considering railing for the back porch, other home improvements, and a vacation. We decided to test the matrix.

First we made our list of desires, and then we plugged each one into its appropriate slot in the matrix. Begrudgingly, I agreed that the entertainment center only merited a *nice to have/future* ranking. We placed the topsoil and sod under *important/present* because our kids were tracking a lot of dirt into the house from the yard and ruining the new carpet. We were both surprised, although we shouldn't have been, to discover that the porch railing was a *vital/present* need. There was a five-foot drop from the back porch to the cement patio below—clearly a safety hazard for our little ones. While we had recognized that we needed the railing, we hadn't previously seen the importance of this purchase in relation to other things we wanted to buy. We were both disappointed that our personal wants weren't the highest priorities, but we were also glad to have seen a real need before an emergency arose.

Seeing your expenses prioritized in this way can dramatically change your purchasing decisions. The Spending Matrix helps put emotional impulses in a proper perspective and helps couples avoid contention. In our marriage, it has helped us create *our* spending plan rather than *his* and *hers.* We have come to a unity of priorities.

ADD A FRUGAL-FILTER TO THE MATRIX

The Spending Matrix needs a third dimension for wise decisions—a *frugal-filter,* if you will. This is used to determine the appropriate level of spending within a category given the family's overall needs and resources. It is needed to determine what is *sufficient* versus what is *desired* and what is affordable versus what might create unnecessary debt. Three examples:

- **Transportation** is universally considered a *vital/present* expenditure, but public transportation may suffice in some situations, while others may require a vehicle. If a vehicle is necessary, a reliable used car or an economy car might be a *vital* expenditure, a midrange automobile might drop down to the *important* category, and a luxury car might drop it to a *nice-to-have* expenditure. And if it causes you to go into unnecessary debt, the midrange or luxury classification might even bump it into the *wasteful/worthless* category.
- **A home**—how much living space is *vital* or really necessary? How many more square feet would be *important* or would contribute to your family's happiness in a significant way? How

many more square feet would be *nice to have*? And when is a home so big or grandiose that it becomes a burden and a detriment? To a certain degree, the square-foot calculation will depend on whether you go with a linoleum, tile, or marble budget (passing it through the frugal-filter).

- **A vacation**—it could be argued that a vacation, or time for rest and relaxation, is vital for one's mental health. A trip close to home or within driving distance could fit that bill. More expensive vacations would likely drop into the *important* or *nice-to-have* categories, but if you can do it without going into debt and it is one of your family's priorities, that's great!

FAMILIES ARE UNIQUE, AND THERE ARE NO ABSOLUTES

The spending matrix is different for every family. There are no right answers—no absolutes. A pet and its associated expenses may be considered a *vital/present* for one family and a worthless expense for another. Some families may consider an education fund for their children a *vital/future,* but I have known parents who believe that the best education they ever received was to finance their *own* schooling through hard work and scholarships, and therefore they don't plan on education spending. Only you can determine your priorities; no one else can do it for you.

One of the major challenges you will face as you begin to fill in the matrix with your needs and wants is the urgent nature of the *important/present* versus the non-urgent *vital/future.* With limited resources, which do you fund first—your children's music lessons or your retirement fund? *Vital* should certainly trump *important,* but the present *urgent* often preempts the *vital/future.* Because there will always be urgent expenses, be careful to defend your *vital/future* expenses from the encroachment of the constant flow of *important/ present* expenses. The easiest way to do this is through automatic withdrawals like a retirement savings program.

The power of the Spending Matrix is in its ability to help bring decisions about money and spending into conscious awareness, giving you greater financial control and more unity in your marriage.[13]

CONSIDER YOUR WAYS[14]

In the Old Testament the Lord condemned the human fault of "excess" (covetousness) and the tendency to spend everything we make: "Now therefore thus saith the Lord of hosts; Consider your ways. Ye have sown much, and bring in little; ye eat, but ye have not enough; ye drink, but ye are not filled with drink; ye clothe you, but there is none warm; and he that earneth wages earneth wages to put it into a bag with holes. Thus saith the Lord of hosts; Consider your ways" (Hag. 1:5–7). This was the Lord's rebuke against those who consumed everything they produced yet were never satisfied and were forgetful of Him. These many centuries later, "consider your ways" is still a good reminder to those who are never quite able to say, "I have sufficient for my needs."

In early Church history, members were constantly on the move—from New York to Ohio to Missouri and then to Illinois and beyond. Building new homes was a frequent chore. Many of the homes were modest by today's standards, sometimes measuring just twelve feet by twelve feet. However, when Mary Richards moved into her new log cabin at Winter Quarters after spending the winter in a tent, she remarked, "Our little house seemed to me almost like a palace."[15] Interesting how grateful her attitude was with so very little.

Today Mary Richards's cabin would be dwarfed by most homes.

The irony is that while the average home has increased in size, the average family has decreased in size; and while homes have more time-saving devices, the average family spends less time together. Affluence is up, but happiness is down, as indicated by today's divorce rates. Why isn't more money buying greater happiness?

WHAT IS SUFFICIENT FOR OUR NEEDS?

In his book *How Much Is Enough?*, Alan Durning says that in the 1990s, people were "on average four-and-a-half times richer than their great-grandparents were at the turn of the century, but they [were] not four-and-a-half times happier."[16] The authors of the book *Your Money or Your Life* suggest that happiness or *fulfillment* seems to increase during the initial stages of spending, when one is buying necessities and some nice things, but actually begins to decrease with excess spending.[17] If that is true, one of life's most fundamental questions should be, "What is sufficient for our family to be happy?" Our success will depend not only on answering that question, but also on answering its corollary, "What *don't* we need to be happy?"

Because the natural man's perceived needs are forever expanding, *"sufficient"* is forever elusive, and his time is increasingly devoted to money and the things of this world. Take the extreme case of Prince Jefri Bolkiah, brother of the Sultan of Brunei, for example. According to the *New York Times* News Service, the Prince "frittered away $15 billion on luxury hotels, casinos, a fleet of jets, thousands of cars including over 100 Rolls Royces, parties, race horses, yachts, etc." His panicked brother finally had to cut the purse strings and limit him to a monthly allowance of $300,000."[18] For the natural man, there is never enough.

Along with obeying the law of tithing and avoiding unnecessary debt, one of the most oft-repeated financial principles taught by the prophets is to live within our means, regardless of our income. If Satan can tempt us to over-purchase, we risk not only becoming a time-slave to unnecessary debt but also being "time-consumed" with too many things of this world. The result is less time for the Lord and for our family.

MORE MONEY EQUALS LESS TIME

Juliet B. Schor, a Harvard professor, says that due to improvements in productivity, Americans could work a 22-hour workweek if they were satisfied with a 1948 standard of living. While we are certainly grateful for the progress made since 1948, that would give many of us at least 18 extra hours per week![19]

In the book *Your Money or Your Life,* the authors convincingly illustrate how everything we buy consumes a part of our life—hence the title of their book. Applying simple math to an hourly wage, for example, can illustrate how upgrading to a bigger home (or an unnecessary home equity loan on an existing home) could cost an extra 5 or 10 years of life to purchase, depending on its cost. And if not 10 years of the father's life, then perhaps 10 years of the mother's life as a second wage earner. When we spend beyond what is sufficient, the trade-off is less time.

It has been said that a rich man doesn't own his things; rather, his things begin to own him. "A thatched roof once covered free men; under marble and gold dwells slavery."[20] This self-imposed slavery is seen not only in the form of time-debt, but also in the form of time-clutter.

In his book *Clutter's Last Stand,* Don Aslett gives us additional insight into this self-imposed slavery. Each item we accumulate, he says, "stifles us and robs us of freedom because it requires so much of our time to tend." He writes further: "We have to pay for it, keep track of it, protect it, clean it, store it, insure it, and worry about it. . . . Later we have to move it, hide it, apologize for it, argue over it. . . . But these things are valuable, you say? What about the value of the life and time to store, to clean, to insure, to transport, to protect—what does that cost? More than money."[21]

CHOOSING TO BE CONTENT

One antonym for *greed,* and perhaps the antidote to it, is *content-ment.* The Apostle Paul stated, "I have learned, in whatsoever state I am, therewith to be content" (Philip. 4:11). Contentment and grati-tude are essential if one is to be truly satisfied and happy.

The ability to be content was one of Benjamin Franklin's great-est traits. It had a profound impact on his life and upon the new nation he helped to found. Author Catherine Drinker Bowen writes of Franklin: "He was forty-two when he retired. . . . Had Franklin stayed in business there is little doubt he could have amassed a for-tune . . . the kind of estate built up in America by royal governors. . . . Once assured of a competence, he showed no desire for increasing it; Franklin never changed his simple style of living and seemed to have no ambition for outward show." [22]

For Franklin, "outward show" was dangerous. He said: "The eyes of other people are the eyes that ruin us. If all but myself were blind, I should want neither fine clothes, fine houses, nor fine furniture."[23] He discovered that *time* is the one thing you acquire *by not spending money.* With more time, he was available to help establish a free land where the gospel could be restored (see D&C 101:80).

President Brigham Young also understood the value of spending his time on that which is most important. After gaining a testimony of the restored gospel, "he gave away many of his possessions and reduced his business." This downsizing gave Brigham Young a gift of time that he could devote to building the kingdom. "He served a series of missions. He held meetings and baptized in the country-side surrounding Mendon. He also traveled into upper New York and Ontario, Canada, to preach the gospel and bear witness that Joseph Smith was a prophet of God."²⁴ Later President Young preached what he here practiced when he said, "Work less, wear less, eat less, and we shall be a great deal wiser, healthier, and wealthier people than by taking the course we now do."²⁵

Of course, the Savior Himself is the greatest example of proper prioritizing. With few possessions to distract Him, He focused all of His time and effort on His mission. The Lord doesn't expect us to be impoverished, but His counsel is direct: "Thou shalt lay aside the things of this world, and seek for the things of a better" (D&C 25:10) and "A man's life consisteth not in the abundance of the things which he possesseth" (Luke 12:15).

PUTTING THE FAMILY FIRST

Benjamin Franklin said, "When you buy one fine thing you must buy ten more that your appearance may be all of a piece; . . . 'Tis easier to suppress the first desire, than to satisfy all that follow it.'"²⁶ This is especially true with today's tendency to purchase the biggest home possible, which requires not just 10 more "fine things" but hundreds to fill it. Families with barely affordable mortgage payments often turn to credit cards or a second wage earner to pay for these fine things. Too often the result is ever-increasing debt, manifest by record numbers of people filing for bankruptcy.

The pioneers had to discern what their true needs were. As they hurriedly left Nauvoo, they took with them essentials such as food, clothing, blankets, cooking utensils, and perhaps a few extras that weren't life sustaining but were nevertheless precious, such as a favorite rocking chair. They tearfully left other keepsakes behind.

The trek that lay before the pioneers was not easy, but with faith they began their westward march. Then they came to the slopes of the Rocky Mountains. The trail that was manageable before seemed almost insurmountable now. Many had to lighten their load and again face the difficult process of choosing what to leave behind. Subsequent travelers migrating west on the same trail would come across tools, chairs, and other valuables left to decay and rust on the plains at the foot of the Rockies.

The Saints who had to make these sacrifices must have made many longing backward glances as they continued their journey. Yet while they left many cherished items behind, they didn't leave behind their most precious asset: their children. That would have been unthinkable.

Now, some 165 years later, we are facing different challenges but a similar choice. Tragically, this time it isn't furniture and fineries that are being left behind but our children. Believing that possessions and "personal fulfillment" are paramount, many parents are leaving the primary care of their children to day-care centers. Some may have no choice, but others do. The Savior tells us:

"Lay not up for yourselves treasures upon earth, . . .

"But lay up for yourselves treasures in heaven, where neither moth nor rust doth corrupt, and where thieves do not break through nor steal" (3 Ne. 13:19–20).

Surely we should consider our family to be among our greatest treasures.

In "The Family—A Proclamation to the World," we learn that the "Family is central to the creator's plan for the eternal destiny of His children." [27] Since the family is central, the most important work we do in kingdom building, according to Harold B. Lee, "is within the walls of our own home." [28] Note the word *within*. Parents earn money outside the home to make a *living*, but they spend time inside the home to make a *life*.

There are multiple case studies in history showing how affluence results in pride and its many negative consequences, something repeatedly depicted in the Book of Mormon and known as the *pride cycle*. The Lord warns us, "The riches of the earth are mine to give; but beware of pride, lest ye become as the Nephites of old" (D&C 38:39). We would be wise to avoid the Nephites' mistakes by being wary of "outward show," learning what is sufficient for our true happiness, and discovering how to be content. These principles are deserving of our sincere pondering and prayer.

A fitting conclusion to this chapter on love, unity, and finances comes in some well-known words from President David O. McKay: "No other success can compensate for failure in the home. . . . The poorest shack . . . in which love prevails over a united family is of greater value to God and future humanity than [any other riches]. In such a home God can work miracles and will work miracles. . . . Pure hearts in a pure home are always in whispering distance of Heaven."[29] And when they are in whispering distance of heaven, they are well on their way to *living happily ever after.*

SUMMARY

- The Lord was the true founder of the United States and the City of Enoch. Both societies were established on the principles of righteousness and unity. A successful family should be established on these same principles.
- One of Satan's foremost battle strategies to destroy marriage and family is to divide and conquer.
- The First Presidency and the Quorum of the Twelve make decisions based upon the unanimous voice of the entire group. A husband and wife would be wise to follow the same principle.
- Finances are divisive in many marriages. Unity with finances means "our" money and "our" spending plan.
- Two helpful tools to avoid divisiveness are a Financial Constitution and a Spending Matrix.
- The more money we spend, the less time we have for the Lord and family.

NOTES

1. "E pluribus unum," Wikipedia, last modified January 8, 2015, http://en.wikipedia.org/wiki/E_pluribus_unum.
2. "Symbiosis," Wikipedia, last modified January 14, 2015, http://en.wikipedia.org/wiki/Symbiosis.
3. "Divide and Rule," Wikipedia, last modified January 17, 2015, http://en.wikipedia.org/wiki/Divide_and_rule.
4. Spencer W. Kimball, *The Miracle of Forgiveness* (Salt Lake City: Bookcraft, 1969), 250–51.
5. Gordon B. Hinckley, "Cornerstones of a Happy Home" (pamphlet, 1984), 8.
6. Benjamin Franklin.
7. "Are You Prepared?" *Ensign*, Aug. 2007, 30–33.
8. Benjamin Franklin, *The Way to Wealth* (Applewood Books, 1986), 18.
9. Years ago I read a study that indicated that the foremost financial problem husbands have is spending money elsewhere (often on "big-boy toys") when the

money was needed at home. For wives it was excessive credit card expenditures. Both challenges were divisive to marriages.

10. Franklin, *The Way to Wealth,* 20.
11. Ibid., 19.
12. Ibid., 28.
13. For further insights on these and many additional financial principles, see my book *Uncommon Cents* (1989).
14. Adapted from Lynn G. Robbins, "The Cost of Riches," *Ensign,* June 2003, 24–28.
15. Quoted in William W. Slaughter, "The Strength of Sacrifice," *Ensign,* Apr. 1997, 38.
16. Alan Durning, *How Much Is Enough?* (New York: W.W. Norton and Company, 1992), 23–24.
17. Joe Dominguez and Vicki Robin, *Your Money or Your Life* (New York: Penguin, 1992).
18. Seth Mydans, "Gluttony Is Undoing of Brunei," *Deseret News,* August 17, 2001.
19. Juliet Schor, *The Overworked American: The Unexpected Decline of Leisure* (New York: Basic Books, 1992).
20. Seneca, quoted in John de Graaf and others, *Affluenza—The All-consuming Epidemic* (2001), 125.
21. Don Aslett, *Clutter's Last Stand* (1984), 4, 5, 46.
22. Catherine Drinker Bowen, *The Most Dangerous Man in America* (1974) , 59.
23. Quoted in Andrew M. Allison and others, *The Real Benjamin Franklin* (1987), 364.
24. *Teachings of Presidents of the Church: Brigham Young* (1997), 3.
25. Ibid., 212.
26. *The Autobiography of Benjamin Franklin, Poor Richard's Almanac, and Other Papers,* 227.
27. "The Family: A Proclamation to the World," *Ensign,* Nov. 2010, 129.
28. *Teachings of Presidents of the Church: Harold B. Lee* (2000), 149
29. J. E. McCulloch, *Home: The Savior of Civilization* (Washington, D.C.: The Southern Co-operative League, 1924), 42, quoted in David O. McKay, in Conference Report, Apr. 1964, 5.

CHAPTER 9

FAMILY HOME EVENING HELPS

A survey conducted by the Research Information Department of the Church found that a surprising number of active families were not holding regular family home evening (FHE). One of the most common excuses given for letting FHE slide was a lack of ideas. Focusing time and attention on Christlike virtues provides a family with wonderful ideas for many successful family home evenings.

If you have an Aaronic Priesthood-age son, consider dedicating at least one FHE per month to his Duty to God program. The Duty to God program is primarily focused on Christlike attributes. If you have a daughter who is in Young Women, consider devoting at least one FHE per month to her Personal Progress for the same reason. It will simplify your life by accomplishing two things at once and will help you raise a Christlike son or daughter. There are also eighteen or so wonderful lessons you can design around the virtues found in the *For the Strength of Youth* booklet.

Another wonderful possibility is to select a Christlike virtue from the list in the Appendix, and develop a lesson around that virtue.

With 100 groupings, you will have material for many family home evenings. The following are elements that might be considered or included in your personal study or FHE outline (see below). There may be too much material for little ones, but you are encouraged to adapt the resources to fit your family's needs. The suggestions included here will help you gain a more comprehensive understanding of any of Christ's virtues in your personal gospel study or in preparing a talk or a lesson.

BEGIN WITH THE DEFINITION—Before we can fully develop a virtue, we must understand its correct meaning. Definitions could come from several excellent sources: the Guide to the Scriptures; the Bible Dictionary; *Preach My Gospel*, chapter 6; *Teachings of Presidents of the Church* (Priesthood and Relief Society manuals); or the dictionary.

CREATE A T-CHART with the synonyms of the attribute on the left side and the corresponding antonyms on the right side.

- **Synonyms**—Studying like-kind character traits can give us interesting insights and add clarity to the definition. For example, we would consider *grateful* and *thankful* to be synonyms and often use them interchangeably. However, the 1828 Webster's dictionary gives us this interesting insight and distinction:
  - **Thankful**—"a feeling or expression of appreciation."
  - **Grateful**—also means "a feeling or expression of appreciation," but goes one step beyond *thankful* to include "a sense of reciprocation."
- **Antonym(s)**—Prophets have explained why the antonym of each virtue is helpful. Joseph Smith said, "By proving contraries, truth is made manifest."[1] And Brigham Young explained,

"All facts are proved and made manifest by their opposite."[2] The antonym not only helps define the virtue, but reveals the wisdom, power, and truth of it. For example, you could not understand nor appreciate health if you had never been sick. It has been said that "sickness is felt, health not at all."

Use the scriptures—Using the Topical Guide, look for scriptural passages on the attribute. Some passages help to define the virtue and establish its importance, while others help frame the virtue and put it in context. Still others identify promised blessings.

Ponder—Questions and pondering are virtually synonymous. You can't ponder without questions. Personal revelation comes as we seek, ponder, and pray. Write down questions that come into your mind as you study the virtue. These very questions may be stimulating questions to ask the family during family home evening discussions.

Use stories—Parables of the Savior, other scripture stories, children's books that teach values, or even fables may work. The Lord nearly always illustrated His teachings with a parable or an example of the things He taught.

Pray for the Lord to help you develop the attribute. Chapter 6 of *Preach My Gospel* states that "Christlike attributes are gifts from God. . . . Ask your Heavenly Father to bless you with these attributes; you cannot develop them without His help."[3]

On the topic of prayer, President George Q. Cannon shared this wonderful insight: "If any of us are imperfect, it is our duty to pray for the gift that will make us perfect. Have I imperfections? I am full of them. What is my duty? To pray to God to give me the gifts that will correct these imperfections. If I am an angry man, it is my duty to pray for charity, which suffereth long and is kind. Am I an envious man? It is my duty to seek for charity, which envieth not. So it is with all the gifts of the Gospel. They are intended for this purpose. No man ought to say, 'Oh, I cannot help this; it is my nature.' He is not justified in it, for the reason that God has promised to give strength to correct these things, and to give gifts that will eradicate them."[4]

POSTER—Consider putting a virtue of the week on a poster on the wall near the dinner table or other common area. Include the definition with synonyms and antonyms. Let the chart be a daily reminder to stimulate some dinner-time conversation of what each family member did that day to apply that virtue in their life or where they could have done better. For example, "In what way did you show kindness today? patience? gratitude?"

NOTES

1. *History of the Church*, 6:428.
2. *Discourses of Brigham Young*, sel. John A. Widtsoe (1954).
3. *Preach My Gospel: A Guide to Missionary Service* (2004), 115.
4. George Q. Cannon, "Discourse by President George Q. Cannon," *Latter-day Saints' Millennial Star* 56, no. 17 (23 Apr. 1894), 260.

FAMILY HOME EVENING OUTLINE
FOR DEVELOPING CHRISTLIKE ATTRIBUTES

SELECT AND DEFINE AN ATTRIBUTE: _____

_____

SYNONYM(S)	ANTONYM(S)
_____	_____
_____	_____
_____	_____

SCRIPTURES ABOUT THE ATTRIBUTE: _____

_____

_____

PONDER: Write down questions and look for answers.

_____

_____

USE STORIES: Parables, scripture stories, children's books, or family stories.

PRAY: In family prayer, ask the Lord to help you develop the attribute.

FOLLOW UP: Use reminders and share additional scriptures and family experiences about the attribute throughout the week. Catch each other *being* that virtue.

CHRISTLIKE VIRTUES

We learn in the *Lectures on Faith* that an understanding of Christ's attributes is fundamental in order to exercise faith in Him. "Let us here observe, that three things are necessary in order that any rational and intelligent being may exercise faith in God unto life and salvation. First, the idea that he actually exists. Secondly, a correct idea of his character, perfections, and attributes. Thirdly, an actual knowledge that the course of life which he is pursuing is according to his will."[1]

The purpose of this chapter is to help increase faith in Jesus Christ by reviewing His attributes, which we can also refer to as Christlike virtues, with a desire to more fully develop them in our own lives.

"Christlike attributes are gifts from God," but "they come as you use your agency righteously. Ask your Heavenly Father to bless you with these attributes; you cannot develop them without His help"[2]

The development of spiritual strength is not unlike acquiring physical strength. A prayer for good health would be in vain if we weren't striving to achieve it through healthy eating, exercise, and sleeping habits. We cannot expect to reap where we have not sown. Similarly, we cannot expect a virtue without effort. Prayer by itself is insufficient. The Lord's love for us and His desire to bless us is always balanced with the principle of self-reliance and His respect for our agency. To access His grace, or divine help, He expects us to do everything in our power, or to pray and act in faith (see D&C 123:17).

Once you identify the Christlike virtue you want to more fully develop, be mindful of behaviors that would help you grow in that virtue, including action items on your to-do list.

Let's say that you wanted to become more patient. Here are some to-dos you could work on based on scriptural guidance. They will help you to *be* a patient person.

- I resist the temptation to get angry when the children misbehave (see 3 Ne. 11:29–30; Col. 3:19, 21; D&C 121:41, 42).
- I resist the temptation to lash out at my spouse when I feel criticized (see Prov. 15:1).
- I wait patiently for the blessings and promises of the Lord to be fulfilled (see 2 Ne. 10:17).
- I am able to wait for things without getting upset or frustrated (see Rom. 8:25).
- I am patient and long-suffering in challenges (see Alma 17:11).
- I am patient with the faults and weaknesses of others (see Rom. 15:1).
- I am patient with myself as the Lord helps me overcome my weaknesses (see Ether 12:27).
- I face adversity and afflictions calmly and hopefully (see 1 Ne. 19:9; Alma 34:40–41).

Earlier in this book, the chapters "Agency and Virtue" (chapter 3) and "Even as I Am" (chapter 4) shared ideas on teaching and practicing Christlike virtues in the home and how to help children develop them.

Chapter 9, "Family Home Evening Helps," has an outline for selecting, studying, and focusing on specific Christlike attributes for a wonderful family home evening.

I invite you to become familiar with the list of virtues below. The more you focus on them in the many ways mentioned in this book, the more "virtue [will] garnish thy thoughts unceasingly" (D&C 121:45), and the more you will become "even as I am" (3 Ne. 27:27).

Virtues

According to the Church's official website, "Virtue is a prerequisite to entering the Lord's holy temples and to receiving the Spirit's guidance. Virtue 'is a pattern of thought and behavior based on high moral standards.'[3] It encompasses chastity and moral purity. Virtue begins in the heart and in the mind. It is nurtured in the home. It is the accumulation of thousands of small decisions and actions. *Virtue* is a word we don't hear often in today's society, but the Latin root word *virtus* means 'strength.' Virtuous women and men possess a quiet dignity and inner strength. They are confident because they are worthy to receive and be guided by the Holy Ghost. President Monson has counseled: '*You* be the one to make a stand for right, even if you stand alone. Have the moral courage to be a light for others to follow. There is no friendship more valuable than your own clear conscience, your own moral cleanliness—and what a glorious feeling it is to know that you stand in your appointed place clean and with the confidence that you are worthy to do so."[4]

Although there are hundreds of virtues, I have chosen to condense them to a list of 100. Omitted virtues are generally included as synonyms in the definitions given. Antonyms also help to define and cherish the virtue by contrasting the virtue with its opposite: "They taste the bitter that they may know to prize the good" (Moses 6:55). The antonyms are the "Thou shalt nots" of life. The development of virtue is a simultaneous quest to develop the positive and to make a concerted effort to eliminate the negative. The negative of a virtue, or its antonym, will generally be obvious to us through our remorse of conscience. However, sometimes these antonyms are not so obvious due to our pride, which can blind us to weak points in our character. These are only discerned through humility and prayer.

Each of these admirable Christlike attributes is deserving of its own chapter; however, an in-depth treatment of each is not practical for this book. There are so many virtues that they may seem overwhelming at first, but which virtue would we leave out? As you review this list, you will realize that your progress in the development of virtues is much further along than you may have supposed. Because Heavenly Father wants us to become like Him, we may expect that He will help us. Remember to select and focus on only one or two virtues at a time rather than becoming overwhelmed by all one hundred.

The Savior often said, "Be ye therefore perfect, even as your Father which is in heaven is perfect" (Matt. 5:48). A careful review of the footnote on that scripture reveals that the Greek meaning of the original translation for the word *perfect* is **complete, finished, fully developed**. Perhaps when you hear this scripture in the future, you could mentally substitute one of those descriptions for the word "perfect" and remind yourself that you are a "work in progress" and that God is not finished with you yet.

I have listed the virtues in a logical sequence rather than

alphabetically to better illustrate their overlapping and interdependent nature. It isn't a perfect sequence; it's just my way, beginning with agency and self-governance. Each virtue is presented in two formats, the noun and the imperative form of the verb *be,* such as *gratitude* and *be thankful.* Pairing them in this way will help you to recognize and develop both the to-do and the to-be aspects of any given virtue.

Note: This is intended to be a resource for lifelong study and reference, not a list of qualities you must immediately obtain. Following the guidance of the Spirit, select and focus on the virtue or virtues that will be the most beneficial to your family given your own time and circumstances.

1. THE VIRTUE OF **SELF-GOVERNANCE.** The wise use of moral agency. The ability and privilege God gives us to choose right from wrong and to act for ourselves. "It is given unto men to know good from evil; wherefore they are agents unto themselves" (Moses 6:56); "to act for themselves and not to be acted upon" (2 Ne. 2:26). "Your freedom to act for yourself is so central to your eternal progress and happiness that the adversary exerts extraordinary efforts to undermine it."[5]

   ❧ *Be free:* Find peace and an unconstrained state of being resulting from accepting truth and choosing to follow righteousness. "We are free not because we can choose, but because we have chosen well."[6]

   • SYNONYMS: acting, free, decisive, acting on impressions.

   • ANTONYMS: powerless, incapable, inactive, giving up, frozen by doubt or fear, hesitant, irresolute, indecisive, wavering, weak-kneed.

2. THE VIRTUE OF **RESPONSIBILITY.** Personal responsibility is the basis of self-governance and is to recognize oneself as being the cause for the effects of one's choices. Those who accept

responsibility as a virtue discover that the power is in them to successfully manage and control their own lives.

❧ *Be responsible:* Develop the abilities and talents Heavenly Father has given you. When you make mistakes or commit sins, resist the temptation to excuse, justify, or minimize them. The first step in the repentance process is to responsibly recognize and own up to the sin or mistake. Being responsible is the courage to confront fears, shame, guilt, and insecurities without trying to excuse them—to choose the right and let the consequence follow.

• SYNONYMS: dependable, trustworthy, reliable, mature, capable, competent, honest with oneself.

• ANTONYMS: irresponsible, unreliable, untrustworthy, careless, reckless, unstable, blaming, self-justifying, excusing, covering up, (see the anti-responsibility list in chapter 2).

3. THE VIRTUE OF **ACCOUNTABILITY**. Accountability is being answerable to God, or His appointed servants, for the use of agency including "your thoughts, and your words, and your deeds" (Mosiah 4:30). It includes a willingness to accept responsibility for one's choices. "That every man may act . . . according to the moral agency which I have given unto him, that every man may be accountable for his own sins in the day of judgment" (D&C 101:78).

❧ *Be accountable:* Accountability includes a willingness to confess sins before the Lord or His servants, or to account for one's actions. "By this ye may know if a man repenteth of his sins—behold, he will *confess them* and forsake them" (D&C 58:43; emphasis added).

• SYNONYMS: responsible, submissive, humble, dependable, trustworthy, reliable, answerable.

- ANTONYMS: irresponsible, defiant, obstinate, uncooperative, non-compliant, recalcitrant.

4. THE VIRTUE OF **FAITH IN JESUS CHRIST.** Confidence and trust in Jesus Christ as the Savior and Redeemer that lead a person to come unto Him, repent, be baptized, receive the gift of the Holy Ghost, and faithfully endure to the end. Faith includes a hope for things which are not seen, but which are true. Faith is evidenced by good works.

   ✤ *Be faithful* with an eye single to the glory of God, without hypocrisy or guile or trying to serve two masters. "Thou shalt have no other gods before me" (Ex. 20:3). Have faith in Jesus Christ. By faith you can obtain a remission of your sins and eventually dwell in God's presence.

   - SYNONYMS: believing, hopeful, trusting, confident, reliant, resolute, full of conviction, assured, loyal, devoted, constant, diligent, dedicated, determined, a covenant keeper.

   - ANTONYMS: disbelieving, despairing, distrusting, doubtful, misgiving, skeptical, disobedient, disloyal, undependable, inconstant, unfaithful, distracted.

5. THE VIRTUE OF **SELF-WORTH.** True self-worth comes from knowing one is a son or daughter of God with divine potential and by developing and using gifts and talents in the service of your fellowmen in building up the kingdom of God. The quality of being worthy of esteem or respect.

   ✤ *Be confident:* Know who you are. Surround yourself with people who love you. Make achievable goals for yourself. Focus on the positive, not the negative.

   - SYNONYMS: knowing your individual worth, self-confident.

- ANTONYMS: afraid, doubtful, fearful, indefinite, pessimistic, full of self-pity.

6. THE VIRTUE OF **RIGHTEOUS DESIRES.** A strong feeling of wanting to have or to do something righteous. Deep-rooted longing to rightfully discern truth from error. "Blessed are they which do hunger and thirst after righteousness: for they shall be filled" (Matt. 5:6).

   ❧ *Be desirous:* Let your greatest desire be that the Holy Ghost be your constant companion.

   - SYNONYMS: passionate, hungering and thirsting after righteousness, inspired, zealous.

   - ANTONYMS: averse, opposed, indifferent, uncaring, apathetic, disinterested, inattentive.

7. THE VIRTUE OF **KNOWLEDGE.** Seek learning, by study and by faith (see D&C 88:118; see also 2 Ne. 9:29). Having understanding and comprehension, especially of truth as taught or confirmed by the Spirit. "Add to your faith virtue; and to virtue knowledge" (2 Pet. 1:5). "The glory of God is intelligence, or, in other words, light and truth" (D&C 93:36).

   ❧ *Be knowledgeable:* Progress and grow. Gain knowledge and intelligence through diligence and obedience (see D&C 130:19). Learn line upon line, precept upon precept. "Be smart—you need all the education you can get. Sacrifice a car; sacrifice anything that is needed to be sacrificed to qualify yourselves to do the work of the world."[7]

   - SYNONYMS: studious, pondering, asking-seeking-knocking, educated, instructed, informed.

- ANTONYMS: ignorant, inexperienced, uneducated, uninformed, misinformed, inattentive, lazy, illiterate, uncultured, misled, blind, clueless, misguided, naive, oblivious.

8. THE VIRTUE OF **SILENCE** AND **LISTENING**. Free from noise and distractions. At rest; calm; undisturbed. Considerate of others in conversation. To meditate and think deeply, often upon the scriptures or other things of God.

   ❧ *Be still and attentive:* "and know that I am God" (D&C 101:16). "Let every man be swift to hear, *slow to speak,* slow to wrath" (James 1:19; emphasis added).

   - SYNONYMS: quiet, still, pondering, listening, empathetic, appreciative, seeking to understand.
   - ANTONYMS: boisterous, gossipy, discordant, disruptive, loud, agitated, rowdy, noisy, distracted, selfish, a poor listener.

9. THE VIRTUE OF **MEDITATION**. Ability to consider things carefully and understand what is important. To conceive of in the mind. "And while we meditated upon these things, the Lord touched the eyes of our understandings and they were opened" (D&C 76:19). When combined with prayer, pondering the things of God can bring revelation and understanding. "And when he had sent the multitudes away, he went up into a mountain apart to pray" (Matt. 14:23).

   ❧ *Be thoughtful:* Positively affect your attitudes and behavior by thinking righteous thoughts. Remember that our thoughts are heavily influenced by the things we allow to enter our minds through media. "For as he thinketh in his heart, so is he" (Prov. 23:7).

   - SYNONYMS: pondering, prayerful, contemplative, searching, seeking, studious, questioning, reflective, thinking.

- ANTONYMS: dismissive, neglectful, rejecting, disregarding, ignorant, overlooking, scornful, abandoning, denying, distracted.

10. THE VIRTUE OF **DISCERNMENT.** A gift of the Spirit given "to understand or know something through the power of the Spirit. It includes perceiving the true character of people and the source and meaning of spiritual manifestations" (Guide to the Scriptures). Ability to make good judgments, to tell whether something is valuable, to detect subtle nuances, feelings, and surroundings.

   ❧ *Be observant and perceptive:* Observing and listening must precede the gift of discernment. Allow the Spirit to teach you to discern between good and evil and to identify the Lord's tender mercies in your life. As Sherlock said to Watson, "You see, but you do not observe."

   - SYNONYMS: quick to observe, listening, circumspect, perceptive, discriminating.
   - ANTONYMS: brushing off, discounting, dismissive, ignorant, scoffing, shrugging off, distracted, inattentive, unaware, unmindful, unready, blind, dulled, insensitive, unwise.

11. THE VIRTUE OF **UNDERSTANDING.** To gain a knowledge through experience or to perceive the meaning of some truth, including its application to life. "They had waxed strong in the knowledge of the truth; for they were men of a sound understanding and they had searched the scriptures diligently, that they might know the word of God" (Alma 17:3).

   ❧ *Be enlightened:* Hearken to the voice of the Spirit to enlighten your eyes, enlighten your mind, and fill your soul with joy. Search the scriptures diligently.

   - SYNONYMS: understanding heart, inspired, feeling, enlightened, guided by revelation.

- ANTONYMS: hard-hearted, unaccepting, unbelieving, callous, insensitive, stern, uncaring, unloving, disinterested, indifferent, insensitive, unfeeling, confused, misled.

12. THE VIRTUE OF **WISDOM.** Wisdom is more than knowledge. It is the ability to use good judgment to make good decisions, utilizing knowledge and experience with common sense and insight. In the premortal life, Lucifer acquired great knowledge, but lacked wisdom—the most extreme example we have of the difference between the two. "When they are learned they think they are wise, and they hearken not unto the counsel of God, for they set it aside, supposing they know of themselves, wherefore, their wisdom is foolishness" (2 Ne. 9:28; see also 27:26). Wisdom is a gift from God to the humble to help them judge correctly.

❧ *Be wise:* Gain wisdom through experience, study, and by following God's counsel.

- SYNONYMS: understanding, intelligent, prudent, clever, using common sense, astute, practical, pragmatic, logical, realistic, sensible, rational, judicious, circumspect, informed.
- ANTONYMS: full of foolish pride, ignorant, misguided, unintelligent, unreasonable, unwise.

13. THE VIRTUE OF **SIMPLICITY.** "My soul delighteth in plainness" (2 Ne. 25:4). While Nephi was referring to keeping writing simple, the virtue is also the judicious use of resources to avoid cluttering life. One who has mastered the virtue of simplicity defends the best things in life from the intrusion of too many good but unnecessary things. It is not a matter of time, but priorities. "But one thing is needful: and Mary hath chosen that good part" (Luke 10:42).

❧ *Be judicious and practical:* "And see that all these things are done in wisdom and order; for it is not requisite that a man should run faster than he has strength" (Mosiah 4:27). "And the cares of this world, and the deceitfulness of riches, and the lusts of other things entering in, choke the word, and it becometh unfruitful" (Mark 4:19).

- SYNONYMS: prioritizing, clear, understandable, manageable, wise, sensible, prudent, unassuming, uncomplicated, unpretentious, straightforward, simple, uncluttered, easy.
- ANTONYMS: complex, complicated, convoluted, difficult, intricate, unclear, unintelligible, unmanageable, incomprehensible, cluttered, littered, disorderly, confusing, excessive.

14. THE VIRTUE OF **CLEANLINESS.** The process of keeping yourself, your possessions, and your environment clean. Diligence in keeping clean. (Being clean in a spiritual sense is addressed under a different heading). "And the Lord God took the man, and put him into the garden of Eden to dress it and to keep it." (Gen. 2:15; see also Moses 3:15; Abr. 5:11). Charity "doth not behave itself unseemly" (1 Cor. 13:5).

❧ *Be clean:* Be considerate by leaving a room or place cleaner than you found it. Follow the pattern of the temple, where cleanliness is a sign of respect and gratitude to the Lord and creates a more inviting environment for the Spirit. It is a sign of wise stewardship.

- SYNONYMS: clean, tidy, neat.
- ANTONYMS: cluttered, dirty, disorganized, filthy, sloppy, untidy, slovenly, unkempt.

15. THE VIRTUE OF **ORDER.** A clear arrangement of the way in which a set of things is done. A situation in which everything is well

organized or arranged. A situation in which people obey the law and follow the accepted rules of social behavior. The Lord's house is a house of order and not a house of confusion (see D&C 132:8).

❧ *Be orderly:* "And see that all these things are done in wisdom and order" (Mosiah 4:27).

• SYNONYMS: orderly, decent, decorous, neat, tidy.

• ANTONYMS: chaotic, confused, disorderly, disorganized, sloppy.

16. THE VIRTUE OF **BALANCE.** "Organize yourselves; prepare every needful thing" (D&C 88:119). A balanced person has a sensible and reasonable attitude toward life with all parts combining well together or existing in the correct amounts, including rest and relaxation. "And he said unto them [the Apostles], Come ye yourselves apart into a desert place, and rest a while: for there were many coming and going, and they had no leisure so much as to eat" (Mark 6:31).

❧ *Be balanced and prudent:* Pace your life—a time and a season for everything. Man is that he might have joy. Balance is having the right amount—not too much or too little—of any quality, which leads to harmony or evenness. Virtues themselves are in need of balancing, such as shown in the Savior's candor balanced with tenderness; justice with mercy; charity with self-reliance; being content but progressing; being bold but not overbearing; blessing "immediately" (Mosiah 2:24) as "He trieth their patience (Mosiah 23:21); reverence with sociality; avoiding pride but not burying talents; being no respecter of persons but having a chosen people; etc. Balance requires wisdom and inspiration.

• SYNONYMS: well-adjusted, full of equanimity and equipoise, stable, steady, prioritizing.

- ANTONYMS: conflicted, obsessed, unbalanced, irrational, distracted, insecure, shaky, uncertain, unpredictable, unstable, faltering, hesitant, procrastinating.

17. THE VIRTUE OF **BELIEF**. To think that something is true, correct, or real. To have confidence in the truth, existence, or the reliability of something or someone, even without absolute proof that one is right in doing so.

   ❧ *Be believing:* All things are possible to him that believes (see Mark 9:23–24). When one acts in righteousness, the power comes: "And he took him by the right hand, and lifted him up: and immediately his feet and ankle bones received strength" (Acts 3:7).

   - SYNONYMS: trusting, accepting, assuming, convinced, having faith, positive, not doubting.

   - ANTONYMS: disbelieving, disputing, distrusting, doubtful, rejecting, suspicious.

18. THE VIRTUE OF **TRUST**. Reliance on the integrity, honesty, strength, ability, surety of a person or thing. To rely upon or place confidence in someone or something. In spiritual matters, trust includes relying on God and the Spirit of truth: "He will guide you into all truth" (John 16:13). "And I, Enos, knew that God could not lie; wherefore, my guilt was swept away" (Enos 1:6).

   ❧ *Be trusting:* "Trust in the Lord with all thine heart; and lean not unto thine own understanding. In all thy ways acknowledge him, and he shall direct thy paths" (Prov. 3:5–6)

   - SYNONYMS: confident, expecting, faithful, hopeful, assured, certain, full of conviction.

   - ANTONYMS: critical, cynical, disbelieving, distrustful, doubtful, skeptical, suspicious, uncertain, unconvinced, wary.

19. THE VIRTUE OF **HOPE.** Hope is the confident expectation of and longing for the promised blessings of righteousness. When we have hope, we trust God's promises, made possible through the Atonement of Jesus Christ. "Our God whom we serve is able to deliver us from the burning fiery furnace, and he will deliver us out of thine hand, O king. But if not, be it known unto thee, O king, that we will not serve thy gods, nor worship the golden image which thou hast set up" (Dan. 3:17–18).

❦ *Be hopeful:* Have a quiet assurance that if you do "the works of righteousness," you "shall receive [your] reward, even peace in this world, and eternal life in the world to come" (D&C 59:23).

- SYNONYMS: optimistic, expectant, assured, confident, faithful, trusting, enthusiastic, persevering.
- ANTONYMS: comfortless, dark, depressed, desperate, despondent, hopeless, miserable, pessimistic, unhappy.

20. THE VIRTUE OF **OPTIMISM.** A general disposition to expect the best in all things. The belief that good will eventually triumph over evil. Optimism goes forward, while pessimism gives up.

❦ *Be optimistic:* "In the world ye shall have tribulation: but be of good cheer; I have overcome the world" (John 16:33).

- SYNONYMS: confident, upbeat, self-assured, self-confident, waxing strong in the Lord, idealistic, trusting, bright, positive, of good cheer, enthusiastic.
- ANTONYMS: uncertain, discouraged, gloomy, hopeless, pessimistic.

21. THE VIRTUE OF **VISION.** The ability to think about and plan for the future using intelligence, imagination, and inspiration. Someone's idea or hope of how something should be done or how it will be in the future. For a vision to have power, it needs to answer the question "why?" "And it came to pass that he rent his coat;

and he took a piece thereof, and wrote upon it—In memory of our God, our religion, and freedom, and our peace, our wives, and our children—and he fastened it upon the end of a pole" (Alma 46:12).

❧ *Be purposeful:* Live up to your privileges. With His help, become all that Heavenly Father has envisioned you to be.

- SYNONYMS: visionary, purposeful, goal-oriented, creative, having foresight, farsighted, inventive, enthusiastic.
- ANTONYMS: rash, shortsighted, not careful, unthinking, unwise.

22. THE VIRTUE OF **FORESIGHT** AND **ANTICIPATION.** Spiritual insight. Making or indicative of timely preparation for the future. The ability to see what will or might happen in the future. To give advance thought, discussion, or treatment to. To meet an obligation before a due date. To be prepared. To foresee and deal with in advance. The act of looking forward.

❧ *Be provident and proactive:* Acting in anticipation of future needs, problems, or changes. A patriarchal blessing helps an individual "look forward" in anticipation and preparation. Act on promptings, which increases the likelihood of receiving further promptings. If you don't make decisions in time, time makes decisions for you.

- SYNONYMS: having foreknowledge, farsighted, following promptings, prepared, prudent, circumspect, provident.
- ANTONYMS: neglectful, procrastinating, delayed, dawdling, living for the moment, shortsighted, improvident.

23. THE VIRTUE OF **VIGILANCE.** Watching a person or situation very carefully so that you will notice any problems or signs of danger immediately. The process of paying close and continuous attention.

❖ *Be watchful and prepared:* "Be watchful unto prayer continually, that ye may not be led away by the temptations of the devil, that he may not overpower you, that ye may not become his subjects at the last day; for behold, he rewardeth you no good thing" (Alma 34:39).

• SYNONYMS: vigilant, diligent, prepared, attentive, alert, careful, cautious, walking circumspectly, farsighted, remembering, record keeping, sentimental.

• ANTONYMS: careless, heedless, inattentive, unobservant, negligent.

24. THE VIRTUE OF **EARLY RISING** AND **RETIRING**. "And in the morning, rising a great while before day, he went out, and departed into a solitary place, and there prayed" (Mark 1:35). "And early in the morning he came again into the temple, and all the people came unto him; and he sat down, and taught them" (John 8:2).

❖ *Be a wise sleeper:* "Retire to thy bed early, that ye may not be weary; arise early, that your bodies and your minds may be invigorated" (D&C 88:124). Revelation comes early.

• SYNONYMS: invigorated, awake, refreshed, revived, rejuvenated.

• ANTONYMS: sleeping in, staying up late, lazy, lethargic, tired, weak of resolve.

25. THE VIRTUE OF **PUNCTUALITY**. The quality or habit of adhering to an expected or appointed time. A kind and considerate gesture to others involved.

❖ *Be prompt:* Respond positively, with little or no delay, to the Lord's counsel. Arrive a few minutes early.

• SYNONYMS: punctual, prompt, dependable, timely, immediate, speedy.

• ANTONYMS: tardy, late, belated, inconsiderate.

26. THE VIRTUE OF **WORK.** Something produced or accomplished through the effort, actions, or agency of a person or thing. A manifestation of energy. Our primary means of both growth and happiness.

   ✤ *Be industrious:* Experience the joy of success that comes from a firmly developed habit of hard work. "Thou shalt not be idle; for he that is idle shall not eat the bread nor wear the garments of the laborer" (D&C 42:42).

   • SYNONYMS: industrious, full of initiative, striving, a self-starter, diligent, self-reliant, independent.

   • ANTONYMS: idle, lazy, inactive, dependent, having a lack of initiative, a freeloader.

27. THE VIRTUE OF **INDEPENDENCE.** The ability to make decisions and live your life free from the control or influence of other people. The state of quality of being independent. A state in which a person does not rely on others for subsistence; ability to support one's self. "*Self-reliance is* . . . an essential element in our spiritual as well as our temporal well-being. . . . Salvation can be obtained on no other principle."[8]

   ✤ *Be self-reliant:* Develop the ability, commitment, and effort to provide for the spiritual and temporal well-being of yourself and your family.

   • SYNONYMS: self-reliant, independent.

   • ANTONYMS: dependent, co-dependent, subordinate, subservient, entitled.

28. THE VIRTUE OF **CONTENTMENT.** The happiness you feel when you have everything you need and you enjoy your life. Happiness with one's situation in life. Not comparing yourself to others. Gratitude precedes contentment. Paul "learned, in whatsoever state

I am, therewith to be content" (Philip. 4:11). Wanting more than is needful is covetousness, which is "a sore curse" (D&C 102:4). Do I have sufficient for my needs?

❧ *Be content:* Avoid the temptation to become time-strapped and cash-poor due to unnecessary purchases. Avoid unnecessary debt. "But lay up for yourselves treasures in heaven, where neither moth nor rust doth corrupt, and where thieves do not break through nor steal" (Matt. 6:19).

- SYNONYMS: envying not, content, satisfied, sufficient.
- ANTONYMS: disappointed, dissatisfied, troubled, unhappy, agitated, envious, covetous.

29. THE VIRTUE OF **PROVIDENT LIVING.** While we strive for self-reliance, we recognize that we are also dependent on the Lord. "For behold, are we not all beggars? Do we not all depend upon the same Being, even God, for all the substance which we have, for both food and raiment, and for gold, and for silver, and for all the riches which we have of every kind?" (Mosiah 4:19). Being frugal and careful is wise use of our resources and one way to show gratitude to the Lord for our earthly blessings. Our first priority with resources is to pay our tithes and offerings.

❧ *Be frugal:* Do not be wasteful. After miraculously feeding the 5,000, the Savior had the disciples "gather up the fragments that remain, that nothing be lost" (John 6:12). Avoid unnecessary debt. Be modest in your expenditures and live within your means.

- SYNONYMS: frugal, provident, providing, thrifty, resourceful, conservative, not wasteful.
- ANTONYMS: careless, improvident, a spendthrift, wasteful, ungrateful.

30. THE VIRTUE OF **COMPETENCE**. The ability to do something successfully or efficiently. Developing skills and talents. A particular ability that involves special training and experience. An art, trade, or technique, particularly one requiring use of the mind, hands, or body.

❧ *Be capable and proficient:* Develop skills and qualifications to do things well. When coupled with a desire to serve God and your fellowmen, it becomes one of the sources of happiness in life.

• SYNONYMS: experienced, expert, talented, adroit, skilled, capable, practiced, able, proficient, accomplished, adept, professional.

• ANTONYMS: incapable, incompetent, inefficient, inept, inexperienced.

31. THE VIRTUE OF **CREATIVITY**. From early childhood there is something inherent in each of us to create. Children create art with crayons, forts out of cardboard boxes or blankets, and snowmen each winter. There is a reason building blocks are timeless toys—there is a deep sense of satisfaction and happiness that comes through creating. The greatest creation is to be co-creators with God in creating a home and family, that the earth might answer the end of its creation" (D&C 49:16; see also 88:19–20).

❧ *Be creative and a problem-solver:* Especially in using gifts and talents in the service of God and your fellow man. Remember the story of the brother of Jared in solving problems. Ask the Lord for help, but be creative with possible solutions (see Ether 2–3). Identify the problem, study possible options, and then decide and act. If at first you don't succeed, try, try again. "Success is going from failure to failure without any loss of enthusiasm" (Winston Churchill).

- SYNONYMS: a problem-solver, innovative, inventive, adept, adroit, skillful, able, capable, practiced, competent.
- ANTONYMS: destroying, critical, cynical, skeptical, scoffing, giving up, surrendering.

32. THE VIRTUE OF **EXCELLENCE**. A high degree or grade of worth. A feature of a person's character, especially when it is a positive one such as honesty, kindness, or a special ability. "A man of understanding is of an excellent spirit" (Prov. 17:27). Excellence does not need to proclaim itself; its reputation precedes it.

   ❖ *Be excellent:* Pursue excellence. "Forasmuch as ye are zealous of spiritual gifts, see that ye may excel to the edifying of the church" (1 Cor. 14:12).

   - SYNONYMS: excelling, high-quality, thorough, meticulous, careful, methodical, of superior value.
   - ANTONYMS: common, inferior, insignificant, not noteworthy, mediocre, cutting corners.

33. THE VIRTUE OF **COMMITMENT**. A strong belief that something is good and that you should support it. A promise to do something. A duty or responsibility that you have accepted. "And ye shall bind yourselves to act in all holiness before me" (D&C 43:9). Doing the things the Lord requires of us is a good indication of the virtue of commitment: daily family and personal prayer and scriptures, family home evening, home and visiting teaching, temple attendance, etc.

   ❖ *Be resolved:* "Resolve to perform what you ought; perform without fail what you resolve."[9]

   - SYNONYMS: a covenant maker, magnifying, endowed, a promise keeper, Sabbath-keeping.
   - ANTONYMS: disloyal, inconstant, a quitter, unfaithful, fickle.

34. THE VIRTUE OF **DETERMINATION**. The refusal to let anything prevent you from doing what you have decided to do. Firmness of purpose. Resolve. "No man, having put his hand to the plough, and looking back, is fit for the kingdom of God" (Luke 9:62).

❧ *Be determined:* Persevere toward difficult goals in spite of obstacles.

• SYNONYMS: determined, resolute, tenacious, strong-minded, earnest, full of grit, zealous, fervent.

• ANTONYMS: weak, yielding, indefinite, undecided, unfixed, wavering, easily discouraged.

35. THE VIRTUE OF **DILIGENCE**. Diligence is steady, consistent, earnest, and energetic effort in doing the Lord's work. It is an attitude or behavior of someone who works very hard and very carefully. Persistent exertion of body or mind. "For he that diligently seeketh shall find; and the mysteries of God shall be unfolded unto them, by the power of the Holy Ghost" (1 Ne. 10:19).

❧ *Be diligent:* Give consistent, valiant effort, especially in serving the Lord and obeying his word. "It is an expression of your love for the Lord."[10] "And if a person gains more knowledge and intelligence in this life through his diligence and obedience than another, he will have so much the advantage in the world to come" (D&C 130:19).

• SYNONYMS: diligent, enduring, perseverant, steadfast, unweary, tireless, relentless, driven, constant, taking initiative.

• ANTONYMS: careless, idle, having a lack of initiative, inattentive, lazy, neglectful, unconcerned, giving up, a quitter.

36. THE VIRTUE OF **CONSTANCY**. Loyalty to a person or belief. The quality of being faithful and dependable. "For do we not read

that God is the same yesterday, today, and forever, and in him there is no variableness neither shadow of changing?" (Morm. 9:9).

❧ *Be firm and steadfast:* Stand firm against the mocking and scorn of the world. Live and defend principles of virtue, integrity, chastity, worthiness, and obedience. "The Lamanites . . . were converted unto the true faith; and they would not depart from it, for they were firm, and steadfast, and immovable, willing with all diligence to keep the commandments of the Lord" (3 Ne. 6:14). "Family home evening doesn't have to be perfect, just consistent. It is a process, not a product" (David A. Bednar).

- SYNONYMS: steady, unchanging, unwavering, unfailing, undeviating, constant, consistent, habitual, energetic, productive, vigorous, enduring.

- ANTONYMS: doubtful, hesitant, unstable, uncertain, unsteady, irregular.

37. THE VIRTUE OF **PROGRESS.** The process of changing, developing, or improving. One cannot progress without change, and "when we are through changing, we are through" (Boyd K. Packer). Striving for the best within you and moving forward with worthy goals. Gradual improvement or growth or development. In His life, the Savior progressed or "continued from grace to grace, until he received a fullness" (D&C 93:13). "When they were slothful, and forgot to exercise their faith and diligence . . . they did not progress in their journey" (Alma 37:40–41).

❧ *Be progressing:* Interested in learning from the best books and growing especially in the development of Christlike virtues with the desire to become "even as I am" (3 Ne. 27:27). "He that receiveth light, and continueth in God, receiveth more light; and that light groweth brighter and brighter until the perfect day" (D&C 50:24).

- SYNONYMS: advancing, improving, penitent, accomplished, hardworking, productive, earnest, purposeful, goal-oriented, enduring, achieving, ambitious, anxiously engaged, eager, a doer.
- ANTONYMS: declining, decreasing, defeated, stagnant, stopped, unrepentant, giving up, idle, distracted, forfeiting.

38. THE VIRTUES OF **RESILIENCE** AND **ENDURANCE.** The ability to achieve something, even in a difficult situation. The property of being physically or mentally strong. Permanence by virtue of the power to resist stress or force. To be resilient is the ability to recover from or adjust easily to misfortune or change.

✿ *Be strong and resilient:* "In the strength of the Lord we can do, endure, *and* overcome all things."[11] "After much tribulation come the blessings" (D&C 58:4). "Let us run with patience the race that is set before us" (Heb. 12:1).

- SYNONYMS: strong, resilient, unshaken, immovable, sturdiness, stable, stalwart, firm.
- ANTONYMS: cowardly, idle, inactive, unstable, weak.

39. THE VIRTUE OF **VALOR.** The qualities of a hero or heroine; showing exceptional or heroic courage when facing danger (especially in battle). "And they were all young men, and they were exceedingly valiant for courage, and also for strength and activity" (Alma 53:20). Strength of mind or spirit that enables a person to encounter danger or opposition with firmness.

✿ *Be valiant:* Be true at all times, especially in difficult situations. Be anxiously engaged in a good cause (see D&C 58:27).

- SYNONYMS: fearless, firm, showing fortitude, heroic, tenacious, ambitious, enduring.
- ANTONYMS: cowardly, fearful, irresolute, timid, weak, surrendering.

40. THE VIRTUE OF **MORAL COURAGE.** Moral courage consists of a willingness to stand for principles of truth and righteousness even when it is unpopular to do so, especially when confronting sin. The life of Jesus Christ reveals many such examples. Perhaps most visible was His public condemnation of hypocrisy among the religious elites of His day. "He never wavered nor flinched. He met every accusation with silent serenity, faced every danger with equanimity."[12] "God has not given us the spirit of fear" (2 Tim. 1:7).

✤ *Be fearless:* "Have the courage to say no when you should, the courage to say yes when that is appropriate, the courage to do the right thing because it is right."[13] A willingness to occasionally stand alone.

- SYNONYMS: courageous, brave, daring, intrepid, gallant, stoic, undaunted, bold, uncompromising, composed.
- ANTONYMS: cowardly, fearful, weak, faint-hearted, timid.

41. THE VIRTUE OF **BOLDNESS** AND **CANDOR.** The quality of standing out strongly and distinctly, with confidence. Fairness and freedom from prejudice or malice. The trait of being willing to undertake things that involve risk or giving offense. The Savior was fearless. Because of His knowledge of His Father's plan and His knowledge of His own identity, He went forth boldly and confidently in everything He did, with purpose and authority: "But, lo, he speaketh boldly, and they say nothing unto him" (John 7:26).

✤ *Be bold and forthright:* Needful correction is a bold and loving act. The Savior was never silent is such situations, whether it was boldly condemning hypocrisy or tenderly correcting the

Martha-judging-Mary error of judgment. "I speak with boldness, having authority from God; and I fear not what man can do; for perfect love casteth out all fear" (Moro. 8:16). Don't let silence imply tacit approval. Parents are firm in disciplining children, but without anger. Balance boldness without becoming overbearing (see Alma 38:12).

- SYNONYMS: confident, frank, forthright, righteous, having authority.
- ANTONYMS: afraid, cowardly, fearful, timid, weak, cynical, critical.

42. THE VIRTUE OF **CHARITY.** Charity is the pure love of Christ (see Moro. 7:47). It is the love that Christ has for the children of men and that the children of men should have for one another. It is the highest, noblest, and strongest kind of love and the most joyous to the soul (see 1 Ne. 11:23). When you are filled with charity, you obey God's commandments and do all you can to serve others and help them receive the restored gospel. "For all the law is fulfilled in one word, even in this; Thou shalt love thy neighbor as thyself" (Gal. 5:14).

✤ *Be loving:* "Wherefore, cleave unto charity, which is the greatest of all" (Moro. 7:46). Go about doing good. Treat others *better* than you would like to be treated. We are to "pray unto the Father with all the energy of heart that [we] may be filled with this love" (Moro. 7:48).

- SYNONYMS: loving, compassionate, affectionate, embracing.
- ANTONYMS: hateful, hurtful, malevolent, mean, unkind, cruel.

43. THE VIRTUE OF **COMPASSION** is a sympathetic consciousness of others' distress, with a desire to alleviate it. In the life of the Savior, it was more than simple empathy. It meant to "suffer with." Christ's compassion for others came from the depth of His soul, with complete identification for the suffering of others. Jesus wept

as He was about to raise Lazarus from the dead; He wept when blessing the Nephite children. "Jesus was moved with compassion" (Matt. 9:36).

🍀 *Be compassionate:* "Succor the weak, lift up the hands which hang down, and strengthen the feeble knees" (D&C 81:5).

- SYNONYMS: caring, concerned, empathetic, comforting, sympathetic, understanding, full of pity.

- ANTONYMS: neglectful, forgetful, hurtful, uncaring.

44. THE VIRTUE OF **AFFECTION.** Expressing love, benevolence, and tenderness as the affectionate care of a parent. For the Savior, this included the human touch. He allowed others to see, feel, and touch. Embraces and hugs would not have been uncommon to Him. "Now there was leaning on Jesus' bosom one of his disciples, whom Jesus loved . . . He then lying on Jesus' breast saith unto him, Lord, who is it?" (John 13:23, 25). "Handle me, and see" (Luke 24:39); "a time to embrace, and a time to refrain from embracing" (Eccl. 3:5).

🍀 *Be affectionate:* Show genuine warmth and love. "Paul called unto him the disciples, and embraced them" (Acts 20:1).

- SYNONYMS: loving, warm, embracing, touching, comforting, endearing.

- ANTONYMS: cold, distant, aloof, remote.

45. THE VIRTUE OF **KINDNESS.** The quality of being warm-hearted, considerate, humane, and sympathetic. The act of being caring or warm in spirit. A kind act. "My kindness shall not depart from thee" (Isa. 54:10).

🍀 *Be kind:* "Be kindly affectioned one to another with brotherly love" (Rom. 12:10). Remember the good Samaritan. Look for opportunities to perform acts of kindness each day. Be kind to those who deserve it least.

- SYNONYMS: kind, loving, kind-hearted, merciful, tenderhearted, angelic.
- ANTONYMS: cold, cruel, harsh, mean, rude, violent.

46. THE VIRTUE OF **FRIENDSHIP**. A state of mutual trust and support. The relationship between people who like each other and enjoy each other's company. "Ye are my friends, if ye do whatsoever I command you" (John 15:13).

❧ *Be friendly and amiable:* Be a good friend. Show genuine interest in others; smile and let them know you care about them. Treat everyone with kindness and respect.

- SYNONYMS: friendly, affable, amiable, amicable, brotherly, close, agreeable, pleasing, pleasant, buoyant, good-natured, likable, appealing, warm, warm-hearted.
- ANTONYMS: disliking, hateful, an enemy, opposing.

47. THE VIRTUE OF **TENDERNESS**. Concern for the feelings or welfare of others. A positive feeling of liking. Very loving and gentle. The tendency to express warm, compassionate feelings.

❧ *Be gentle and peaceable:* Be "peaceable, gentle, and easy to be entreated, full of mercy and good fruits, without partiality, and without hypocrisy" (James 3:17).

- SYNONYMS: gentle, tender, mild, peaceable, kind-hearted, soft, warm.
- ANTONYMS: cruel, harsh, indifferent, mean, callous, unkind.

48. THE VIRTUE OF **MINDFULNESS** AND **SENSITIVITY**. A state of awareness. The Savior was supremely aware of people around Him and considerate of their time, property, feelings, and comfort—such as providing wine at the marriage in Cana (see John

2:1, 11); seek first to understand before being understood. It is better to suffer wrong than to do wrong. Be conscious of your movements and acts so that nothing that goes on in you escapes your attention.

❧ *Be considerate and thoughtful:* Being considerate is being aware of and sensitive to the time, feelings, emotions, and property of others, especially members of your family. Speak and act in a kind and unselfish manner. Being thoughtful implies acting on the thought, being there for someone, showing love, concern, and care.

- SYNONYMS: considerate, sensitive, mindful, conscientious, circumspect, aware.

- ANTONYMS: inconsiderate, uncaring, careless, inattentive, negligent, unaware, unobservant, stealing, covetous, envious.

49. THE VIRTUE OF **HOSPITALITY.** Friendly and generous behavior toward visitors and guests, intended to make them feel welcome.

❧ *Be easy to be entreated:* To receive, be approachable. Treat others in such a way that they feel welcome, safe, and relaxed in your presence; they will want to be with you.

- SYNONYMS: welcoming, warm, accommodating, approachable, neighborly, accepting.

- ANTONYMS: cold, incompatible, unfriendly, aloof, unsociable, rejecting, snubbing.

50. THE VIRTUE OF **POLITENESS** AND **CIVILITY.** The act of showing regard for others. A courteous manner that respects accepted social usage. Jesus Christ was a gentleman in every way, showing respect especially for women, children, and the elderly. "Suffer little children, and forbid them not, to come unto me" (Matt. 19:14).

❧ *Be courteous:* Put the needs and comfort of others before your own: let them go first, say please and thank you, open and hold doors, stand when someone enters the room. The Savior would have used words of courtesy and respect common among the Jews. The Savior, while on the cross, asked John to care for His mother (see John 19:25–27).

- SYNONYMS: chivalrous, cordial, nice, gentlemanly, ladylike, gallant, genial, polite, proper, selfless, well-mannered, well-behaved.
- ANTONYMS: aloof, cool, discourteous, impolite, rude, unsociable.

51. THE VIRTUE OF **REFINEMENT.** The quality of being very polite and well educated. Excellence in thought, manners, and taste.

❧ *Be gracious:* Treat others with tact, kindness, and respect. Be generous of spirit and pleasant, cordial, and affable. Care more about listening than talking. Make time for others. Use your time to improve the lives of people in need.

- SYNONYMS: noble, gracious, distinguished, dignified, becoming, reputable, respectable, revered, graceful, genteel, delightsome, fair.
- ANTONYMS: crass, harsh, rough, uncultured, unsophisticated, crude, foul, rude, uncouth.

52. THE VIRTUE OF **CULTURE.** Activities involving music, literature, and other arts. The tastes in art and manners that are favored by a social group. All the knowledge and values shared by a society. Enlightenment and excellence of taste acquired by intellectual and aesthetic training. "Praise the Lord with singing, with music, with dancing" (D&C 136:28).

❧ *Be cultured:* Be a person who is well-read. Develop an appreciation for art, history, languages, music, literature, world cultures.

- SYNONYMS: a connoisseur, virtuosic, musical, singing, dancing, artistic, seeking beauty.
- ANTONYMS: ignorant, rude, uncivilized, uncultured, unrefined.

53. THE VIRTUE OF **VITALITY.** A zest for life. The Savior loved life: "I am come that they might have life, and that they might have it more abundantly" (John 10:10). "He loved the vitality of nature. Time and again Christ sought solace in the outdoors: in the green hills west of Galilee, the fields and meadows surrounding Jerusalem, the rural byways outside Nazareth. All his days were spent in the open air. His parables, replete with allusions to the intricacies of the plant and animal kingdoms, reflected his love of all things living. . . . He loved dinners and feasts . . . supping and commingling with people all around."[14]

   ❧ *Be sociable and vibrant:* Enjoy what you do. Surround yourself with likeminded people who bring out the best in you. Appreciate others. Move. Expose yourself to new ideas and ways of thinking. Ask questions. Explore. Discover. "The Son of Man came eating and drinking, and they say, Behold a man gluttonous, and a winebibber, a friend of publicans and sinners. But wisdom is justified of her children" (Matt. 11:19). "That same sociality which exists among us here will exist among us there, only it will be coupled with eternal glory" (D&C 130:2).

   - SYNONYMS: sociable, festive, enlivened, sporting, vibrant, adventurous.
   - ANTONYMS: apathetic, inactive, lethargic, dull, indifferent.

54. THE VIRTUE OF **ENTHUSIASM.** Passionate feeling of interest in something or excited by it. A lively interest. The origin of this word means 'God in us.'

❧ *Be enthusiastic:* Discover yourself. Find your passion, your inspiration. Find what excites you. Laugh. Try new things. Find the wonder in the world around you. Keep learning.

- SYNONYMS: enthusiastic, vivacious, quick, exuberant, excited, zealous, fervent, ardent.
- ANTONYMS: apathetic, dispassionate, indifferent, unconcerned, uninterested, bored.

55. THE VIRTUE OF **HEALTH.** "Know ye not that your body is a temple?" (1 Cor. 6:19). The condition of being strong and well. A healthy state of well-being, free from disease.

❧ *Be fit:* Obey the Word of Wisdom. Take care of your body: eat nutritious food, exercise regularly, and get enough sleep. Avoid activities or substances that could harm your body or put your body at risk.

- SYNONYMS: healthy, fit, active.
- ANTONYMS: apathetic, feeble, infirm, lazy, lethargic, unhealthy, weak.

56. THE VIRTUE OF **HUMOR.** The ability to know when something is funny and to laugh at appropriate humorous situations. The trait of appreciating (and being able to express) the humorous. Good humor is medicine to the soul. The Savior appreciated and used puns, enigmas, and paradoxes—all evidence of His sense of humor. For example, "Ye blind guides, which strain at a gnat, and swallow a camel" (Matthew 23:24). The imagery seems like a ludicrous exaggeration until one understands that the Aramaic word for gnat is galma and for camel—gamla. The Pharisees were careful to observe petty rules (the gnat), but were blindly guilty of huge sins (the camel). The Savior was brilliant and witty!

❧ *Be pleasant:* Be full of good humor. Humor can ease tension, relieve uncomfortable or embarrassing situations, change attitudes, generate love and understanding, and add sparkle to life. A properly developed sense of humor is sensitive to others' feelings and is flavored with kindness and understanding.

- SYNONYMS: humored, humoring, smiling, laughing, witty, bright.
- ANTONYMS: unpleasant, depressing, gloomy, grouchy, dour, boisterous.

57. THE VIRTUE OF **JOY**. A condition of great happiness and peace coming from righteous living. The purpose of mortal life is for all people to have joy. Full joy will come only through Jesus Christ.

✤ *Be happy:* "Men are, that they might have joy" (2 Ne. 2:25). Live after the manner of happiness: "Love your family, keep the commandments, regularly study the scriptures, work with your hands, attend the temple, give meaningful service, remain steadfast in Christ.[15] "These things have I spoken unto you, that my joy might remain in you, and that your joy might be full" (John 15:11).

- SYNONYMS: joyful, joyous, glad, cheerful, merry, smiling, blissful, gleeful, peaceful, gregarious, jovial, convivial, lighthearted.
- ANTONYMS: full of melancholy, miserable, sad, sorrowful, unhappy, light-minded.

58. THE VIRTUE OF **GOOD WORKS**. Acts of charity, kindness, or good will. Activities that you do to help other people. "He went about doing good" (Acts 10:38). Be a good Samaritan.

✤ *Be helpful:* Help others. Build the kingdom through righteous service. "Therefore let your light so shine before this people, that they may see your good works and glorify your Father who is in heaven" (3 Ne. 12:16).

- SYNONYMS: helpful, benevolent, altruistic, a humanitarian, succorer, serving.

- ANTONYMS: stingy, uncharitable, selfish, unsacrificing, unmindful, lazy.

59. THE VIRTUE OF **GENEROSITY.** The trait of being willing to cheerfully give of your money or time. Showing kindness, especially in sharing resources with the needy. "Verily I say unto you, Inasmuch as ye have done it unto one of the least of these my brethren, ye have done it unto me" (Matt. 25:40).

   ✤ *Be giving:* "Never suppress a generous thought."[16] Cheerfully donate until it feels good and right. Experience the joy and satisfaction of giving.

   - SYNONYMS: an almsgiver, offering, generous, liberal, sharing, big-hearted, magnanimous, selfless.

   - ANTONYMS: greedy, inattentive, selfish, small, stingy, thoughtless, unmindful.

60. THE VIRTUE OF **NURTURING.** To promote growth or improvement over a period of time. Aiding in the process of maturing. The care and attention given to others in helping them grow and develop.

   ✤ *Be a nurturer:* Listen and observe as others share their feelings and challenges. Empathize and validate their feelings. Encourage and assure them. Help and empower them. The Savior believed in the potential of those close to Him and nourished them physically and spiritually.

   - SYNONYMS: trusting, believing, seeing potential, delegating, supportive, encouraging, praising.

   - ANTONYMS: neglectful, depriving, ignoring, withholding, doubtful.

61. THE VIRTUE OF **PRAISE.** To express strong approval or commendation. The Father publicly praised the Son on at least three

occasions: "This is my beloved Son, in whom I am well pleased" (Matt. 3:17).

✤ *Be supportive:* Look for and find the good in others, and acknowledge it. "Even harder to bear than criticism, oftentimes, is no word from our leader on the work to which we have been assigned. Little comments or notes, which are sincere and specific, are great boosters along the way."[17]

- SYNONYMS: praising, complimentary, supportive, sustaining, encouraging, attentive.
- ANTONYMS: blaming, censuring, critical, disapproving, neglectful.

62. THE VIRTUE OF **SERVANTSHIP.** Jesus Christ came to serve His Father and His fellow man. "He went about doing good" (Acts 10:38); "And there are also many other things which Jesus did, the which, if they should be written every one, I suppose that even the world itself could not contain the books that should be written" (John 21:25). "For Him, lordship was servantship."[18] "An unselfish spirit is essential to happiness."[19]

✤ *Be serving:* Selflessly look for others in need. Look for ways to help. Charity without serving, like faith without works, is dead.

- SYNONYMS: ministering, giving, comforting, caring, a servant.
- ANTONYMS: neglectful, disregarding, ignorant, overlooking, avoidant, refraining, inattentive, withholding.

63. THE VIRTUE OF **RESCUING.** The process or act of saving someone from danger, pain, anguish, or harm. Recovery or preservation from loss or danger. The act of regaining or saving something lost (or in danger of becoming lost). The act of setting someone free.

✤ *Be a rescuer:* "Jesus always looked to lift people, to change their condition from suffering and hopelessness to a place of peace and reconciliation with God. He urged repentance, but He offered practical help too—cleansing the lepers and healing the sick. He urged people everywhere to have faith, obey the commandments, love their Father in Heaven, and sin no more. Some of His most powerful redemptive moments include teaching the adulterous woman, talking with the publican Zacchaeus, or relating the parable of the prodigal son."[20]

- SYNONYMS: liberating, ministering, redeeming, fellowshipping, healing.
- ANTONYMS: neglectful, inconsiderate, apathetic, uninterested, lazy, indifferent.

64. THE VIRTUE OF **DIPLOMACY** AND **TACT.** Having a desire for peace and harmony and skillfully handling affairs without creating offense, taking offense, or arousing hostility. "Offense cannot be given; it must be taken. One has to choose to be offended."[21]

✤ *Be a peacemaker:* "And blessed are all the peacemakers, for they shall be called the children of God" (Matt. 5:9). Contention, especially between members of the Lord's Church or between family members, is not pleasing to the Lord. Pride causes contention. The Lord commands men not to contend with one another (see 2 Ne. 26:32). The devil is the father of contention and stirs up men to contend with one another (see 3 Ne. 11:29).

- SYNONYMS: considerate, discreet, appeasing, listening, sensitive, thoughtful, polite, tolerant, careful.
- ANTONYMS: contentious, disagreeing, discordant, agitated, disharmonious, distressed, tactless.

65. THE VIRTUE OF **POISE** AND **SERENITY.** A disposition free from stress or emotion. A feeling of being calm or peaceful and showing gracious tact in coping with difficult circumstances and

handling tense situations. "Be not disturbed at trifles, or at accidents common or unavoidable."[22]

✤ *Be calm:* The Savior was not a nervous, tense, or uneasy individual. In tense situations, like the time when the sinner woman was about to be stoned, or when Peter cut off the centurion's ear, the Savior acted rather than reacted. He diffused the confrontational feelings of others with wisdom and perfect poise. He was a master at eliminating tension and fear. Charity is not easily provoked.

- SYNONYMS: calm, poised, peaceful, serene, sportsmanlike, composed, patient.
- ANTONYMS: agitated, annoyed, loud, nervous, upset, angry.

66. THE VIRTUE OF **FORGIVENESS.** The action or feeling of forgiving someone. As people forgive each other, they treat one another with Christlike love and have no bad feelings toward those who have offended them.

✤ *Be forgiving:* Forgive those who offend or hurt you for their offenses or misdeeds. "As you look to God for the strength to forgive and set aside your pride, fear, resentment, and bitterness, you will feel hope and peace."[23] "But if ye forgive not men their trespasses, neither will your Father forgive your trespasses" (Matt. 6:15). Trust in the Lord's justice.

- SYNONYMS: forgiving, pardoning, guileless, patient.
- ANTONYMS: condemning, accusing, blaming, censuring, punishing, bitter.

67. THE VIRTUE OF **LONG-SUFFERING.** Forbearance to punish; clemency; patience. Long-endurance, not being easily provoked. Charity "beareth all things . . . it endureth all things. . . . Charity never faileth" (1 Cor. 13:7–8).

❖ *Be tolerant:* Every successful marriage and family is dependent to some degree on mutual toleration.

- SYNONYMS: patient, forbearing, lenient, tolerant, understanding, not easily provoked.

- ANTONYMS: agitated, troubled, frustrated, impatient, intolerant, ill-tempered, angry.

68. THE VIRTUE OF **PATIENCE.** Having the quality of enduring evils without murmuring or fretfulness; sustaining afflictions of body or mind with fortitude, calmness or Christian submission to the divine will. Not easily provoked; calm under the sufferance of injuries or offenses; not revengeful. Persevering; constant in pursuit or exertion; calmly diligent. Not hasty; not over eager or impetuous; waiting or expecting with calmness or without discontent. The ability to put your desires on hold for a time and trusting in the Lord's timetable.

❖ *Be patient:* Follow the Savior's example of facing injustices with poise and equanimity. Actively work toward worthy goals without getting discouraged when results take extra time and effort. "One cardinal lesson of the parable of the wheat and tares . . . is that of patience, long-suffering, and toleration—each an attribute of Deity and a trait of character that all men should cultivate."[24] "Tribulation worketh patience" (Rom. 5:3).

- SYNONYMS: long-suffering, forbearing, lenient, tolerant, bearing all things.

- ANTONYMS: agitated, troubled, frustrated, impatient, intolerant, unwilling, seeking instant gratification.

69. THE VIRTUE OF **MERCY.** The spirit of compassion, tenderness, forgiveness, and leniency. "And blessed are the merciful, for they shall obtain mercy" (3 Ne. 12:7). Jesus Christ offers mercy to us

through His atoning sacrifice. "The tender mercies of the Lord are over all" (1 Ne. 1:20).

❧ *Be merciful:* Follow Heavenly Father's example of mercy in your relationship with others. Remember that to obtain mercy, you must be merciful.

- SYNONYMS: compassionate, empathetic, reasonable, pardoning, forgiving, thoughtful, slow to anger.
- ANTONYMS: cruel, harsh, mean, merciless, severe, unkind, unfair, unreasonable.

70. THE VIRTUE OF **JUSTICE.** Treatment of people that is fair and morally right. The quality of being just or fair. The unfailing consequence of blessings for righteous thoughts and acts, and punishment for unrepented sin.

❧ *Be just and fair:* Tell the truth. Play by the rules. Don't blame others for your mistakes. Treat others the way you want to be treated.

- SYNONYMS: just, equitable, fair, circumspect.
- ANTONYMS: corrupt, dishonest, inequitable, partial, unfair, unjust, dishonest.

71. THE VIRTUE OF **INCLUSION.** The act of including others even if you feel they are somehow lacking. "Of a truth I perceive that God is no respecter of persons" (Acts 10:34). "Jesus's habit of inclusiveness may be one of His most striking characteristics. He counted among His associates both rich and poor, men and women, the elderly and children, righteous and sinners, sick and healthy. He challenged the conventions of the day by associating from time to time with Gentiles, including the Roman occupiers of Judea. But He did all this without ever compromising His own standards, always being ready to teach and lift and bless His listeners."[25]

❧ *Be unprejudiced:* Look for others who are alone or not participating. Smile and encourage them to join in. If they do, let them know that you are glad they did. If they don't, let them know they are always welcome.

- SYNONYMS: inclusive, impartial, unbiased, unprejudiced, objective.
- ANTONYMS: abandoning, exclusive, forgetful, separating, denying, rejecting, shunning, segregating.

72. THE VIRTUE OF **OPEN-MINDEDNESS.** Willing to consider different ideas or opinions. "That when all have spoken that all may be edified of all, and that every man may have an equal privilege" (D&C 88:122).

❧ *Be approachable:* "Encourage family love by being approachable even when you feel you have reason to turn away."[26] Smile. Put down electronic or other distracting items, which may send the message that you are busy and don't want to be bothered.

- SYNONYMS: broad-minded, open-minded, thoughtful, a listener.
- ANTONYMS: biased, prejudiced, partial, intolerant, hasty, too busy.

73. THE VIRTUE OF **DISCIPLESHIP.** Christian discipleship is exercising faith in Jesus Christ and His Atonement. A disciple follows the teachings and example of the Savior by repenting, being baptized, receiving the gift of the Holy Ghost, and striving to overcome the pressures and trials of this present life to become more and more Christlike. To be a true disciple, we must follow Him in word and deed. "But be ye doers of the word, and not hearers only, deceiving your own selves" (James 1:22).

❧ *Be a disciple. Diligently strive to follow the Savior and do as He did and be as He is (see 3 Ne. 27:21, 27).* "By this shall all men know that ye are my disciples, if ye have love one to another" (John 13:35).

- SYNONYMS: advocating, believing, a good example, full of light, adherent, following, studious, loyal.
- ANTONYMS: disloyal, murmuring, rebellious, faithless, unfaithful, duplicitous, having enmity.

74. THE VIRTUE OF **TESTIMONY**. Something that you felt, saw, know, or experienced. Proof or evidence that something exists or is true. A testimony begins with a seed of desire and is then nourished with faith and hope. When it bears sweet and joyous fruit, faith becomes dormant, as it is replaced by knowledge from many validating experiences, line upon line and precept upon precept (see Alma 32). A testimony is confirmed by a spiritual witness given by the Holy Ghost, the strongest witness possible.

   ✤ *Be a witness:* Happiness in this life and throughout eternity depends largely on whether or not you are "valiant in the testimony of Jesus" (D&C 76:79). "Freely ye have received, freely give" (Matt. 10:8).

   - SYNONYMS: witnessing, testifying, teaching, sharing.
   - ANTONYMS: silent, fearful, timid, denying, opposing.

75. THE VIRTUE OF **EXAMPLE**. A person or way of behaving that is considered a model for other people to copy. A representative form or pattern. "Behold I am the light; I have set an example for you" (3 Ne. 18:16).

   ✤ *Be a leader:* "Be thou an example of the believers, in word, in conversation, in charity, in spirit, in faith, in purity" (1 Tim. 4:12).

   - SYNONYMS: exemplary, a light, shining, leading, inspiring, praiseworthy, guiding.
   - ANTONYMS: bad, dishonorable, unideal, wrong.

76. THE VIRTUE OF **TEACHING**. Educating or instructing; activities that impart knowledge or skill. The responsibility to teach the

doctrine of the kingdom by the Spirit through word and example, even if you don't have a formal assignment or calling as a teacher. "Teaching is the very essence of leadership" (Gordon B. Hinckley). "What did Jesus have as an occupation? There is only one answer. He was a teacher. . . . The gospels say so. Of some ninety times He is addressed in the four gospels, sixty times He is called 'Rabbi,' which means 'teacher.'"[27]

❧ *Be a teacher and enlightening:* "Seek ye diligently and teach one another words of wisdom; yea, seek ye out of the best books words of wisdom; seek learning, even by study and also by faith. . . . Establish a house . . . of learning" (D&C 88:118–119).

- SYNONYMS: teaching, inviting, demonstrating, mentoring, instructing, coaching, testifying.
- ANTONYMS: ignorant, neglectful, dictating.

77. THE VIRTUE OF **HONOR** AND **RESPECT.** We first honor and respect God and then our fellow man. To show reverence and honor; to esteem as possessed of real worth and good qualities.

❧ *Be respectful:* "If ye love me, keep my commandments" (John 14:15). Show admiration to others based on their personal qualities, their achievements, their eternal potential, or their status (parent, sibling, leader, teacher). Treat them in a kind, polite, and loving way.

- SYNONYMS: esteeming, estimable, respectful, deferential.
- ANTONYMS: disrespectful, rude, ill-mannered, impolite, discourteous, insolent, critical.

78. THE VIRTUE OF **SOLEMNITY.** "Call upon the Father in solemn prayer" (D&C 20:76). Having or showing serious purpose and determination. Involving serious behavior or serious attitudes.

❧ *Be solemn:* Take upon you the name of Christ and speak and walk in the ways of truth and soberness. "Declare whatsoever thing ye declare in my name, in solemnity of heart" (D&C 100:7).

- SYNONYMS: sober, serious, mature, thoughtful, meditative.
- ANTONYMS: coarse, crude, frivolous, light-minded, weak-minded, flippant, trivial.

79. THE VIRTUE OF **WORSHIP.** A feeling of profound love and admiration. To worship God is to give Him our love, reverence, praise, service, and devotion. Worship not only shows our love for God and commitment to Him, it gives us strength to keep His commandments and to strive to become like Him. Through worship we grow in knowledge and faithfulness. "Remember the Sabbath day, to keep it holy" (Ex. 20:8). Reserve it for worthy and holy activities. Attend your meetings and "offer up thy sacraments upon my holy day" (D&C 59:9). Avoid the temptation to participate in activities that much of the world accepts and promotes on the Sabbath.

❧ *Be reverent and prayerful:* Honor God and obey His commandments. Confess His hand in all things (see D&C 59:21). Make a habit of approaching God in prayer to come to know Him and draw ever nearer to Him. "Yea, and when you do not cry unto the Lord, let your hearts be full, drawn out in prayer unto him continually for your welfare, and also for the welfare of those who are around you" (Alma 34:27). The object of prayer is not to change the will of God, but to secure for ourselves and for others blessings that God is already willing to grant, but that we must ask for in order to obtain.

- SYNONYMS: reverent, worshipful, devout, grateful.

- ANTONYMS: dishonoring, disregarding, disrespectful, disdainful, scornful, agnostic, irreverent, unholy, apathetic, lazy, slothful, indifferent, forgetful.

80. THE VIRTUE OF **GRATITUDE.** A feeling of being grateful to others because they have given you something or have done something for you. An uplifting, exalting attitude. People are generally happier when they have gratitude in their hearts. You cannot be bitter, resentful, or mean-spirited when you are grateful. A gracious person is not too proud to accept help when it is truly needed, thereby allowing another to enjoy the fruits of service and giving.

   ❧ *Be thankful:* Regularly express your gratitude to God for the blessings He gives you and to others for the kind acts they do for you. "Live in thanksgiving daily" (Alma 34:38).

   - SYNONYMS: thankful, grateful, appreciative, pleased, content.
   - ANTONYMS: abusive, mean, thankless, unappreciative, ungrateful.

81. THE VIRTUE OF **MEEKNESS.** Mild of temper; soft, gentle, not rough. Not easily provoked or irritated; given to forbearance under injuries or provocations.

   ❧ *Be meek:* "Being meek does not mean weakness, but it does mean behaving with goodness, gentleness, and kindness, showing strength, serenity, healthy self-worth, and self-control."[28] "For I am meek and lowly in heart" (Matt. 11: 28).

   - SYNONYMS: mild, gentle, calm, tender, soothing, mellow, peaceful, humble.
   - ANTONYMS: harsh, rough, overbearing, arrogant, impertinent, proud, unyielding.

82. THE VIRTUE OF **HUMILITY** AND **SUBMISSIVENESS.** Be willing to submit to the will of the Lord and to give the Lord the honor for what is accomplished. "Do always those things that please

[God]" (John 8:29). Show gratitude for His blessings and acknowl-edgment of your constant need for His divine help.

❧ *Be humble and submissive:* "Whosoever therefore shall humble himself as this little child, the same is greatest in the kingdom of heaven" (Matt. 18:4). "Be thou humble; and the Lord thy God shall lead thee by the hand, and give thee answer to thy prayers" (D&C 112:10). "Acknowledge that you are in the Lord's hands. Surrender to Him on His terms—not yours. Make it a total sur-render, no negotiating; yield with no conditions."[29]

* SYNONYMS: lowly of heart, childlike, submissive, broken-hearted, contrite, dutiful, teachable, willing, unpretentious, anonymous.

* ANTONYMS: arrogant, boastful, conceited, egotistical, proud, rich, showy.

83. THE VIRTUE OF **REPENTANCE.** To feel sorrow and pain for sins or offenses. To be committed to a change of mind, heart, and behavior. A change of course. A turning away from sin and a turn-ing to God for forgiveness. It includes faith in God, sorrow for sin, confession, abandonment of sin, restitution, and righteous living.

❧ *Be penitent:* Be willing to acknowledge your weaknesses and im-perfections, and humbly express sorrow and ask for forgiveness of sins or offenses committed, including from those you have offended or hurt. Change your behavior in such a way so that you feel the peace of the Lord Jesus Christ. "Yea, and as often as my people repent will I forgive them their trespasses against me" (Mosiah 26:30).

* SYNONYMS: remorseful, contrite, conscience-stricken, apologetic, re-gretful, sorry, willing to change.

* ANTONYMS: unashamed, impenitent, unrepentant, unapologetic.

84. THE VIRTUE OF **OBEDIENCE**. The act of obeying; dutiful or submissive behavior with respect to another person. Doing God's will. Showing our willingness to obey Heavenly Father's commandments. Obedience is something that should be freely given. "Though he were a Son, yet learned he obedience by the things which he suffered" (Heb. 5:8).

> ✤ *Be obedient:* "If ye love me, keep my commandments" (John 14:15). "If ye be willing and obedient, ye shall eat the good of the land" (Isa. 1:19).

- SYNONYMS: submissive, hearkening, heeding, following, God-fearing, respectful, dutiful, law-abiding.
- ANTONYMS: contrary, disobedient, neglectful, unfaithful, obstinate, rebellious.

85. THE VIRTUE OF **LOYALTY** is a feeling of devotion, duty, or attachment to somebody or something. To rely upon or place confidence in someone or something. In spiritual matters, loyalty includes relying on God and his Spirit.

> ✤ *Be true and loyal:* true to your faith, spouse, and family. Be "true to the faith that our parents have cherished, true to the truth for which martyrs have perished." "Faith of our fathers, holy faith, we will be true to thee till death" (*Hymns,* nos. 254, 84). Endure to the end.

- SYNONYMS: trustworthy, faithful, dependable, devoted, allegiant, reliable, keeping confidences, constant.
- ANTONYMS: unfaithful, disloyal, dishonest, false, irresponsible, unreliable, undependable, betraying, treacherous, dishonest.

86. THE VIRTUE OF **TRUSTWORTHINESS**. While loyalty is given by you to somebody or something, trustworthiness indicates that you deserve the trust and confidence of another. It includes being

able to keep covenants, commitments, and confidences. "Not keeping confidences constrains revelation" (David A. Bednar).

❧ *Be trustworthy and dependable:* Earn and be deserving of the Lord's trust. The Lord gave Nephi His complete trust and sealing power: "Blessed art thou, Nephi, for those things which thou hast done; for I have beheld how thou hast with unwearyingness declared the word. . . . And now, because thou hast done this with such unwearyingness, behold, I will bless thee forever" (Hel. 10:4–5).

• SYNONYMS: faithful, dependable, devoted, allegiant, full of integrity, reliable, keeping confidences.

• ANTONYMS: unfaithful, disloyal, dishonest, false, irresponsible, unreliable, undependable, betraying, treacherous.

87. THE VIRTUE OF **SINCERITY.** An honest way of behaving that shows that you really mean what you say or do. The quality of naturalness and simplicity. The quality of being open and truthful; not deceitful or hypocritical.

❧ *Be sincere and guileless:* Be the same person when you are alone as you are when you are with others. Say and do good things that are genuinely in your heart. Avoid excesses and pretensions. Be slow to take offense and quick to forgive. Look for your own fault first. "Blessed is the man . . . in whose spirit there is no guile" (Ps. 32:2).

• SYNONYMS: earnest, genuine, honorable, innocent, guileless, having no pretense.

• ANTONYMS: counterfeit, deceitful, devious, dishonest, fake, false, cunning, full guile, duplicitous.

88. THE VIRTUE OF **INTEGRITY.** The quality of always behaving according to the moral principles that you believe in. Incorruptibility. An unimpaired condition; soundness. The quality

of being complete or whole. "Till I die I will not remove mine integrity from me" (Job 27:5).

✤ *Be honest:* Be true to yourself, your country, and your God at all times, in all things, and in all places that you may be in, even until death. Do the right thing at the right time for the right reason. Make righteous choices even when no one is watching. Be honest in all your dealings with your fellow man.

- SYNONYMS: honest, truthful, sure, honorable, true, principled, grounded, scrupulous, credible, ethical, inscrutable.
- ANTONYMS: deceitful, dishonest, corruptible, dishonorable, lying, unfaithful, corrupt, false, anti-social, misanthropic, traitorous, apathetic, indifferent.

89. THE VIRTUE OF **FAMILY**. As used in the scriptures, a family consists of a husband and wife, children, and sometimes other relatives living in the same house or under one family head. A family can also be a single parent with children, a husband and wife without children, or even a single person who enjoys familial relationships. "No success can compensate for failure in the home" (David O. McKay).

✤ *Be family-oriented:* "Honour thy father and thy mother: that thy days may be long upon the land which the LORD thy God giveth thee" (Ex. 20:12). Appreciate your family. Remember that successful marriages and families are established and maintained on principles of faith, prayer, repentance, forgiveness, respect, love, compassion, work, and wholesome recreational activities.

- SYNONYMS: familial, fatherly, motherly, grandfatherly, grandmotherly, loving.
- ANTONYMS: alone, withdrawn, exclusive, distracted.

90. THE VIRTUE OF **UNITY**. The quality of being united into one. A situation in which people, groups, or countries join together or agree about something. "And the Lord called his people Zion, because they were of one heart and one mind, and dwelt in righteousness" (Moses 7:18). "I say unto you, be one; and if ye are not one ye are not mine" (D&C 38:27).

❦ *Be united:* "The Saints can accomplish any purpose of the Lord when fully united in righteousness."[30] "And he commanded them that there should be no contention one with another, but that they should look forward with one eye, having one faith and one baptism, having their hearts knit together in unity and in love one towards another" (Mosiah 18:21).

• SYNONYMS: united, one, cooperative, unanimous, interdependent, adapting, adjusting.

• ANTONYMS: contentious, divided, separate, uncoordinated, full of enmity.

91. THE VIRTUE OF **PATRIOTISM**. Having or showing great love, respect, and duty toward your country or cause and a willingness to sacrifice for it. A feeling of pride for your country and the values it represents. "He caused the title of liberty to be hoisted upon every tower which was in all the land" (Alma 46:36).

❦ *Be civic-minded:* Be a good citizen. Participate in civic affairs. Educate yourself on the issues. Vote. Support measures that strengthen the moral fabric of society, particularly those designed to maintain and strengthen the family as the fundamental unit of society.

• SYNONYMS: patriotic, civic-minded, loyal, devoted.

• ANTONYMS: traitorous, conspiring, apostate, a renegade, rebellious.

92. THE VIRTUE OF **SACRIFICE.** In ancient days, to sacrifice meant to make something or someone holy. It has now come to mean to give up or suffer the loss of worldly things for the Lord and His kingdom. Joseph Smith taught that "a religion that does not require the sacrifice of all things never has the power sufficient to produce the faith necessary unto life and salvation." In the eternal perspective, the blessings obtained by sacrifice are greater than anything that is given up.

❧ *Be selfless:* Be more concerned about the happiness and well-being of others than your own convenience or comfort. "Be willing to serve others when it is neither sought for nor appreciated, even service to those you may dislike."[31] "For whosoever will save his life shall lose it: and whosoever will lose his life for my sake shall find it" (Matt. 16:25).

• SYNONYMS: sacrificing, self-sacrificing, selfless, altruistic, generous.

• ANTONYMS: self-serving, stingy, selfish, miserly, refusing, rejecting, withholding, greedy.

93. THE VIRTUE OF **FASTING.** To fast is to go without food and drink voluntarily for a certain period of time. Fasting combined with sincere prayer can strengthen us spiritually, bring us closer to God, and help us prepare ourselves and others to receive His blessings. "Nevertheless they did fast and pray oft, and did wax stronger and stronger in their humility, and firmer and firmer in the faith of Christ, unto the filling their souls with joy and consolation, yea, even to the purifying and the sanctification of their hearts, which sanctification cometh because of their yielding their hearts unto God" (Hel. 3:35).

❧ *Be self-denying:* "Deny yourself of all ungodliness. Put off the views and appetites of the natural man."[32] "If any man will come after me, let him deny himself, and take up his cross daily, and follow me" (Luke 9:23).

- SYNONYMS: abstaining, forbearing, refraining, having self-control.
- ANTONYMS: overindulgent, gluttonous, gorging, binging, carnal.

94. THE VIRTUE OF **SELF-MASTERY** AND **TEMPERANCE.** Conquering the natural man. Shunning the forbidden and avoiding excesses of good things—passions, appetites, and desires. Exercising self-control over thoughts, actions, and behavior. "Can we imagine the angels or the Gods not being in control of themselves in any particular? The question is of course ludicrous."[33]

❧ *Be disciplined and temperate:* Remove and avoid temptations. "And every man that striveth for the mastery is temperate in all things" (1 Cor. 9:25). "The highest achievement of spirituality is gained when we conquer the flesh."[34] "Spirituality, our true aim, is the consciousness of victory over self and of communion with the Infinite."[35]

- SYNONYMS: bridled, disciplined, controlled, restrained, moderate, abstinent, self-denying.
- ANTONYMS: overindulgent, angry, impulsive, decadent, fanatical, extreme, excessive.

95. THE VIRTUE OF **MODESTY.** The tendency not to talk about yourself, your achievements, or your abilities even if you are successful. Freedom from vanity or conceit. Behavior or appearance that is humble, moderate, and decent. A modest person avoids excesses and pretensions. "Let all they garments be plain" (D&C 42:40).

❧ *Be modest:* Do not draw undue attention to yourself. Dress, groom, and behave in such a way that you would feel comfortable in the Lord's presence.

- SYNONYMS: simplicity, plainness, humility, comeliness.

- ANTONYMS: brazen, forward, indecent, lewd, ostentatious, boastful, risqué.

96. THE VIRTUE OF **CHASTITY.** Chastity is sexual purity. Those who are chaste are morally clean in their thoughts, words, and actions. Chastity means not having any sexual relations before marriage. It also means complete fidelity to husband or wife during marriage. Physical intimacy between husband and wife is beautiful and sacred. It is ordained of God for the creation of children and for the expression of love within marriage.

   ❧ *Be chaste:* Do not have any sexual relations before marriage, and be completely faithful to your spouse after marriage.
   - SYNONYMS: chaste, moral, respectful, appreciative.
   - ANTONYMS: adulterous, lewd, licentious, promiscuous, unchaste, dishonorable.

97. THE VIRTUE OF **MORAL PURITY.** A pattern of thought and behavior based on high moral standards. A way of behaving in which you do what is morally right and avoid things that are morally wrong. "Can ye look up to God at that day with a pure heart and clean hands?" (Alma 5:19).

   ❧ *Be clean and virtuous:* "Let virtue garnish thy thoughts unceasingly; then shall thy confidence wax strong in the presence of God; and the doctrine of the priesthood shall distil upon thy soul as the dews from heaven" (D&C 121:45) "Be clean—in language, in thought, in body, in dress."36 He that hath clean hands and a pure heart shall stand in the Lord's holy place (Ps. 24:3–5)
   - SYNONYMS: clean, light, radiant, aglow, pure, wholesome.
   - ANTONYMS: vile, wicked, corrupt, immodest, impure, indecent, polluted, vulgar, sinful.

98. THE VIRTUE OF **SPIRITUALITY.** Concern with the things of the spirit. Spiritual gifts are blessings or abilities given by God to His children through the power of the Holy Ghost. To God, all things are spiritual (see D&C 29:34). "Every noble impulse, every unselfish expression of love, every brave suffering for the right; every surrender of self to something higher than self; every loyalty to an ideal; every unselfish devotion to principle; every helpfulness to humanity; every act of self-control; every fine courage of the soul, undefeated by pretense or policy; every being, doing, and living of good for the very good's sake—that is spirituality."[37]

❧ *Be righteous:* Fill your mind with righteous ideas, concepts, and images. To be spiritually minded is life, peace, and eternal life (see Rom. 8:6; see also 2 Ne. 9:39).

- SYNONYMS: holy, godly, righteous, worthy, upright, good, divine, pious, saintly.
- ANTONYMS: corrupt, immoral, irreverent, unspiritual.

99. THE VIRTUE OF **CONSECRATION.** To dedicate, to make holy, or to become righteous. The law of consecration is a divine principle whereby men and women voluntarily dedicate their time, talents, and resources to the establishment and building up of God's kingdom. Sacrifice precedes consecration.

❧ *Be consecrated:* Find true success in this life by consecrating your time and choices to God's purposes.

- SYNONYMS: consecrated, devoted, dedicated, wholehearted, committed.
- ANTONYMS: apathetic, neglectful, lazy, dispirited, desecrated, profane, sacrilegious.

100. THE VIRTUE OF **SANCTIFICATION.** The process of becoming perfect in Christ, free from sin, pure, clean, holy, without spot.

"Yea, come unto Christ, and be perfected in him, and deny yourselves of all ungodliness; and if ye shall deny yourselves of all ungodliness, and love God with all your might, mind and strength, then is his grace sufficient for you, that by his grace ye may be perfect in Christ; and if by the grace of God ye are perfect in Christ, ye can in nowise deny the power of God. And again, if ye by the grace of God are perfect in Christ, and deny not his power, then are ye sanctified in Christ by the grace of God, through the shedding of the blood of Christ, which is in the covenant of the Father unto the remission of your sins, that ye become holy, without spot" (Moro. 10:32–33).

❖ *Be purified and cleansed:* "But no man is possessor of all things except he be purified and cleansed from all sin. And if ye are purified and cleansed from all sin, ye shall ask whatsoever you will in the name of Jesus and it shall be done" (D&C 50:28–29).

• SYNONYMS: blameless, unspotted, spotless, favored, pure, perfect.

• ANTONYMS: filthy, unclean, impure, stained.

NOTES

1. *Lectures on Faith* (Deseret Book Company, 1985), 38.
2. *Preach My Gospel: A Guide to Missionary Service* (2004), 115.
3. *Young Women Personal Progress* (booklet, 2009), 70.
4. LDS.org, Gospel Topics, "Virtue." Note: Much of the material in this chapter is taken from the official website of The Church of Jesus Christ of Latter-day Saints. Due to space limitations, many individual attributions have been omitted. In some cases, slight changes have been made for the focus of this book.
4. LDS.org, "virtue."
5. Russell M. Nelson, "What Will You Choose?" *Ensign,* Jan. 2015, 32.
6. David Hart, "Freedom and Decency," *First Things,* No. 144, June/July 2004, 33–41.
7. Gordon B. Hinckley, "A Prophet's Counsel and Prayer for Youth," *Ensign,* Jan. 2001, 2–11.
8. Thomas S. Monson, "Guiding Principles of Personal and Family Welfare," *Ensign,* Sept. 1986, 3.

9. Benjamin Franklin, "13 Virtues."

10. *Preach My Gospel,* 121.

11. David A. Bednar, "In the Strength of the Lord," *Ensign,* Nov. 2004, 76–78.

12. Bruce D. Porter, *The King of Kings* (Deseret Book, 2007), 72.

13. Thomas S. Monson, "Be Strong and of a Good Courage," *Ensign,* May 2014, 66–69.

14. Porter, *The King of Kings,* 70–71.

15. Marlin K. Jensen, "How to Be Happy," *New Era,* Aug. 1999, 4–7.

16. Camilla Kimball, quoted in Bonnie D. Parkin, "Personal Ministry: Sacred and Precious," BYU Devotional, Feb. 13, 2007.

17. Ezra Taft Benson, *God, Family, Country: Our Three Great Loyalties* (Deseret Book, 1975), 140.

18. Porter, *The King of Kings,* 85.

19. Boyd K. Packer, "Called to Serve," *Ensign,* Nov. 1997, 6–8.

20. *Church Communication Guide,* 12.

21. *Church News,* Nov. 9, 2014, 16.

22. Franklin, "13 Virtues."

23. Benjamin F. Call, "Choosing to Forgive," *Ensign,* Jan. 2014, 68–71.

24. James E. Talmage, *Jesus the Christ* (Salt Lake City: Deseret Book, 1973), 287.

25. *Church Communication Guide,* 11.

26. Marvin J. Ashton, "While They Are Waiting," *Ensign,* May 1988, 62–64.

27. Boyd K. Packer, *Teach Ye Diligently* (Salt Lake City: Deseret Book, 1975), 17.

28. Ulisses Soares, "Be Meek and Lowly of Heart," *Ensign,* Nov. 2013, 9–11.

29. Neal A. Maxwell, "Willing to Submit," *Ensign,* May 1985, 70–72.

30. Henry B. Eyring, "Our Hearts Knit as One," *Ensign,* Nov. 2008, 68–71.

31. H. Burke Peterson, "Selflessness: A Pattern for Happiness," *Ensign,* May 1985, 65–67.

32. Neal A. Maxwell, "Deny Yourselves of All Ungodliness," *Ensign,* May 1995, 66–68.

33. Kimball, *The Miracle of Forgiveness,* 28.

34. Spencer W. Kimball, *Liahona,* Dec. 1984, 5.

35. David O. McKay, in Conference Report, Oct. 1956, 5–6.

36. Gordon B. Hinckley, "I Am Clean," *Ensign,* May 2007, 60–62.

37. David O. McKay, *True to the Faith,* comp. Llewelyn R. McKay (1966), 245.

INDEX